T0157433

The Way It Was

The Way It Was

Dolores Palà

THE WAY IT WAS

iUniverse books may be ordered through booksellers or by contacting:

iUniverse
1663 Liberty Drive
Bloomington, IN 47403
www.iuniverse.com
1-800-Authors (1-800-288-4677)

ISBN: 978-1-4917-6631-6 (sc)
ISBN: 978-1-4917-6632-3 (e)

Print information available on the last page.

iUniverse rev. date: 05/05/2015

There would be no book without the magic of Kathleen Grosset and Thierry Mignon who, for the second time, took my sheaf of scribbles and turned it into a book. Thanking them properly is beyond me.

A special word of thanks to Mallorie Kaskubar who took on the enormous task of trying to put grammar back into my lexicon.

If this were a Corrida I would offer the ears to Suzy, my magical daughter, who has whisked order out of chaos in our private Twilight Zone, bringing us calm and comfort and paving the way to laughter when none seemed remotely in view.

And, raising a glass of Sherry, I salute those who left the ring too early: Ann, Barbara, Cocotte, Susie O. and my valiant young cousin, Mono, who are still close by, waiting.

The Way it Was

Chapter 1

The reason I have begun this is to avoid the next generation the confusion I find in figuring out my parents' lives and times. Everyone's background is rich and each of us is sure of his own uniqueness. All lives are worth sharing. When they involve cross points from Ireland to Canada to New York and Paris or Estremadura in Spain to Bogota in Colombia through to New York with the help of Barcelona and to Paris for good, perhaps they are a little more unique than others. In any case, they are harder for others to pin-point. Which is the reason for what follows.

Anyone who knows me even slightly knows I'm American and even the shortest further acquaintance will reveal that I am a New Yorker, too. After a half century in France the accent has lost little of the Hudson, of strong nuns' elocution tests or, even, a deep association with the Maritimes in Canada. It disturbs me that Americans all seem to talk the same way now; the regional differences have been blurred by homogenized nasal passages, a surfeit of grunts and a vocabulary built around the word *awesome.*

Not only am I a New Yorker but I am inordinately fond of the part of the city I grew up in, the top part left of the island, which has not been physically removed in the intervening years but which has been so altered as to be a totally different place. It is called Washington Heights, it is north of the wonderful museum complex on Broadway at 156th Street, next to Trinity Cemetery where Clement Moore, author of *'Twas The Night Before Christmas*, is buried and where there is a candlelit Christmas Eve vigil every year for children. Then north to the George Washington Bridge and up to Fort Tryon Park and The Cloisters.

While I was growing up in the late 1930s, through the war and the end of the '40s, Washington Heights was something on the order of a small town. It had been a battleground during the revolution and still maintains the rough contours of its militant past in hills and rock faces, unexpected frame houses dating from the nineteenth century, and amazing views of the river's sweep. It was a walker's paradise.

In the mid '30s the buildings were relatively new. Growth in upper Manhattan was mostly post WWI. The houses were made for families and they were built to last. There were parks galore. Riverside Drive was wild and ridged so the streets curved, rose to hills perfect for sleds in winter, produced ponds that were instant ice skating rinks by Christmas, and in spring the sparse traffic and relative calm allowed for bikes and roller skates, a rare advantage in New York City at any time.

It was a part of Manhattan where neighborhood meant friendliness and community. There was all the innocence one seeks in a place to raise children. I am grateful now to my father's disregard for labels and his quest for clean air (already!) in the Depression years that made him move from 85th Street and Riverside Drive where we had lived before. That was the reason he gave. Not the fact that rents, way uptown, were about half what he paid and that, in moving, he got something like a six month's concession on paying the rent at all. He wasn't broke yet and money was never his main concern, so it might well not have been that at all. He always found it pretty, even in 1963 when he was dying; he enjoyed the breeze from the Hudson and the presence of trees.

As I grew into a prickly teenager, of course I tackled him on his choice of addresses. It would have been a lot more suitable to have a Riverside Drive address when going off on a Princeton weekend where the other girls, pale blondes with uncommitted eyes, might murmur, *"I live in Pound Ridge. Where do you live?"* When that happened I seethed underneath. I hated them. But I learned to snap back: *"Pound Ridge?"* I would echo, shuddering a little. *"That's really far!"* It took me time to perfect it but it worked. They were wary of The Dark Stranger from then on.

Washington Heights was a misunderstood address even then, when it was American-born, upwardly mobile, college-educated, slightly Jewish, a tiny bit Greek, and leafier by far than the rest of our sweet island put together.

The building my parents chose was red brick with a court in the front. There were eight wide front steps and it was forbidden to leave carriages or bikes in the court. There was a foyer with well-polished brass bells and nameplates. The bells had a buzzer so that no one could enter if not admitted by a tenant. The floor was well-scrubbed marble. It opened onto a wide lobby with a pay telephone, more brass mailboxes and a directory of the tenants. Lots more marble. There was a long table along one wall with a huge brass vase containing fresh flowers in season or a nice bouquet of branches in winter. There was a back door, with another brass nameplate reading Yard, which led to a staircase going down into a wide, spacious yard with an array of tubs of flowers, evergreen bushes, small trees placed here and there.

The house-proud superintendents—we avoided the word janitor—were a Hungarian family, Mr. and Mrs. Shirokman and their children, Andy and Olga, who were my age. Looking back, the Shirokmans were inventive immigrants who provided their American-born children with instant playmates by creating an informal community center. A few non-building kids were included but they had connections with the tenants. It was a private playground, idyllic for urban parents. And for the only child that I was, it precluded even the notion of loneliness. I had a built-in social structure, a child's parliament, a toy-pool and a storyteller's workshop without leaving home. Coming from the anonymity of 85th Street, it was like walking into heaven.

Most of the families in the building were American-born, aside from the Greek ones. The Chukalases lived on our floor. There were Eugenie and Jimmy, my age, and their cousins, who had shortened their names to Morris, in the adjacent flat, with three handsome older sons whom all the girls in the building had crushes on. Mrs. Chukalas was a beautiful woman with two older daughters, Nita and Peachy, also beautiful. There was an oil portrait of a distinguished gentleman on their living room wall. He was Mr. Stephanopolis, the older girl's late father. All my childhood I wondered how the mild mannered Mr. Chukalas, the second husband, managed to live in the shadow of his haughty predecessor. I never asked. They were kind, concerned neighbors, discreet as diplomats, and all were pleasing to look at.

Greek-Americans were very Greek then, which was no doubt a matter of painful complexity to their American children, who frequently were sent to Greek schools. It wasn't 'til the third generation that inter-marriage was tolerated. All the Chukalas children married within their community, if not someone from Greece itself. Eugenie, whom I met in later life, married a chemical engineer from Athens. Her children, American-raised, broke the chain. But by then the majestic Mrs. Chukalas had been long gone from her post as guardian of the temple.

I was fond of our Greek neighbors; I loved their food, their discretion, their restraint, their other-ness. They were exemplary neighbors. Their notion of being Americans was different from other immigrants, but their generosity to others made me reluctant to criticize them in the way I felt quite free to criticize other communities. Even at a tender age, I was opinionated.

But when we met some twenty years later in Paris, the first thing Eugenie asked me was, "How did you get away?"

The other children in the building were second or third generation American and, though mostly Jewish, knew few words of Yiddish—the words that most New Yorkers know no matter what their persuasion. Kvetch, schlep, yenta, smatas, schmuck—basic New Yorkese. I once heard one of the nuns at Incarnation shout in anger to a lazy van driver delivering text books, "You don't expect me to schlep this box myself do you!"

And no one batted an eyelid.

The Alexanders had two children, Gloria and Martin, who became fixtures in my life as soon as we met. Mr. Alexander had been gassed in WWI and was left with a peculiar disorder. He pursed his lips and breathed in, then blew out with the frequency of a normal person's breathing. It was disfiguring, disconcerting and it must have been hell for him. His family behaved as though there was nothing wrong, which set the tone for others. No one mentioned it, no one asked questions, no one stared. He was a mild man who "went to business" every day with a briefcase, as my father did, he dressed quietly and carefully and they lived a perfectly normal life. Looking back, I wonder how they managed to retain such dignity with apparently no visible effort. "A war injury," was the first and last explanation. So be it.

Gloria was exactly my age and was bright, sharp, blonde, and blue-eyed. She was a very pretty girl. She and her brother Martin were excellent students, had also skipped, and were musical. Martin found us too young and seldom came down to play in the yard. Both were good pianists, both had good minds.

Gloria and I were close. We told each other secrets, we exchanged confidences, we passed each other favorite books. And we were both jealous of Joan Levy who was exquisite, not just pretty. And very grand.

The whole Levy family was distinguished. Joan was their after-thought child; they had a grown son and daughter. All were handsome and from Boston. There was a class difference at play here, which even the kids knew. Coming from Boston they spoke with that flat r-less cadence which somehow implied culture. And they had a Steinway piano, not an upright like the Alexanders. Mr. and Mrs. Levy played duets, Joan had a European teacher and gave recitals with his other pupils in Town Hall once a year. That in itself was a class advantage to die for.

Joan was smallish, with perfect features, dark wavy hair never out of place and almond shaped blue eyes. She looked like a nine-year-old Paulette Godard. When she ate an Oreo after school with the others in the back yard, she nibbled at the white, coaxing it with her tongue while the others crunched their way through half a dozen. She was poised, removed; she was a princess. I loved her. Gloria didn't. It made for an interesting situation.

There were other kids, but we three, along with Olga and Andy, the Super's children, were the cores. The others were either younger or boring and I scarcely remember their names. But the crowd was considerable even if they all didn't live in the building, and we played out our own lives with little interference from the parents.

We played a game no one else seems to know of so I assume it was invented by one of the kids. It was called *I declare war on:* You drew a circle on the ground, then drew lines dividing in into slices, like a pie. Each slice was a country—France, England, Germany, etc. One day I wrote in Ethiopia. Everyone howled. Who ever heard of a place with a name like that? I insisted, they shouted, I won, and I bellowed at the top of my voice, "I declare war on Ethiopia."

That night I listened to the news with my father and heard, to my horror, that Italy had declared war on Ethiopia. I let out a cry. My father, who enjoyed discoursing on world events to me, looked surprised. "I told you they would," he said mildly.

Yes, he had. He had told me all about Mussolini, all about fascism, about National Socialism in Germany, about the madness of dictators. He told me all the many things he would have told his friends, if he had any friends. But he seemed not to. I was his public, his audience and I only half-digested what he told me in such detail and with colorful intellectual baggage I was far too young to absorb. So, I had said Ethiopia just to show off in the back yard! By playing Miss Know-it-all I brought disaster on a poor, faraway Christian country and it was invaded by Italians in heavy boots as a result. Shame.

I wasn't old enough to laugh at myself, nor to imagine how it happened. The unlucky Negus had been in the news, of course, but this was pre-television news. Only my father, among the other parents, brought me into his radio circle. I was the only child who shared a parent's commentaries on world crises. I was probably Ed Murrow's youngest listener. Only I, among the other kids downstairs, knew of the possibility of Italy's little war but, by showing off, I had precipitated it. I was convinced that it was I who had brought the invasion to Ethiopia, and I was sick with remorse.

My mother took me to church every Saturday to go to confession. I was happy to do it. I loved the ceremony of the Confessional, the waiting, the penance. It gave me a sense of belonging to a family beyond my own. It was a sense of comfort and safety, and, especially, of forgiveness.

I went to confession that Saturday and told the priest what I had done. I expected release, redemption.

If it had been a movie the priest would have spoken gently to the child and dispelled her fears. It wasn't a movie, it was Incarnation, a parish church on 175th Street and St. Nicholas Avenue. The priest merely grunted, gave me two Hail Marys and an Our Father, and planted a seed of doubt and resentment in my heart that would take half a lifetime to work out.

Chapter 2

The rise of Hitler and the flight of European Jews changed the neighborhood even more than the Depression had. Our building was suddenly bilingual. German-speaking families filled the apartments before one knew they were vacant, my mother was heard to say to Mrs. Adelman of the ground floor. Like most of the other tenants, the Adelmans were American-born. Their empathy with the refugees was emotional and instantaneous. However, when confronted with tall, heavy set people, well dressed and swiftly employed at a time when their own economic reality was still dicey, these refugees fell short of the sympathy mark.

For starters, they failed to connect with the American Jewish families. They did not seem to even seek to adapt. They shocked the whole building when they referred to the handyman as the Schwartzer in his own hearing. They mocked American guilelessness while they took its generosity. In the local schools their children excelled because, they claimed, European education was miles ahead of culture-less America. It was hard to make friends with these newcomers; worse, it was harder still to admit it.

Most of those families soon moved on. The ones that stayed tended to be Viennese. The German children hadn't made friends with us. But we all had learned the meaning of the word *scheisse*.

Henry Kissinger was one of those boys. I have a faint memory of him and another Henry, who was pale and wore golf pants, and a third, square-headed Herbert Hirsch who came to the Alexanders' apartment to listen to some new recording of a Sibelius symphony Martin had just acquired. Martin was a serious boy with a deep sense of music. All of his spare money went in to an enviable record collection. The Three Hs sat on dining room chairs, straight backed and intent. I remember finding the atmosphere in the room taut, unnerving. There was a moment when I feared a rush of *fou rire*, which I fought down only by divine intervention.

At the end all three rose noisily from their chairs, breaking the spell. They walked around the living room for a minute or two and then, clearing his voice Herbert said, "Inconsequent." The two Henrys nodded their heads in approbation. Martin was openmouthed. I, who knew nothing about music, was amazed at the word. The silence was like ice. Eventually Martin attempted an argument but they stood their ground haughtily. I was stunned by their arrogance.

It seemed inconceivable to us that these Jewish boys would want to appear so German: their stubborn accents, their dress, their attitude. It took me a very long time to understand that, of course they seemed German: *That's what they were.* How deep their humiliation must have been. They had been rejected by their own. It would have called for great strength to admit it to others.

It was this prickly invasion that brought several welcome additions to New York's West Side, wryly dubbed The Fourth Reich: good pastry shops and the lending library. For that alone I am much indebted.

There were several lending libraries scattered through the neighborhood, all run by Central Europeans of immense culture, men with sad faces and Olympian memories who organized poetry readings, debates, readings from translations, exhibits of drawings or etchings because the shops were too cramped for paintings.

I had been a regular at the public library almost all my life beginning with the Story Lady. My parents were readers and the house was filled with books. But the cozy little lending library on Broadway near 181ˢᵗ Street was a different planet. It was intimate. On a table in the back there was a coffee pot, cups and a plate of cookies that seemed to replenish itself by magic. If there was a little Beethoven playing it was not background music, it was being listened to by a couple of elderly men with attentive expressions.

The flavor was distinctly foreign, and as such it produced immense curiosity in me about the world they had been forced to flee. I saw it as a romantic world of the dispossessed. The survivors. I became infatuated not only with Paris but Vienna, Prague and, oddly, Krakow with its looming Vevel Castle. They had been turned into cities of failed magic in my adolescent's mind. I fell in love with Europe then, moseying around the secondhand bookshops of upper Broadway, trying to picture winding ancient streets and faded palaces in a war which was devouring our heritage as I grew.

When I was eleven my father lost his job. That was on Columbus Day, 1939. His job, much like himself, was an odd one. He had come to New

York in 1914 from Bogota just before the war because his older brother, don Alberto, was there. Don Alberto was with the Colombian Consulate. He had married an American, Margaret Murphy, a tall elegant New Yorker and something of a fashion plate.

He came to New York, then, because Alberto was there and he revered his older brother. He never had any intention of settling down for good. In his own mind, he was always going home next year.

To try to explain my father, one has to take a careful look at who he was when he started out and then attempt to make sense of the rest.

To say he came from a prominent Colombian family would be an understatement because his family is far more than that. And that includes the side that is only Colombian by chance.

The Sotos, or De Sotos as he preferred to call himself in New York— just as his irascible grandfather did, who had a seat on the Stock Exchange and lived part of every year in New York—for the simple reason that they thought that Soto sounded Japanese and that displeased them enormously. De Soto, on the other hand, was a household word thanks to the explorer, who was a long ago ancestor in any case, and eventually the automobile.

More in the present, the first Soto to appear in Colombia was Buenaventura Soto who arrived in what was then called Nueva Granada, the upper left hand side of the South American continent which comprises the present Venezuela, Colombia and Ecuador plus Panama which used to be part of Colombia 'til the US decided to build a canal and annex it. Which brought about a bit of a tremor in their good neighborliness.

Buenaventura Soto and his brother Bartomeo came from Extramadura, which is where the Conquistador came from, too. Family legend has it that the brothers came to the New World with a land grant thanks to their ancestor. We descend from Buenaventura who married the Madrid noblewoman Montes de Oca and settled in Cucuta, in Colombia. He established a thriving business which included trading a variety of commodities, especially coffee and chocolate but also gold and silver, emeralds and grain. He became a leading figure in Colombian economics and so did his brother Bartolomeo.

The Montes de Oca family was already established and helped, presumably, in the rise in the fortunes of their enterprises. All this is documented thoroughly and easily available on the Net.

The Sotos became leading figures in what evolved as Colombian politics, eminences in the Liberal Party, and within one generation, were leaders in the movement for independence from Spain under Simon Bolivar.

Francisco Soto Montes de Oca, the son of the first generation, was Bolivar's secretary and his first general. He was called the Thomas Jefferson of South America and wrote the first Constitution. He was also the leader of the subsequent plot to overthrow Bolivar when The Liberator began to turn into The Despot late in his career. It was General Soto who organized the uprising which did not depose him but which jarred Bolivar loose from his helm, ruined his health and, subsequently, caused his retirement.

The Soto family were among the founders of the Partido Liberal and remain so 'til the present time, even down to the half dozen US Sotos who are ardent, active Democrats.

Through the nineteenth century all the Sotos thrived in business, banking and public service. They were rich, true, but they were forward-looking, highly educated, philanthropic and devoted to intellectual as well as public advancement. There have been four Soto Ministers of Foreign Affairs in the nineteenth and twentieth centuries. It is also true, they own the Banco de Bogota but there are high schools named after Jorge Soto del Corral, my father's first cousin whom I knew and was in awe of at the United Nations, where he was Ambassador.

Don Jorge was an eminence, a brilliant diplomat, a mentor. He had been Ambassador to France just at the outbreak of the war, then Ambassador to the UN in its infancy at Lake Success and Senator in Bogota, as well as an outstanding professor of Constitutional Law.

In 1949 a lunatic got up one day in the Senate, brandished a gun around, fired it before anyone could get to him, and managed to hit Jorge in the ankle. This was followed by a sudden stroke which left him only half-alive for the next year or so. The Colombian government flew him to New York for a ground-breaking brain operation which did not work and he died, stupidly in mid-life. He had been a hero of mine and I was devastated by his absurd death.

His brothers, Luis, Alvaro and Camilo lived out their lives as prominent members of the community with the Banco de Bogota and Luis Soto hijos, the stock brokerage with a seat on NY Exchange, but Jorge left no heirs.

The rest of the Soto tribe in Bogota is similar in scope and influence. They are descended from the second son of Francisco Soto Villamizar, Luis. The first was Francisco Soto Landinez, my grandfather. And that makes all the difference because he married my grandmother, Soledad Castillo Aranza, who was not quite Colombian.

Briefly, Francisco-my-grandfather, being the eldest, got to go to Europe for his education and then to take the grand tour that went with it. The 19th century was nothing if not generous with the firstborn.

If his brother Luis had a way with money, Francisco had a way with living. He lived well. He enjoyed living. He was handsome, a story teller, a reader of poetry and a friend of poets, admirer of paintings, architecture, scenery, theater... of cafés and what they served. He enjoyed life.

He went to Louvain University in Belgium to study agronomy because he liked the countryside, but not banks so it was decided that he would be in charge of the Soto agricultural and mining holdings, which went from coffee and cocoa to silver mines. Louvain has a world famous agronomy faculty. He did that, but then decided he should do medicine as well. In case the cattlemen got sick, so to speak.

His grumpy father, who was well into a second marriage—his first wife having died—let him stay in Europe. His father had begun a new batch of children to complicate everyone's score card. These were called Soto Hoyos. The Hoyos, though noble, had insanity in their genes. We are not Hoyos, all the Soto Landinez, including myself, are quick to point out.

My branch, the earlier Soto Landinez ones, had no insanity. They did it one better: they had a fabulous rogue who was Colombia's first financial scoundrel. He began as a financial hero in that he lent money to the emerging Republic during its War of Independence but later swindled the whole continent with a pyramid scheme similar to Bernie Madoff's.

I must note that I only learned this through the Net, to my immense surprise, because all the annotations I have ever seen around his name in family documents have been smudged with erasures and scribbled over. I thought that had had something to do with his first name which was Judas Tadeo Landinez...not many people have a forebear they can call Grandpa Judas, after all. Also, he had been Minister of Foreign Affairs in the 1840s. Who would have guessed that he was a world class scoundrel?

So, my grandfather, Francisco Soto Landinez, returned to Bogota after more than ten years of learning and of traveling through Europe and even the Middle East. These travels included a longish stay in Egypt, where he visited the tombs and the excavations that were bringing us Tutankhamun at the time.

He returned to Bogota that was, in good Spanish tradition, a city with a cultured core that welcomed travelers and their stories especially if the traveler was vivid, handsome and gracious. My grandfather was all this and more, his younger son told me. He was an enchanting companion by all accounts.

He promptly fell in love with Soledad Castillo Aranza, who was the granddaughter of one of the two sons of the Spanish Governor General of Cuba at the time of Bolivar's War of Independence of continental South America from Spain. The Governor General's sons wanted Independence for Cuba. This was a good hundred years before Freud started talking about the need to kill the father.

And Cuba? It would seem that that particular little island in the sun nurtures a long line of extravagant soldiers of independence.

The two young Castillo brothers left their father's house and headed for Cartegena de las Indias in Colombia, Bolivar's headquarters, to ask his financial help for the revolution that was about to begin in Havana. In the time that it took them to get to Cartegena, however, that Cuban revolution had been nipped in the bud and all its leaders either executed or imprisoned.

The two Castillo Escobar brothers were left high and dry to fend for themselves in the newly independent Colombia. I can find no record of what their father, the Spanish Governor General of Cuba, had to say about this. Pity; I would love to know.

Unable to return to their family, they remained. According to my father, not usually trustworthy about strict fact but fairly accurate about mood, they remained a bit apart and continued to call themselves Cuban, a nationality that did not yet exist.

My grandmother, Soledad, married the elegant heir to a family heritage that was kept firmly in the hands of the seemingly eternal Francisco Soto Villamizar, her husband's father, busy in his late middle years making money and attending to a new family tarred with mental peculiarities, thus with little time for his eldest son who did nothing much but tell stories to a loving entourage.

But my grandparents' house was a happy one, everyone tells me, with interesting friends and an ever open door for guests from abroad.

I find an air of Gabriel Garcia Marques about this but I am assured that the great Colombian master's rich characters were all drawn from other parts of the country, not Bogota. Pity. But then perhaps the whole country is blessed by particularly titillating mountain winds, for Bogota is one of the highest capitals in the world.

Sadly, however, the master of the house died when his eldest child, my uncle Alberto, was fourteen, and the youngest, my father, was five. Soledad, the bereft widow, was left with four children and was at the mercy of her irascible father-in-law whose often peculiar second family, about the same age as her children, proved a handful.

In addition, he cast a querulous eye at her rather odd relatives, the brainy Castillos, who were still not quite Colombian.

Meanwhile, her brother and sister had both married Colombians and for all intents and purposes they were all integrated, no longer Spanish and certainly not Cuban. Yet they considered themselves Cuban. I suppose being a failed revolutionary leaves traces. My father always claimed he had Cuban connections, somewhat to my annoyance as a child. In my eyes Colombia had a touch of class whereas Cuba was rumbas, cigars and dancing girls, not at all the image I had of all my august ancestors.

The Castillo brothers who remained in Colombia furnished South American letters with two fine poets. One, Guillermo Valencia Castillo, was one of the foremost poets of the first part of the 20th century, not only in his own poems but also his translations from the French, particularly Victor Hugo and Gerard de Nerval. His son became President of Colombia in the 1960s, a brilliant member of the Liberal Party.

Eduardo Castillo was the son of my grandmother's brother, a poète maudit, who, according to my father who revered him, wore a Cordobes hat and cape and died young. My father did not say so but it would seem that cocaine had a great deal to do with the body of Eduardo Castillo's work as well as with his early death. His poetry is still in print. So, of course, is Guillermo Valencia's. Castillo's poetry is recommended to anyone interested in the way the mind streaks itself out in the best and worst of cases.

They were two faces of one muse. I am particularly proud of them.

So, when my father, the boy whose father died when he was five and who looked up to his older brother pursuing a brilliant diplomatic career on post in New York when he failed medical school and had no idea of what to do with himself in 1912, he went to New York to join him.

His grandfather would have taken him into the brokerage office, he used to say, but he had no sense of money. That was an understatement. He settled in, his brother made him comfortable, and he had some sort of job somewhere. I never knew where, but he lived agreeably at the Hotel Roosevelt.

In the early 1920s Alberto, by then married to his glorious Irish-American called Margaret Murphy, who was soon called Margot and whom I loved when I got to know her in Paris in the late 1940s, took his family back to Bogota where he remained in the Ministry of Foreign Affairs, a career diplomat, 'til he retired to become a full-time writer. He died in 1946. It was the only time I saw my father cry—when I handed him the letter from his wife, Aunt Margot.

He was then the editor of a political satire magazine called *El Sapo* and wrote a charming book of memoires called *Fullerias*, which I treasure. He died in 1946.

My father said he went to New York on a whim, because Alberto was there. It was an arbitrary move; he might just as easily have stayed home.

He never explained why he remained or what happened to the young man whose first cousins were poet laureates or presidents of the Jockey Club or the Senate, whose forebears had won and lost wars of liberation, whose father had ridden camels in the Egyptian desert.

In the long run, I think he did not know. I believe he must have grown comfortable in the anonymity New York allowed him. No one knew the prominence of his family in New York. No one told tales about him. No one chastised him when he got drunk. No one knew or cared. He was young; he lived in the Hotel Roosevelt in mid-town Manhattan. He was having a wonderful time. There would always be time.

The Roosevelt, where he had lived since he arrived in 1913, offered him a job as public relations for a new and rising South American clientele. Don Paco was by way of being a greeter, a smoother-over of situations, a go-between. He loved it. He was happy in his element.

South American visitors became a serious hotel target, with the decline of Europe in the 1930s. Business boomed. My father was free to hire an assistant. He chose badly. A clever polyglot Greek, who had lived in Argentina as well as Paris and who spoke their languages fluently, took the job. He was charming. Beware of Greeks bearing gifts, we are told. Don

Paco didn't see it coming. It took a good ten years, but in 1939 the wily Mr. Vallis eased him out and lived happily ever after.

By then my father was 51. He no longer lived in the hotel but in an apartment in Washington Heights. After his marriage in 1923, he had gradually turned into Frank De Soto. The dashing don Paco had slowly taken his leave. Like everyone else he saw most of his investments crash in 1929 and the trickle of inheritances that fell to him from time to time dried up.

In 1923 he acquired a red-headed Irish-American wife called Laura Collins who was just as ill-advised as he was. She was dazzled, she said vaguely many years later, by his manners, his lifestyle, his difference. She soon set about to change that difference. By the time I was around ten years old he was someone altogether different. I only have the vaguest recollection of don Paco.

Frank De Soto was a much-loved burden.

My mother was born in Montreal and was brought up in a variety of places: New York and Montreal, principally, but also in Philadelphia and the West of Ireland. She remained hazy about her early years but her older sister affirmed that she had gone to Westmount High School and a small college in Quebec. When we visited Ireland together in 1963, I learned that she had attended the Sisters of Mercy school there, but she was unclear as to how long; neither she nor her numerous re-found friends nor the relatives I met during her six year stay in Castlebar at the end of her life were any more precise. She wanted it to be vague; she worked hard at drawing a veil over her exact age and, although my aunt told it to me on a number of occasions, I never really remembered. Her need to veil it must have been stronger than my need to know.

Aunt Birdie, ten years older than my mother according to her, was an immense figure in my childhood. Elizabeth Collins Reicker, her parents' oldest child, was elegant, well-groomed, blonde and a snob. She was the antithesis of my mother. Her clothes were stylish, her house carefully furnished with the early American pieces she managed to spirit away from her father's house on East 94th Street in New York when he died in 1923. She was active in the community; she fit in. My mother stuck out. And she knew it.

I spent all the summer holidays with Aunt Birdie and her husband in Digby, Nova Scotia throughout my childhood. I owe her much. Through her I had a sense of belonging in that small, graceful town snuggled on the shores of the Bay of Fundy. Green hills, craggy cliffs, carefully tended white houses with magnificent hydrangeas in manicured gardens; Digby was a picture post card come alive. The sea that battered the coast admirably scented the air, gave sustenance to the birch groves and ever-present maple trees. Even as a child I was taken by its charm.

There were lakes as well. Aunt Birdie and Uncle Harold had a cabin on a small lake with only seven houses around it. A cabin in Canada is a three-bedroom house and a sleep-in porch with half an acre of woods and a pier with a couple of boats at the end of it. Hidden in among the tall trees the lake looked, to this city child, like a toy amid dollhouses, a plaything come to life by a sorcerer's wand. I fell in love with Digby when I was ten years old. I still am today.

If I had lots of playmates in New York, I had at least as many in Digby. Different sorts, perhaps, but the difference was piquant. I realized right away that I was privileged to have access to two worlds, two countries—for all their sameness—and two vantage points. In Canada I met people who had known my mother when she was young, had known my grandfather J.P Collins and admired him, had greeted Birdie when she decided to settle there in 1923 when J.P. died in New York. Snobbish, social Birdie who did the 5th Avenue Easter Parade and was the first woman to graduate with a degree as a hospital dietitian at NYU, was 40ish in 1923. She was popular, had beaux, traveled. She astonished everyone when she announced she was going to Digby, where she had spent family summers only, and open a hat shop.

She designed hats, raised dachshunds, bought a big white house and married a man ten years younger, Harold Reicker. From St. John's, New Brunswick. Who wasn't a Catholic and who wouldn't "change" either. Moreover, he looked exactly like Oliver Hardy, the fat one in Laurel and Hardy. Exactly.

If my parents' marriage was peculiar, this one defied logic. Birdie, the social doyenne of Digby, spent a great deal of her time keeping Harold from being rude to people. Like farting in the kitchen knowing it would be heard in the living room where her bridge club was having tea. Like saying "he don't." Like bursting in on a whist drive, poking around the tea things and demanding, "Any decent grub here?"

His own father "got religion" when Harold was fourteen, left his wife and three children, taking the bankbook with him and went off to preach the gospel. He doused his flock in cold Canadian rivers for the glory of God, leaving Harold to support his mother, brother and sister. Which he did well. George, his brother, and Zena, his sister, were both handsome, well-spoken and eternally grateful to the rough-edged curmudgeon Harold had become. I was very fond of him. He didn't fart when I was around. He taught me how to mess around with a sailboat, how to row when the lake was rough, how to hold a fishing rod. The only disappointment I ever caused him, I think, was to grow up. But I did that to all concerned.

Growing up in any decade is a handful, but growing up in a World War ensured a sense of outrage, of heightened drama, a nose for subterfuge and a sharpened sense of the ephemeral. An imaginative child, left on her own more than the others, would acquire a taste for superlatives with no coaxing.

No one gave me much guidance about schools. Mother and her bosom friend, Muriel Alger, a dotty woman of uncertain age, who invented much of her life, was to have been the final source of wisdom as to deciding where I should go to high school. Over Danish or whole wheat donuts and cups of coffee in our living room, Muriel and Mother decreed that George Washington High School, a handsome building set down in a rolling grassy campus around it and built in the colonial style not far from our house, was out of the question. A girl was known to have had a baby in the tower, one said while the other nodded vigorously in delectable reprobation. I was twelve years old and knew nothing about how babies were made and even less as to why a tower would make it worse.

I remember those dowagers in the living room with a bit of the George Washington Bridge behind them, casting that handsome school where most of my friends were to go, into the darkness of doubt and shame. When I turned to my father he merely became Colombian again, a device he had perfected over the years. He had had tutors 'til it came time for the *liceo* and after that he went to college. High schools, like most things Yanqui, were suddenly beyond his grasp.

I do remember him making one suggestion during that time, but it was shot down by my mother with a single scathing glance. He said, "Why doesn't she go to Sacred Heart? That's where girls go in Bogota." As soon as he said it, of course, he realized his thoughtlessness and as far as I recall, he never enquired about my schooling again.

That was in February, 1941. I was always a mid-term student because I had skipped 1B. From the beginning I was just a little out of step.

From 1939 'til the winter of 1941 my father was out of a job. The Hotel Roosevelt had fired him in October, 1939. By Thanksgiving my mother, who had stopped working when I was born, had found herself a job as a floor clerk at the Hotel Commodore, on 42nd Street between Lexington and 3rd. She remained the sentinel on the 22nd floor 'til she retired in late 1962, weeks before my father's death. It was, I am convinced, one of the happiest ventures of her life. The Commodore was her kingdom, she was surrounded by friends. Her work world was varied, colorful and thick with intrigue. She met famous people, could drop names. Her fellow floor-clerks were accomplices, there was an *esprit de corps*. Not to mention an *esprit d'escalier*. She bloomed.

There are no floor clerks in big hotels now. There are not even keys. But in that more intimate world, the floor clerk in a "good" hotel was seated behind a desk in front of the bank of elevators and she was the first person the new guest would deal with. She took the keys when the guest went out, returned them when he came back, took messages, kept the housekeepers on their toes after the maids, chatted with the bell hops, ran an empire of transients. Often used in fiction as a microcosm of life and times, the hotel was the sum of its floors and at the Commodore, the lady at the desk was the Regent. She knew it all. Mother had the kind of face that suggested confidence and she became the confidante of hundreds. Her discretion was enviable. She told me only snippets of what went on in her almost private world.

Many of her colleagues were widows with grown families. They were a clan. Only big hotels still kept the service: The Commodore, The New Yorker, The Waldorf Astoria. The ladies knew each other, met often in the oyster bar in Grand Central Station. They had hen dinner parties at the Martha Washington on 23rd Street where Veronica Lake ended up as hostess in the restaurant. They adored that.

Many of the other floor clerks were gentlewomen alone in life, and they tended to live at the Murray Hill Hotel. Dorothy Parker, the most unlikely of lonely ladies of slender means, lived there and immortalized the experience in her play *Ladies of the Corridor*.

The profession is extinct. The class of women is not. I have no idea of what has replaced the floor clerk or even the Murray Hill, but I would bet it has little to do with computers.

My taste for walking around cities with no particular plan, of taking buses to explore neighborhoods where I had nothing to do, was acquired then, at the age of eleven. I was especially attracted to the Hudson and would follow its course past Fort Tryon Park, frequently stopping at the little red lighthouse for a look around. I had visions of inhabiting it.

Lighthouse keepers existed in the Maritimes, didn't they? Wasn't part of our family, the Myricks of Cape Race, Newfoundland, in the business of lighthouse keeping? Wasn't it Uncle Jim Myrick who received the message from the Titanic and wired it through to St. John's where Aunt Daisy, his sister, took it and then informed the whole wide world? No one lived in the little red lighthouse on the bank of the Hudson but, at eleven, I filed it away for future reference.

High school separated the children on the block. Gloria Alexander sensibly went to George Washington along with almost everyone else. I went to Wadleigh. Lydia F. Wadleigh School for Girls. That sounded perfect. It wasn't. The address was Central Park West. But it was on 103rd Street, not quite Harlem but not quite *not* Harlem, either.

At the age of twelve I had been brought up by parents with no racial prejudice, with tolerance for others that bordered on sanctity in my Father's case and was simply good manners on my mother's. Never be hurtful to people; I think it was the only golden rule she ever passed on. It went well with "what they don't know won't hurt them," another safeguard she practiced. The other side of her coin. My father considered Americans odd Democrats. They treated their Negroes like slaves or objects of laughter. *Amos 'n' Andy*, a favorite on the radio, was a matter of curiosity for him. Why did they poke fun at themselves?

"But it is endearing," I would answer, not seeing anything wrong with laughing at yourself. He shook his head.

Central Park West and 103rd meant taking the subway to 125th Street, the A train, then change for the local for two more stops. Instead of the ten-minute walk through familiar streets to George Washington High where a sunny new building surrounded by lawns and trees would have cosseted me, I had to face the 8th Avenue subway rush hour with one change at 125th Street and a sea of black faces.

If there was racial tension in February 1941, I was blissfully unaware of it. I only saw differences that were literally skin deep. There were no taboos. I made friends because I liked someone, not because she was white, black or a mixture of both. And there were more of the latter than anything else. Because of my Spanish name I was a point of interest to Puerto Rican or Cuban girls who soon backed off when they learned that I didn't know a word of Spanish and the only foreign connection I had was with Canada.

Despite our innocence, and none of the handful of Incarnation girls who went on to Wadleigh were capable of conscious racial discrimination, we gravitated to other white girls. There were several Italian girls, there were even more Irish and if I was guilty of snobbery here it would certainly be with the Irish-Americans. They were everything I rejected in Incarnation or in the neighborhood. Dumb, church-ridden, interested in nothing that I was interested in, they didn't read books, they didn't ask questions. Nothing penetrated those heads. Even the girls struck out with a fast slap rather than argue a point. They fomented trouble with the black girls; they held the class back in English or History because of their thickness. Their book reports were dismal and their English coarse.

At twelve I was a fine, fiery bigot, but on a different target. I had no problem making friends with black girls, even less with the Italian-Americans (some of whom were clearly related to the Sopranos) but I couldn't stand the Micks.

My mother was amused. My father was perplexed. "All your friends seem to be Jewish," he mused. New York was an endless riddle to him. But by then he was used to perplexity.

No one told me much about racial injustice. Yet what little they said and however they said it, the values set out were wise ones. Tolerance was not a goal, it was a practice. Small neighborhoods, like small towns, should engender mutual inclusion—if given half a chance.

The way we were at Wadleigh in those early 40s seems light years away from the anger that followed. Or, if that anger was already sparked, I might have been too young to register it. It seemed nothing out of the ordinary at the time to be invited to a birthday party at the home of a jolly black girl called Shirley Luncheon and to have my mother's permission to accept. What was exceptional was that a chauffeured car came to my door to pick me up, picking up other classmates on the way, to drive us to a Greystone house on Sugar Hill and be greeted by Shirley's mother, a judge. What was odd was the chauffeured car and the townhouse, not the interracial civility.

Or so I thought. I was, of course, far off the mark but it was fortunate for me to have understood that girls of other colors and I could be friends. I was forced to temper that certitude but it was already engrained in my mind. I have Wadleigh to thank for that.

There was a left-over gentility about the school from a not-too-distant past that I only recognized after I left it. As public schools go, it had advantages I didn't appreciate 'til I missed them sorely. We had, for instance, a glee club led by the music teacher, Miss Goetz, who stepped out of an Edith Wharton novel.

A tall woman in late middle age, who wore beads and a paisley shawl, she taught us songs by Victor Herbert or Stephen Foster and told us romantic stories about the great composers. She lisped. Generous and concerned about her pupils, this kindly soul divided the class among voice tones and listeners. With my tin ear, I was a listener. She managed this without hurting my feelings or making me feel monstrous, which the redoubtable Sister Winifred did at Incarnation. Even though I thought Miss Goetz's choice of songs a bit woebegone in the age of Bing Crosby, I still melt at the strains of Flow Gently Sweet Afton.

Like Miss Goetz, there was an art teacher who took us to museums and extolled the paintings of American masters: Mary Cassat, Remington's memorable horses, the beloved Whistler. And there was a very young teacher who put on a play she had devised from an O. Henry short story, *The Onion*. She spurred me on to reading O. Henry and precipitated my long love affair with the short story. In my second year she vanished into the war and I thought of her from time to time in cloaks of spyery, winning the world back from Hitler's mayhem. Her name was Helen Geffin.

I met her again in 1947 at the United Nations where we both worked. I recognized her voice, suddenly. Wheeling around, I said to her "Did you ever put on a play called *The Onion*?" She stared at me. Her brief career in teaching must have seemed like in another life to her by then.

"Yes," she said finally. And I took her in my arms. We remained close ever since. She died recently, in her late nineties and 'til the end she supervised translation work at the UN decades after retirement. She was a monument to New York and what it offered its children.

Wadleigh's position as a school with a large black student body gave it certain prerogatives which I probably wouldn't have found in other public high schools. I certainly never encountered them after.

W.C. Handy, the great man of music, paid a visit to the school and I remember him walking down the Assembly Hall aisle, a straight-backed, very old man wearing dark glasses and a hat, flanked by four black girls proudly escorting him. He carried a cane and I believe he was totally blind. The school band played his music as he made his way to the stage. His young escorts skillfully led him to the stairs and over to the microphone in the center. There was resounding applause which, after a bit, he silenced by stretching out his hands. The quiet that followed was awesome. A girl on my right sucked in her breath and seemed to shiver. I saw she was crying.

W.C. Handy spoke firmly in a soft voice that had a taste of the south. He told the girls that they were the vanguard of their people and were blessed with the gift of opportunity. He hadn't even imagined going to a school like this when he was a boy, he said. Don't waste your gifts, he warned. I remember that.

At the time Wadleigh looked shabby to me, old fashioned, a poor substitute for Mount St. Vincent or George Washington. I realized how differently people judged luck and how painless my life was. The black girls' faces were taut with emotion, while most of the white girls looked only mildly curious.

The concept of gifts opened a whole new window for me. However, I knew that pretending there was no racial tension, was no real solution. It blurred the issue, it didn't solve it. It was easy to be friends with middle class black girls. It was something else to maintain space between tough street kids who were in school only because they would have been arrested if they weren't. These were kids who didn't come from homes conducive to study, who had no parents to help them. There was a scale of deprivation at play in the neighborhoods adjacent to Wadleigh that I couldn't have imagined at that age. It had nothing to do with the other poor of New York.

And then there was Esther Toppin. Esther was a noisy girl, built like a small boxer, solid, firm, rounded and full of bounce. She was dark, had big sparky eyes in a pretty, genderless face. She talked all the time and verged on the uncontrollable. Just at the edge. Yet, she was smart, and a few of the teachers took her on as a challenge. Others ignored her presence, which amazed me.

She picked me out as a pal. I was more than a little scared of her because her muscular body wanted me to be scared of her. It was part of her language. Inchoately, I knew that. I talked to her, joked with her and tried to keep her at a distance. When she would occasionally burst into a group of us in the cafeteria, she would aim at me, lifting her chin a little, with a smile that could have snapped into violence at any moment. I kept her at bay. I liked her although I was afraid of her, too. She came to epitomize all that I did not understand in getting along with others.

Of course, I lost track of her when I left Wadleigh in January, 1943. Years later, in the early 1970s, I was waiting for a light to change on East 59th Street and noticed a black woman peering at me on the other side. I crossed the street, she remained where she was 'til she could see me better. When she was sure, she shouted out, "Hey you… Wadleigh High School… I remember you!" And amazingly, I remembered her. Esther Toppin.

I said her name and she laughed out loud in pleasure. "That's me, Esther Toppin. Man, where d'you come from like that?"

I wasn't about to say I lived in Paris, because it would make an instant gulf so I mumbled about having moved away from New York a long time ago. She bubbled on, telling me she had two good boys and a wonderful mother-in-law, brushing aside the husband. She asked me my children's' names and what my husband did. I said he was a welder, which in a way, he was since many of his sculptures were in metal. She liked that and she liked my children's names. I asked her where she was going and she said, "Hey, I work down there," pointing to a hospital.

I blurted out, "Oh you're a nurse?" And then it happened. The change in her eyes was instantaneous. We were as far apart now as we were then, as we would always be.

Of course, she wasn't a nurse. She did something menial, she wouldn't have had the education to be a nurse. I had forgotten that, unforgivably. The light in her eyes was altered, a little sharper. She nodded her head slightly and said "Yeah, yeah, a nurse… I remember you… you were a nice kid… I remember you."

I felt then the depth of my failure. It was not enough to close your eyes to differences, to the reality of social scars. Closing your eyes proved more hurtful still, in the long run.

Chapter 3

The next step came as a downer. We are in February, 1943. Wadleigh moved its students from the 103rd Street school at the beginning of the junior year to another building, on 116th Street. I don't know why, perhaps it had something to do with wartime overcrowding. The handful of girls from Incarnation opted for transfers. If white girls were only a slight majority at the junior school, they were a distinct minority on 116th Street. I recall asking my parents if there was any way I could go back to Mount St. Vincent, the by-now idealized school of my early years, but they seemed unable to take on the expense. I understood that. Two years of unemployment had been a grueling experience for them, though I never felt deprived. I also understood that there was a peculiar chasm between them and my school life. It was as if when I left the house in the morning I went into a world they had little part or even interest in.

Except for report cards. If my grades were poor, my mother made a scene. When I got the occasional A she mentioned it in passing to a neighbor or bragged to Muriel or Dot, her other friend. My losing battle with mathematics was seldom mentioned; I was always tops in History. She talked about my history classes with pride. Numbers became a minefield even after my father admitted that his problems with medical school had a great deal to do with numbers.

I'm not sure why, but I ended up with the least interesting of my neighborhood school friends in Textile High School. It is hard to believe. Wadleigh was far from where I lived, some sixty blocks, but Textile was all the way downtown on West 18th Street in a semi-industrial part of Chelsea. There wasn't a tree to be seen. The air had a peculiar odor. I learned that it came from the Nabisco cookie factory up the block. The air reeked of Oreos.

It was a grim prison-like structure, as though it was geared for wizened candidates for the sweatshops in an earlier age. Or, perhaps, a detention center.

I was fourteen years old. How could anyone have thought of sending me to a school with severe race problems, a reputation for gang fights, drop-outs, and English deficiency, an hour's trip from my home? I have no recollection of why I ended up there but I remember vividly how isolated I felt. The classes were overcrowded, which was the first shock. But there was much worse. I had just spent two years in a girls' school and suddenly there were boys.

Not only boys but looming hulks long past puberty. Textile was my introduction to urban want, though no one used that kind of language then. It wasn't just black and white elements, it was something I'd never heard of: ethnic rivalries. Poles and Swedes, for instance. I was unaware that there were that many Poles or Swedes in New York at all, but apparently Brooklyn had whole neighborhoods where they cohabited in unsteady truces. Why they came in to Manhattan to bring havoc to Textile, I never learned. Perhaps it was just that sort of school.

Boys brought teasing, heavy handed goatish behavior. Boys attempted to grope you in the staircases. Not seriously but demeaningly. They made salacious cracks as a girl walked by. They destabilized us. Their attitude was perhaps just gross fun but it was also humiliating. The presence of boys meant a new nervousness, a new and wobbly vanity, a keener rivalry among girls. I was unprepared for most of this.

The January to June term was close to hell for me but I recall no conversations with my mother that might have changed things. Why wasn't I rescued? Perhaps I never called for help. My mother occasionally mentioned George Washington High as the local den of iniquity. What, I wonder, would she have made of the zoot-suited thugs leaning against Textile's grey walls hissing obscenities at the hapless girls walking by? But she never saw them and I stayed on for the next two years 'til graduation.

Summers in Digby brought me back to life. The day after school closed I was on a Greyhound bus for what I called my escape. Everything changed. The accents, the air, the options, the climate, even the cast of characters.

The government of Canada had built the largest Naval Training Station in the British Empire just outside Digby in Cornwallis—primarily, I thought, to redeem my miserable adolescence. Picturesque, bright, good humored and well-behaved, Digby was now miraculously inundated with Naval Cadets.

In 1943, I somehow drifted into the slightly older "in" set in town. The summer that I turned fifteen I was invited by Claire Merkle, the town's socialite, whose mother was one of Birdie's undeclared rivals, and June Knightly, the other town beauty, to afternoons in the Merkle garden with a portable record player, pitchers of lemonade and a very select handful of suitable cadets.

As the summer warmed the air, this grew to evenings of lobster broils on the beach in the company of suitable chaperones. The portable phonograph allowed us the magic of Cole Porter. I was enchanted. The burden of urban deprivation was lifted from my tender shoulders and I floated into a world of tall pines and blue-eyed boys from outer space who couldn't believe they were talking about the bravery of distant Londoners with a funny girl from New York. My fifteen-year-old sophistication, lifted undiluted from the pages of the New Yorker which I all but memorized, was much appreciated in those gracious surroundings. Aunt Birdie invited them out to the cabin on the lake, offering picnics to make Mrs. Merkle's eyes narrow in envy, while I lived out that summer and the next and the one after that, shaking New York and the real world off my shoulders in utter bliss.

All the boyfriends I didn't have in New York were made up for in Digby. I was courted, cosseted, coaxed. My first kiss. My first sense of power over another person. The fact that he was a millionaire's son from Montreal, I like to think, had nothing to do with my secret little pleasure in making him wait. Nor the fact that he kept coming back to Cornwallis every summer. He was the bright icon of my growing up. I would have loved to have fallen in love with him, but it didn't happen. Though I think it did to him, and I cherished that unspoken little secret for a long time after. Summers in Digby allowed me to breathe, and breathing is life.

Classes in Textile were not only crowded, they were also uninspiring. I can only remember one teacher who took the trouble to look for sparks in the classroom and channel the talent she found. Not all the students were louts. To its credit, Textile had a bit of a reputation for its drama classes because the much admired John Garfield had gone there. Long years before my arrival, one of the English teachers started a theater workshop, which attracted bright kids. In my senior year she staged a noteworthy production of *Macbeth*. I played Lady Macbeth. Like most children who grew up in the golden years of "movies," I had harbored niggling ambitions to be an actress. The arduous work involved in even a high school production nipped any such fantasy in the bud. I have only admiration for people of the theater, for their stamina, their patience and their vision. Lady Macbeth was a seminal experience for me in that I to have had nothing but admiration for the theater since. I consider actors on a par with early Christian martyrs. It is the most magical of the arts, as well as the most fraught with pitfalls.

Not much else engaged me, however. The overcrowded classes seemed anonymous, but the streets outside were inviting. I devised a variety of ways to cut classes. Then I set about discovering the world. A few blocks down the avenue and I was in Greenwich Village.

I wandered through it on my own, slowly taking in the shapes of the houses, the winding suddenness of its changes in mood. One street could be as different from its immediate neighbor as night is to day. I moseyed around, feeling their pulses, weighing their pasts. The Village was pristinely old; it hinted of London, and the streets bore their names like banners.

I dreamed of living on Little West 12th Street if only to say its name. I yearned to belong to the little groups seated in the Italian coffee house on the corner of MacDougal Street where, having gathered up the courage to actually go in, I had my first cappuccino.

It was in these truant months that I discovered photography, quite by chance, at a gallery called The American Place. I had never heard of Alfred Stieglitz or even imagined that a camera could be a vehicle of art. Another door had opened and I began a lifelong love affair with photography, thanks to the deficiencies of the New York school system in the middle of a World War.

The war had raged on for what seemed to me most of my life. It had begun in 1939 for us because of the Canadian connection. No family was spared, looking back, not even ours.

My father's brother decided to send his son, nicknamed Mono, to New York to study engineering in September, 1939. I was eleven, the only one on the block who didn't have cousins, who never had Thanksgiving dinners with all the trimming because there was no extended family to share it with. And suddenly I had a cousin.

Mono, who was really called Francisco like almost everyone else in the De Soto family, was tall, fair and possessed of an easy charm that I recall vividly even today. For the first few months in New York he actually lived with us and for a brief autumn I had a big brother.

His spoken English was strange but he understood perfectly. His mother, Aunt Margot, was New York-born. She enthralled me, sitting elegantly in our living room when she brought Mono to New York, explaining that she only spoke English at home. Her husband, my uncle Alberto, their two daughters, Margot Jr. and Alice as well as Mono, answered in Spanish. I must have blinked because I remember her looking at me kindly and saying to my father, lightly, "You should send her to us for a while, she should know what it is to be a Soto." I remember, too, that my father flinched at that.

Whatever their tensions might have been, I was uninterested in them and was totally captivated by having a new Big Brother. Unexpectedly, I got to do things that my friends did and that I so envied: I went to hockey games in Madison Square Garden, I took him ice skating in Central Park, we went to Palisades Amusement Park and, without telling my parents, I took a parachute jump alongside him. We went to the Paramount and saw Harry James on stage. Mono was my dream brother come true.

Eventually he found a studio on Waverly Place in the Village and moved slightly out of my orbit. Only slightly until in 1940, perhaps on a whim, he joined the Royal Canadian Air Force. He was a Colombian citizen, he had been born and brought up in Bogota. He had never experienced a cold winter 'til he came to New York. The RCAF sent him to the Aleutian Islands. The bleak cold and boredom left him defenseless. He was totally ill equipped to deal with it. After the US entry into the war in December 1941, Mono applied for a transfer to US forces. It was offered to him in the middle of the following year on the condition that it be into the parachutes. He accepted. At 21 he took part in the US landings in North Africa.

We saw him after that, in New York on leave. I thought he had grown, but he said no, it was I who had grown and it was about time he taught me to dance. He was gentle and comforting and I had no idea of how to tell him how proud I was of him. Words like that did not come easy; everyone would have squirmed. I remember the few times we talked, in the living room with my parents, a little unsure of the new soldier he had become, that I was disturbed by the needlessness of his bravery. He was unique, his life was special, I thought. Adolescence is a troubled eyeglass.

Mono was killed in the battle for Rome, at Monte Casino, on May 29, 1944. His father, Alberto, sent a cable announcing it and I happened to be alone at home when it came. I was almost sixteen, at the terrible age of half-truths and ill-digested intuitions. Anger filled me then that never entirely faded. There was something wrong with the Canadian military mind that punished an eighteen-year-old's generosity by sending him to a frozen outpost though he had no defense against winter. And there was something wrong with the American military who accepted him on the condition that he join the most perilous of its forces.

Something was wrong. The world as promised in Incarnation by the unshakable nuns bore no resemblance to the one I was opening my eyes to. 1944 was not a year for stilling doubt. My faith, which I had imagined as a matter not open to question, was shaken to the point of rupture. There was no basis for faith, no gates to love. Government was suspect, interests were like caverns, endless. I was angry at all the lies, especially those I couldn't even formulate. It took me another twenty-five years to work my way back.

When events overwhelm you it is astonishing that time does not stand still. But it doesn't; it goes on. Routines continue, little sign of your personal earthquake is sensed in the world around you. That was almost as hard to digest as the cause.

At the end of the June term I got on the Greyhound and went to Digby. Since Aunt Birdie was Mother's sister and knew little of my father's connections, she was barely aware of my loss. Her own nephew, Bill Collins, also my cousin, had been killed in 1943; he was a navigator in the RCAF. He was my mother's godson as well as her nephew and I had met him and his brother, John, when both visited New York briefly. His death had moved me; my mother's grief had startled me. I learned a lesson in loss then. But it was different with Mono. In my mind he was not just a war loss, he was a victim. His loss was a personal wound in my mind.

To her credit, Aunt Birdie was discreet with me. She let it pass, and the summer of my sixteenth birthday was particularly charming. Along with Mrs. Merkle and a few other dowagers, she organized a Sweet Sixteen party for me at the Smith Cove country club. Each of the girls was appointed an escort who came to the house, corsage in hand, and drove her the five or six miles to the clubhouse. There was a band, punch, and delicious little things to eat. There were chaperones. At midnight the world turned into a pumpkin and we all drove home, enchanted.

I tried to describe a Digby girlhood to a few friends in New York but they just stared. I was talking about another planet, another time sphere, nothing they had experienced. Yet, there it was—on the Bay of Fundy tucked into a quiet corner of a real life no one could even guess at in New York. I was blessed.

Returning to school for the eighth and last term, impatient to graduate, I cut classes as much as I could and still get away with it. The Village became my spiritual home. I felt comfortable in the narrow streets with names instead of numbers, with the Italian cafés, the movie houses that showed foreign films, the galleries that hung photographs as well as paintings and the congenial atmosphere I sensed in Washington Square Park, where I often sat on benches and did my homework. I didn't know anyone and seldom exchanged a word. But I kept my eye on Washington Square College, part of New York University, and decided that it would be my destination. It was a point of serendipity that it also offered an excellent course in journalism.

It had never entered my mind that I would not go to college. Everyone went to college. Even my mother had been to college, albeit somewhere obscure in Quebec. I had taken it for granted. When I mentioned it one day when the three of us were at home, I was absolutely astounded when, quite off-handedly, Mother said, "Oh, no. You'll have to get a job. That's why I wanted you to learn shorthand. You don't have to have a college education to be a secretary."

I stared at her. My father saw this and said mildly, "We can't afford college, darling. Anyway, you'll get married." I was sixteen.

I get angry easily and I cry easily, but I did neither. We stood in the middle of a sunny living room and I felt that I had been shot.

Shorthand was one of the courses I cut as often as possible. I vowed that I would never be a secretary, never. Biting off your nose to spite your face is a specialty of the very young. I excelled at it. Not only did I never learn steno, which is a handy skill, but I never learned to type properly, either. Once launched on a road of *my* way, I never strayed.

My father had gradually drifted into the corner he would spend the rest of his life in: expounding to me, his captive audience, on everything from Churchill's speeches to what he saw as Roosevelt's slouching off into dictatorship. What else was he doing with all his reelections? Although he admitted that there were still no signs of the President becoming a dictator yet, that his leadership was still democratic, he clung to parallels with Bolivar, who did become a dictator at the end of his career.

I knew that one of our most distinguished ancestors had been Bolivar's first general, his secretary and the first to back him in fighting against Spain. But when Bolivar voted himself President for life the Ancestor led an uprising in Colombia to unseat him. It failed but it broke the Liberator's health and he died not long after.

My father's fear of dictatorship was so engrained that he applied it to anyone who hung around too long. He even eyed Mayor La Guardia suspiciously.

My father's vision of the world was so blurred by the time of Mono's death that I was able to disengage myself from being at home without much effort. He never mentioned my increasing absence nor seemed to notice my restiveness at his monologues, which he took as conversation.

I went out in the evenings then, to the movies or to listen to records with Gloria downstairs or "hang out" at a drug store called Cardini's because that was the brand of ice cream it served, where a group of boys and girls took to settling in. The boys were mostly Jewish, an additional interdite. Everything fell apart at the same time.

I drifted into boys, along with a plunge into movies that soon evolved as films in our new vocabulary. Reading books like *Point Counter Point* and seeking out answers in the disarray of those tender Jewish boys who were on the edge of maturity, for they would be instantly drafted after graduating from high school. And, though they pretended to be eager to see action, they were terrified by everything from boot camp in places like Georgia to the invasion of Normandy.

They were all a couple of years older than me, but at that point everyone was a couple of years older than me. The war made the difference. They would go from being stringy lads of eighteen, no doubt still virgins, into privates in the army overnight.

I was desperately in love with one such boy, whom I think I terrified with my ill-digested talk of books and theory, of the place of dialogue in politics, of the poetry of T.S. Eliot and the quandaries of Aldous Huxley. My head was a basket of notions, of half knowledge, of words and colors. I loved books; I loved the people I met in them. Who could not love the people in John Steinbeck's *Cannery Row*?

Or the anguish of Tom Wolfe? Or the singularly American demons of Theodore Dreiser?

I was full to overflowing with colors and scents and did nothing but overwhelm my handsome Jewish boy, whose father was a butcher. He was my great love, my nervous passion, my reluctant *objet du désir*.

We wrote deep letters—at least, mine were deep, when he was drafted and sent to someplace which I imagined to be a swamp: Biloxi, Mississippi.

He eventually confessed that he had met a girl and thought we should stop writing and that he would be sent overseas soon anyway. I wrote back that I agreed but what was her name? He answered that her name was Carrie May, that Biloxi was awful, and that he was coming home on leave and maybe we could have a coke at Cardini's. He was barely nineteen.

He was my big broken heart. At that age everyone harbors a big broken heart. Mine was a boy whom I look back on tenderly. I hope he does the same for me.

I already had a long string of after-school jobs. The first had been in Gimbels department store where I addressed envelopes for 25 cents an hour, three hours a day, five on Saturday. I was rich. When Gimbels bored me, I switched to Arnold Constable on 42nd Street opposite the library, a bit further upmarket. There were a dozen large department stores in New York, I must have worked in half of them. The advantage was to receive a discount card, good for a year, allowing a 20% discount on all purchases. I was in heaven.

Eventually I rose to being a telephone operator whereupon I was generally fired within the month for cutting off calls. One hapless lawyer I worked for was courting a well-known operatic diva and I constantly cut him off. He charged out of his office one day and screamed, "You're fired," throwing a handful of bills at me and pointing to the door. He was a small man, red in the face, and I had a terrible urge to laugh. I think he would have smacked me but lawyers are lawyers. The diva's announcement of her engagement to another man made a page-long story in *The Daily News* some months later. I felt guilty, a little.

Chapter 4

I did go to Washington Square College, but through the back door. Night school. I went downtown to register and found myself in a bleak room waiting to talk to a harried-looking woman at a crowded desk who barely glanced at me when I sat down. She pulled out a new folder from a stack, took a pen and began to write my name on the top corner, spelling it Desoto. I hesitated but went ahead. "It is in two words," I said timidly.

She lifted her head slowly and gave me a long displeased look. "Ah, so?"

Then she went back to the papers adding, "You would be better off studying English Literature. Journalism is something you learn by doing it. Get a job as a copy girl, you will learn journalism. But with English literature you will at least know how you should write."

The woman had a German accent and her harshness toward a half-grown girl making a career choice on her own still chills me all these years later.

I remember clearly that she kept looking at her watch. She suggested a couple of courses, most of them given at Commerce, the faculty next door. When I pointed this out, she assured me that the courses were better for freshmen, that if I lasted through six years of night school—which she seemed to consider remote—I could work out the credits with Washington Square. I remember leaving her cubicle dazed, confused. I felt that I had just handed over the rest of my life to a diffident woman who doubted even the concept of tomorrow.

I signed for four courses. The first began at five p.m., the last at eight. The courses stretched over five days, Monday through Friday. I made out a check for $100, and I felt like a giant.

It never crossed my mind that working at an eight-hour a day job, which I didn't have yet, and attending classes another four hours might be something of a long day for a sixteen-year-old. Nor did my parents when I told them that evening. They smiled and said something encouraging like, "How nice, dear." I moved into the world of adults with precious little outside interest.

Jobs were easy to find in 1945. I had had a dozen by then, not only at the major department stores where I stayed long enough to qualify for the discount cards, but others as well. I worked for The Book Find Club, George Braziller's left-leaning publishing house where my colleagues made me join the Union. I had little practice with politics beyond my father's theories and was of two minds about joining the office workers' union. It didn't please me to be considered an office worker, for starters, and it cost money for another. The salary was $25 a week, the union dues took a sizable snip. But I joined and was suddenly uplifted: it was quite a giant step to belong to a union. I had admired picketers' courage, though knowing next to nothing about the labor movement itself. Now it pleased me to be in a legitimate position to contest authority. Yes, I liked that.

Then came United Press. Someone told me they needed a copy girl. I made my way to the Daily News Building on 42nd Street off Third Avenue feeling a tremor of anticipation. It is a handsome structure, by now a landmark, housing not only the *Daily News*, a tabloid I detested even then, but also the famed Scripps Howard News Agency and probably a clutch of other publications, as well.

I had read the books by the great reporters of the war years and the pre-war years as well. Vincent Sheehan, who was called Jimmy to those who knew him and I felt I was one of them if only because of the ardor with which I read his book, *Personal History*, was one. William Shirer, Ernie Pyle, Howard K. Smith—these monuments of integrity and courage all entered here. That building held the hallowed halls of our history, the one in the making, the one I wanted a part in living.

I went up to the Foreign Desk and was interviewed by a gentle, cordial man called Paul Smith who must have noticed my nervous eagerness and was indulgent with me. After a few minutes of conversation he told me that as far as he was concerned, I seemed to fit the bill. He took me over to meet the man with the final say, a huge blond whale of a man who filled his desk rather than sat at it. His name was Gail Wallace. They called him Moose and he terrified me on sight. He had a low voice, an air of massive power, he had no place in my fantasy of the press. But he mumbled his agreement with Smith's choice.

Newspapers of today have nothing to do with the age of the typewriter and teletype machine, which is where the job and its title "Copy Boy" (or girl) originated. The UP newsroom was fast, noisy, the air tinted a yellowish hue because the paper coming out of the machines was yellow and so, apparently, was cigarette smoke. There were calls of "Copy!" here and there when the people at the desk had a finished story to be delivered to the copy desk. There was a buzz and a peppery ballet of quick movement across the crowded space. It took no time to get used to the noise and cigarette smoke; the atmosphere was instantly exhilarating to me. More than that, I was where I had dreamed of being. Paul Smith sensed this and was particularly protective of me, while never hesitating to tell me to get a move on whenever I was distracted from doing what I was supposed to do and was reading the copy instead.

UP fanned the magic I saw in world affairs and gave flesh to the actors I imagined to be major players. I venerated the role of the press. These newsmen were the guarantors of their age, I imagined. Of course, they were. Some of them, in any case. I met a few legends and almost choked with emotion when I first saw Robert St. John. I had read his "Land of the Silent People," a superb account of his experience in Yugoslavia just as war broke out. Cautiously, I asked Paul Smith if I could ask St. John to sign my copy of his book. Smith laughed good-naturedly and said, "Sure, why not. He'll be pleased to know he sold a copy." Then he suggested I join them for a drink in Tim Costello's.

Tim Costello's? I nearly fainted. I would have to cut a class if I went, but sitting with Smith and St. John at that fabled newspaperman's bar was like an invitation to heaven. I went with them, barely breathing. Neither pretended to notice.

Tall, well built, wearing a small beard, St. John instantly put me at my ease. He told stories, exchanged tales with Smith for my benefit, but he also asked me questions and encouraged me to talk. I think back with gratitude on their tender indulgence.

NYU and its classes in Journalism, Current Events, American History and Creative Writing was another kind of passage, though different from United Press. On the first day of classes I met the beautiful girl who was to be my closest friend for the rest of my life, Ann Wallach.

She sat next to me in Journalism under the tutelage of a Mrs. Beatty, who had worked at UP in the past and who knew everyone I worked for. The classroom was large, shabby, high-ceilinged, and overcrowded. It was early February, 1945. Returning soldiers were flooding the education system, thanks to the GI Bill. If I was sixteen everyone in the night school class seemed to be 35, battle scarred and short of sleep. Ann, at twenty, was the closest to my age.

Ann was tall, slender, beautiful, but she was different from other tall, lanky brunettes. Huge dark eyes, a quick smile and her long hair worn in braids over her head, or in a chignon, made her something special. She was arresting. I liked her instantly but was afraid she would dismiss me because I was chatty and overeager and knew it. She didn't mind. Her sister, Lorraine, was exactly my age and was away at Goddard College. Ann, however, was doing her degree at night school while working at a responsible job at NAM, the National Association of Manufacturers. She was much more mature than I, amazingly well read. She had read Faulkner and enjoyed him, which impressed me indelibly. She lived in Brooklyn with her father—whom I grew very fond of—who was a pharmacist, a Grand Street Boy, a race-track fan and a widower since Ann was eleven. Ann's mother had died in her sleep one night and no one had noticed it 'til the afternoon. When she told me that I had goose pimples, I remember a shudder. I must have stared at her. She frowned a little and said, "I don't unusually tell people that." We sat side by side in that unloving classroom and became friends for life.

Not long into my first term on a chilly April night I turned the corner into Greene Street and saw a small group huddled around a car. As I approached, a girl turned to me, pale: "President Roosevelt is dead," she said. Tears were running down her face. I was dumbfounded. President Roosevelt? He couldn't possibly be dead; the war wasn't over.

I recall standing totally still feeling like a pillar of ice, not breathing, frightened. I couldn't remember the world without President Roosevelt's gracious voice, without the wisdom of his words on the radio. My heart pounded. Like most Americans at that moment, I felt orphaned and afraid.

The small group around the car radio listened to the reporter's voice. Their comments were hushed, as though to avoid intrusiveness. Only the girl who had spoken to me first used a normal voice. "Truman is a Southern Cracker," she said. "Everything is going to change. We're going to be all alone now." It was only then that I realized she was black.

I had never heard the word cracker and it distracted me, though I caught its meaning easily enough.

He was a new vice president, this Harry Truman. The other one, Henry Wallace, was more familiar, the handsome corn farmer of Roosevelt's third term. All I knew about Harry Truman was that he played the Missouri Waltz on the piano and used to sell neckties. For some reason, that made everyone laugh.

Standing there in the chill damp night, forgetting to rush to my classroom, I realized that I wasn't sure I knew where the South actually began. Missouri spoke to me of railroads and cattle, not slaves. Then I became indignant. President Roosevelt would not have chosen a cracker for a running mate! I turned toward the building with my heart in mourning but ready to defend Truman as a tribute to the late masterful president's judgment. "He can't be a cracker," I told the older girl. "President Roosevelt would not have allowed it."

Only one President and only one Mayor. Mayor La Guardia had been a fixture of my entire childhood. The stability of my kingdom was rock-like in its imagery. One God, one Church, one President, one Mayor. I shouldn't have had a doubt in the world.

The loss of the President was felt by everyone. My father, who had harbored suspicions of his motives in his third and fourth terms, was now contrite, a little embarrassed. Roosevelt was—had always been—a great statesman, a majestic leader, my father allowed. He leaned on the word majestic, should I not catch the measure of its meaning. Majesty was not necessarily a quality in a Democratic president. Of course, these times had been trying—the Great Depression, the War—not easy years. My father had voted Wilkie. In this hour of national mourning he looked a little pained. Well, he might.

My mother had worn a Wilkie button in the recent elections. I remember my friend Hymie Dolinsky, an intense boy I often took the subway with, saying to me, "Why does your mother wear a Wilkie button?" As though it wasn't enough that she had bright orange hair and a haughty look.

"Because she's a Republican."

Aghast, Hymie said, "Why is she a Republican?"

"Because she thinks she should be rich," I answered and wished we could talk about anti-fascism and Howard Fast, whose books he had lent me, and not my mother's notion of class structure.

Vance Packard, who was later to write an important book in the post-war scene, taught the current affairs class I was scheduled for on the day President Roosevelt died. When I entered the classroom it was almost full yet there wasn't a murmur. He nodded as I took a seat, nodded to the two or three other students who followed me. After a time he said. "This is an exercise in national loss few of us here will have had any experience with. If anyone has anything to say, I'd be glad to hear it. Otherwise, it might be wise to postpone the class till next time."

There was a thoughtful silence broken by a tall ex-GI called Brill who got to his feet and said "I would prefer to deal with this on my own. And I think a lot of other people feel the same." There were murmurs of assent.

Packard nodded his head thoughtfully. He stood up and said solemnly. "There is nothing more to say."

I remember feeling abandoned. There was everything to be said. I would have liked the comfort of their numbers, of their thoughts. I was too young to understand the scope of national disarray in that bleak moment of abandonment.

The UP office was chaotic the next morning, I remember. It remained so for days after. It was a cold spring. The colors of the city seemed muted, dimmed. We saw the funeral procession in the newsreels at the local movies, we followed it on the radio, step by step 'til we finally laid him to rest, that great man who had seemed so utterly present in our world on the banks of the Hudson.

New friends arrived with the winding down of the war, new doors opened. Ann took me to the cinematheque at the Museum of Modern Art for readings and lectures that stunned me. I heard Erika Mann speak of pre-war Germany and her illustrious father. The theater was small and intimate, and everyone in it looked as though Thomas Mann's work was as familiar as Dick Tracy. I was as impressed by the audience as I was by the swashbuckling Miss Mann.

I was just as taken with Ann, who seemed quite at ease in the basement of the Museum of Modern Art. Not long after, she asked if I would like to go again this time to hear Edith Sitwell. She told me about the Sitwell family, their extravagant names, lifestyles and literary eminence. I went with pleasure. The gnome-like English lady looked like a leprechaun, sounded like a man and, to me, was undecipherable, though I couldn't take my eyes off her. English accents were not totally unknown in our house, but this great lady came from an island of her own. I was captivated.

Ann appeared to me like a fountain of multicolored wisdom, a new and heady world of live letters, with a cast including the extravagantly garbed figure of Edith Sitwell trotting up to a small stage and accepting devoted ovations.

I knew nooks and crannies of the city which I introduced her to, including gaping into the window of Mc Sorley's wonderful saloon near the Bowery where women were not admitted, like the Fulton fish market or the winsome house where Edgar Allen Poe had lived in Van Cortlandt Park, which Ann hadn't known about. We exchanged treasures and I brought her into my new universe, delighted to share it.

It was a happy way to wriggle through the teen years; it seem to go in chapters, like a novel. Chapter 2 closed with a bang in June when The Moose, my unpleasant and unloved boss on the Foreign Desk at UP called me as I was rushing from one side of the newsroom to the other with a handful of dispatches.

"Hey, stupid," he called, loud enough for everyone to hear. Paul Smith looked up over his glasses, not at me but at him. I stood still, midway between one desk and another. I was afraid I would cry.

"Don't call me stupid," I said, quietly.

"You're fired," he said and turned back to the papers he had been reading. Paul Smith let out a sigh, as did a woman editor whose name I forget but who was reportedly having an affair with him—an unimaginable prospect—whose desk was adjacent to Smith's.

"Carrajo!" I heard from over to my left where the Latin America desk was and where I had made great friends with the anti-Peronista newsmen who manned it. It is one of the few words I knew in Spanish and it sounds as harsh as it means.

I hadn't been the fastest copy girl in the west, that was probably true but I was certainly the happiest. I had made friends with most of the newsmen, showed my interest in the events they covered in the world as it was unfolding. They enjoyed my enthusiasm, my blatant hero worship, my endless questions, and they were sorry to see me humiliated. I knew that Gail Wallace had worked in South America for some years as bureau chief and had got used to treating those under him as cattle. Paul Smith, who was second in command, often put him in his place with a chill look. The other newsmen took his verbal abuse without a word. No one liked him, all were wary of him, but I hadn't seen him coming. I was crushed, but I learned a lesson. The power wielded by a boss was infinite and fairness seldom entered into wielding it. A boss could change your life. I should have known that: a boss had totally changed my father's.

It was June. I had a little money saved. I went to Digby. I spent my seventeenth birthday surrounded by my summer friends, in the cottony comfort of my alternative life.

History was being made around us. We celebrated V-J Day with a lobster boil on the stony sand of the Bay of Fundy. The war was over!

If anyone was troubled that August day by the nature of the atomic bombs over Japan, I don't remember it. Digby had lost enough boys—I had lost two cousins—to have any second thoughts about the Japanese. It is shameful to say it, but no one I knew was anything but relieved that they finally surrendered.

There was much to be learned on the subject. But not then. The war was over. It was all finished. We had beaten the evil that had gnawed at our world. We had come close enough to touch ignominy when they opened the gates of Auschwitz.

That winter in New York I went through a couple of dreary jobs, but I took my college courses seriously. I learned to love the reference room of the Public Library. It had the grandeur of a palace, the warmth of a haven; it was a pleasure to learn its rules and consult its riches.

New friends took on vital roles during this dicey period of adolescence, not all of them to last through adult years. Bobby Coufos, a bright boy from the neighborhood, became an instant buddy. We were both enamored of the theater, of the city, of the great world out there tantalizingly at our fingertips. This is an age which ideally one shares with a steady boyfriend. I didn't have one. Bobby's complicity was uncomplicated, uncompetitive. There was never a glimmer of physical attraction between us but there was everything else. We both wanted to *go* … to go everywhere … and to go quickly. We were like twins for a while, eager, reassured by the presence of the other. We went to the theater together, we ferreted out art movie houses; Bobby joined Ann with me at the little theaters around the Village, the lectures that stirred the brand new post-war air of New York. I didn't actually know that he was homosexual. I'm not even sure he was convinced of it himself. It didn't matter.

Bobby was the youngest of a family of five. He had three sisters and a brother, George. Their father was Greek and their American mother was half-Indian. If my parents were an odd couple, his were unimaginable. Mr. Coufos was a slightly forbidding man who spoke with a strong accent while his wife was a small, squat motherly woman with a distinctly Indian face, though of fair complexion. She bubbled hospitality and liked me immediately. Her husband owned a flourishing grocery store and imported olive oil. He was a man of substance and was frequently away from home. Mrs. Coufos, however, rarely left the apartment. The two older sisters were married—one to a doctor in Connecticut, the other to a broker in New York—and the third, Dottie, was slightly retarded and much loved. George was a struggling actor in Hollywood. All had high cheekbones, Greek noses, and were handsome. They were brought up as Episcopalians and were the only Greeks I ever came across who did not seek out other Greeks and, more astonishing still, turned their backs on the Orthodox Church.

For whatever reasons both Bobby and I were "outsiders" and we got along perfectly. It took years for me to understand that he was homosexual. It finally became evident when I came back from Europe at Christmastime of 1949—after we had both met the men of our lives. We never discussed it, even then. We had needed each other at a crucial moment in each other's lives and that was bond enough. I bless him still for that.

In the spring of 1946 I got a phone call from the Agence France-Presse bureau in New York asking me if I would be interested in a job as copy girl. Someone from UP had recommended me. My heart flipped. I had applied for jobs at all the newspapers in New York, including the *Hobo News*, but with no luck. Whatever the Agence France-Presse was, I would be delighted to go. It never occurred to me that I might not learn a hell of a lot amid a language I didn't know a single word of.

But it wasn't like that. I learned everything.

The office was on 42nd Street on the corner of 5th Avenue, just opposite my beloved Library. The Commodore Hotel, where my mother worked, was a five-minute walk down to Lexington. The hours I worked—from 9 to 3, coincided every other week with hers. I often met her at the Commodore's Grand Central Station exit and we went shopping together or had an oyster stew at the Oyster Bar before going home. The spring had finally settled in and we were uncommonly close.

Working at AFP was, in my eyes, a privilege. All of the romanticism I grew up with surrounding Occupied France and the valiant Resistance seemed personified by the people in that bureau. In my mind I saw them all as war heroes. The bureau chief, André Rabache and his second, Jean Lagrange, were well-known figures in press circles. Rabache, who spoke English like an Englishman, had covered the Nuremberg trials; Jean Lagrange had covered the Spanish Civil War.

The office was also used by other French journalists in New York. It was there that I met Lionel Durant, the Haitian-born newsman who later worked for *Newsweek* in Paris and who was a much-loved figure. These were real foreign correspondents, some of them even looked it, like Robert Villers who was young, fair and dashing. And there was a stunning girl almost as young as I who would eventually marry him, Aimée Lemercier. It pleases me no end to say that we have remained friends since she turned up in that office, making me understand what they mean by French chic. I was in heaven.

Those months of 1946 are muddled in my mind. There were French lessons with a Mrs. Peck, a charming French born woman who had a son she promptly introduced me to, Tommy Peck. And her fey sister had an even more charming son called Larry Swinburne, a great nephew of the poet. These were ladies of *une certaine société*, as one of their friends put it. For whatever reason, they became interested in me.

Tom and Larry were Princeton freshmen. They invited me to football weekends at Princeton, to the Yale game in New Haven. Tommy, mostly, picked me up at home and drove downtown for dances, sometimes formals: long dress, gardenia in a box, black tie. He was tall, slender, excellent company. He didn't interest me in the least physically but he made little effort to try. I think he probably felt my distance but didn't mind. We got on well together, somewhat mysteriously.

I owe him a comfortable venture into the sort of privilege I so noisily rejected. That was something; unlike Hymie Dolinsy, I knew what I was talking about.

The real world was encroaching seriously into my life, which I welcomed, but when summer struck New York I was a little unprepared for a heat wave without Nova Scotia. Somehow I wrangled my way into a three week vacation. It seemed too soon for me to give up my "other" world. It was too soon to stop being what I had been all along.

I took the bus, stayed again with my loving "little aunties" in St. John and then took the Princess Helena to Digby. I was just in time for the wedding of one of my friends to the young officer from Ontario whom we all met in 1944 for the first time. Claire Merkel was already married to another young officer from somewhere remote, in Alberta I think. The three or four years that separated us now made a serious difference. I was eighteen that August; they were already anchored in adulthood at 21 or 22.

I knew that I envied them their commitment, the love I saw in the eyes of their new husbands. Though I ached to have someone look at me like that, I couldn't imagine settling down as though life was all over.

There was something languid in those three weeks. I didn't go to dances as I used to. I stayed in the garden, reading. We went to the Lake for a few days, but the Wrights next door were not there and there was a sort of fading calm over the water, as though autumn was claiming the year too soon. There was a real or imagined sniff of nostalgia where nostalgia had never been.

Then Uncle Harold fell ill. He had trod on a rusty nail and infected his foot, but he vehemently refused to see a doctor. Birdie was upset, confused. For two days she bowed to his angry wishes and nervously sent me into town to fetch tubes of an unguent he insisted would heal the wound.

Harold had a hat full of nutty ideas, including a blanket rejection of doctors which everyone put down to his father's running off to serve God. He mixed his own mouthwash, cough syrups, indigestion elixirs. He made his own sarsaparilla, too. I never knew where he had learned these recipes but he was full of odd lore. It wasn't altogether out of character for him to refuse to see a doctor.

While in town, I went down to the ship's office to buy a ticket for the St. John's boat. Getting back to the house, I was struck by the strong stench of rotting matter. The day before I had noticed something similar, but Birdie had sprayed the upstairs floor and I didn't pursue the question. Now, however, I was frightened.

"If you don't call the doctor, I will," I told her, a little surprised at my own authority. She nodded and went to the phone. I saw how old she looked and how threatening this situation was going to be. I was terrified that Harold would die, that their pleasant quiet lives would be destroyed.

The doctor came, sent for an ambulance to carry Harold just across the road to the hospital. He was diagnosed with gangrene, with complications caused by diabetes. No one had known he was diabetic. It was hardly a surprise, considering his diet, but I was shocked that no one had ever thought to check on his health because of the way he ate.

I had to leave. It was horrible to leave like that. Harold's sister, Zena, was on her way from Montreal, however. Birdie would not be alone for long.

We embraced, my generous aunt and I, and I remember the sting of the knowledge that this was the end of my childhood. Right there, on the sidewalk in front of her lovely white house with banks of hydrangeas as big as melons on the lawn.

Within days Uncle Harold was taken to Halifax and his leg was amputated. He survived the operation, returned to Digby, but they were forced to sell the house on the hill with the woods and pond and the trees I tried to climb, awkwardly like the city child I was. They bought a three-bedroom, one-story house on Queen Street where he was able to avoid stairs. It was light and airy and Birdie's early American furniture looked splendid, my mother assured me.

But my father told me that Harold was a ghost. He hated his disability and couldn't get used to his loss of independence. He had been driving a car since the age of fourteen, had been a traveling salesman for as long as he could remember. Sitting on a porch passing the time of day with his neighbors was something in the order of hell for him.

On the boat going home I admitted to myself that summers in Digby were at an end. I fell back on Chekov's line: "I am in mourning for my life." But I cannot explain why I never returned to Digby again.

This is the point when I must explain something that made all the difference to what happened next. At both job interviews I was asked if I knew any Spanish, in view of my name. Both times I fudged a little.

"Know any Spanish? You'll have to work on the Latin American desk so it would help if you could read a little," Paul Smith had asked.

I was a little surprised but I answered, "Oh yes, I can read a little." He didn't push it any further and it wasn't quite untrue. I could read a little—possibly by osmosis because there were always Spanish books around the house and I had taken Spanish briefly in school. But I had a good accent and whatever I parroted sounded authentic, so the Latin Americans on the desk actually thought I knew more Spanish than I did.

At AFP the interest was sharper and I didn't try to bluff. I told Jean Lagrange, who spoke fluent Spanish, that my father was Colombian, that the language was familiar, that I frequently met with uncles from Bogota. I was familiar with South American ways. He perked up at that.

As it happened, Jorge Soto del Corral, my father's first cousin, was Minister of Foreign Affairs at the time. Moreover, he had been ambassador to France just before World War II, had negotiated the evacuation of Spanish refugees to Colombia, and was a much-respected professor of Constitutional Law. He was still in his mid-forties and was considered one of the most outstanding liberal voices in Latin America. Jorge was just then named Ambassador to the nascent United Nations. The chief of the delegation was Alfonso Lopez, the crusading former president, a figure comparable to FDR in the United States. He was a close friend of the family and their political mentor. My uncle Alberto had written many long articles on the man and the statesman in El Timepo, Bogota's leading paper.

No wonder Jean Lagrange had a glint in his eye when he hired me and sent me off to the Lake Success headquarters of the United Nations.

Lake Success was the temporary headquarters outside Great Neck on Long Island where the United Nations would begin to change the world as of 1946-7. There had been early meetings held at Hunter College in the Bronx, but none of the newspapers or wire services had opened bureaus there. Correspondents just shuttled back and forth. Lake Success, however, was over an hour's ride on the Long Island Railroad or by bottle-necked road. The temporary headquarters were geared to last however long it would take to build a UN building in Manhattan. At the same time, journalists accredited to United Nations did not necessarily have to have visas for the US. United Nations benefitted from extra-territoriality. That became a vital issue almost immediately.

AFP was pushing its Latin American coverage, a juicy market. All the other agencies were doing the same. Competition among news purveyors can be as sharp as in any other trade. A little influence on the ground is not to be disregarded.

I knew nothing whatsoever of such matters. Though brought up on the lore of my father's illustrious kin, I didn't take the question any more seriously than that. They were a long way from Washington Heights, weren't they? As it happened, they were a lot closer than I'd ever imagined.

When the UN bureau was opened, Lagrange asked me if I would like to work there, rather than in the 42nd Street office. I was thunderstruck! Imagine being right there while history was being made. Imagine sitting in on the creation of world government? I could barely breathe, I was so thrilled.

That brought us up to the February term of 1947. My erratic college courses were in the balance. It was hard enough to juggle a work day in Manhattan plus four subjects requiring reading and written reports. I couldn't do it from far out on Long Island.

Ann and I talked the situation over and, without much hesitation, she persuaded me that I could easily take a break. Being a copy girl was not the greatest job in the world but being a copy girl at the UN just as it opens its doors was an invitation that could not be refused. Whatever wisdom the amiable Vance Packard might impart, it would weigh little next to the creation of a world body with me in attendance. I needed Ann's counsel and I knew she was right.

At home, no one noticed that I didn't sign up for more classes. Clearly, no one was interested in educating me.

My father, when I told him about being sent to Lake Success, raised an eyebrow. Then he said he would arrange for me to meet Jorge with him beforehand. I had met the eldest of the Soto del Corrals, don Luis, frequently, because he was the head of stock brokerage as well as the Banco de Bogota and often had business in the city. He always saw my father.

The year before I had met Luis' daughter, Isabel, who was roughly my age. We had sat around a tea table at the Waldorf eyeing each other uncomfortably. She invited me to her coming out ball, an invitation I would have liked to refuse but which a glacial glance from my father had made me accept. She was in a Latin American Debutante Ball with all the pomp and puffiness I deplored, to the music of Gary Davis's father's society orchestra, for good measure.

Whoever made the arrangements appointed a well-known tennis player as my escort to whom I was passably obnoxious especially after he said jauntily, when he came to fetch me bearing an orchid, "I have never been in The Bronx before."

I hissed out, "This is not The Bronx," as icily as I could, and the poor chap spent the rest of the evening trying to make up for it.

Adolescent pride, when pricked, is seldom forgiving.

So much for my South American connections, I had thought at the time, determined to have nothing more to do with dumb cousins and blundering athletes. But Jorge was something else.

A small, fair, froggish looking man, he had humor, curiosity, interest in this abrasive young cousin who didn't speak a word of Spanish but who didn't hesitate to voice her opinions on Peron, the *Apristas* in Peru, or the role of oil in Mexico. He seemed very startled by me. I didn't tell him that I had read all the dispatches I ferried around the newsroom in UP and had talked frequently to the Argentines on the Latino desk. The result was that I knew a little bit about a lot of things; it has turned out to be a lifelong tendency. And it was a way of making up for my lack of a formal education.

Jorge evolved as a kind but stern mentor. He made it clear that there was a hierarchy to be observed and boundaries to be respected. I was indeed his cousin's daughter, but I was a long way removed from Bogota. And he knew what a copy girl was. Diplomacy has its codes, he taught. Caution is its first component. I am still grateful to him, but I have never been the best of pupils, particularly about caution.

The first thing to say about Lake Success is that it was a wide sprawling disaffected factory that had made gyroscopes during the war. The fact that it was mostly one-storied was its first good fortune. You saw everyone, no matter how august the person, because there were no corners. No elevators, no executive floors, no place to hide.

If only the building Philip Johnson built in New York had been ranch style, the Cold War might have been considerably warmer and a lot shorter.

There was only one parking lot and it was accessible through one exit, so ambassadors waited alongside file clerks while cars were being brought up.

The cafeteria served everyone who wanted a cup of coffee or boeuf bourguignon. Everyone. But the delegates in the dining room did not. Nor should it have. But delegates often needed a little sustenance in the middle of the afternoon or at ten o'clock at night when the sessions seemed endless and the word democracy was served up there in the cafeteria along with donuts or cheese Danish.

Lake Success had artificial light, was far from the city—it was even far from Great Neck. But it was the most auspicious of starting blocks for an exercise in peace on Earth. I learned to love it despite the hours of sleep I missed in getting there and back, not to mention the chronic lack of sun and eyestrain. Because I saw it as a last chance, I believed in its mission.

While doing a modern history course I delved into the League of Nations and saw its frailties, the inbuilt brakes that would shortly cripple it. United Nations had a better start. Its charter was as steel-lined as the Bill of Rights. It had to work. It would work. Men of good will wanted it to work and, stunned by the atom bomb, it was time for men of good will to take command. So said the eighteen-year-old pundit.

In any case, the alternative was inconceivable. Tommy Peck and Larry Swinbourne and I had talked this over at those Princeton weekends. There had to be world government, we all agreed, to ensure the very existence of the world after the bomb. We, the United States, had an obligation to history, as a result of the decision to use it, to lead the movement toward peace under these new circumstances. Otherwise the US was in danger of becoming a rogue state itself.

Moreover, the world had altered course in the wake of the war. The USSR and its ideology had to be reckoned with, had to be given space to rebuild itself after the heroic sacrifice of its men, its land, its resources to destroy fascism. There had to be equity toward the USSR. There had to be a new understanding of the post-war world in the United States where isolationism, mindless anticommunism, ignorance and suspicion of the rest of the world was beginning to be a concern.

We were a country built on checks and balances. There has to be an intelligence community in the United States because there is one everywhere else. Before the war, a "spy agency" was thought to be ungentlemanly, so the US relied on British intelligence, except for small outfits in the US Navy and US Army.

That could no longer be possible. The wartime OSS should be turned into a free, independent agency that would have rigid lines of operation and conduct. It was a decision of honorable men determined to live in the world as it was, serving no interest but the national interest. It had to be above parties, politicians, or vested interests. It was beyond presidential manipulation. It would work for the same goals and aims as the United Nations. We were among honorable men.

That is the way I walked into Lake Success. Those are the ideals I nurtured. Through the decades, as disgraces followed each other in American policy, I often thought of that innocent girl I was, talking daydreams with the likes of Larry Swinburne and Tommy Peck, and I wonder how they accommodated themselves to the real world we all fell heir to, rather than the one we tried to create.

But that was later. And entering into Lake Success as it began was to be something far different.

Chapter 5

This is not the place for a chronology of the United Nations' first year nor am I a historian. In passing, however, it might be noticed that the rest of its career was traced out in 1947. All its failings were determined then. The Marshall Plan remained a purely American venture, Israel was created without a net.

The former solidified the Cold War, the latter entrenched permanent instability. The remarkably generous Marshall Plan, if it were to have remained unassailable above national interests, should have been channeled through the new world body. The world that might have harbored such generosity was not the world that emerged from the ashes of WWII, much as idealistic children like myself would have liked to believe. Generosity is not the same as altruism.

Of course the Marshall Plan came with strings. That is what they mean by *Realpolitik*. It could break your heart.

In 1947 the Holocaust was still an open wound. The creation of Israel was no longer just an option, it had become a foregone conclusion. There had to be a Jewish state; there was no other sensible place to put it but Israel.

Damn the consequences.

I don't pretend I had the kind of wisdom to have thought along those lines at the time. Indeed, when people like newsman Ted Berkman did say precisely that, I was somewhat shocked. His caution remained at the back of my mind, however, while I harbored hearty enthusiasm for the Zionist cause.

The Jewish Agency was represented by an attractive delegation. People like Moshe Sharett, charismatic leaders of a daring cause, fired my admiration. He, too, talked about the rocky future but he talked with humor and humanity and that was as far as I looked. Ted said to him "What are you going to do about the Palestinians? Put them in camps, create a new homeless uprooted people?"

Sharett answered slowly, "We will find a way."

The atmosphere in Lake Success was charged with partisan policies; it was electric. The working agendas were all heavy with consequence. One issue was the status of Franco Spain, its election to membership.

The delegation of the Republic in exile was made up of admirable men who had lost that singular war, Hitler's unchallenged tryout in Spain. They were about to lose the peace. I recall Sir Hartley Shawcross, an elegant Laborite head of the British delegation, who wore a handkerchief stuck in his sleeve, to my cousin Jorge's disdain, clamor that British children could no longer be deprived of oranges, as they had been through the Second World War because of a conscience-salving embargo on a distasteful government that was firmly in power.

So much for noble causes. I remember buying a copy of Arturo Barea's excellent book, *The Forging Of A Rebel*, for Jorge Soto after Colombia voted against Spain's admission to the UN at that time. Jorge was amused principally because I gave him the English translation but also for the partisanship I showed.

There are moments when chance comes galloping into one's life and changes its course smoothly, without a sound.

The woman who was the Press Accreditations Officer with several years' practice in international organizations to draw on decided she wanted to take on a temporary conference, to be held in Cuba at the same time as the General Assembly in Flushing Meadows, outside New York City. Flushing Meadows was a leftover of the World's Fair of 1939.

Mary Ronay was an odd, somewhat sour person who did her job capably but with no real enthusiasm. She mixed with the others in that Press Room with more of a frown than a smile and was far more attracted to the prospect of dark young men on Havana beaches than she was to the notion of being a spectator to history in the making. She cleared it with the Press Division personnel and then came to me and asked me if I would like to take her place during the General Assembly, and a little while after while she went to Cuba.

The salary was enormous, I thought, but the position was enormous. I would be the person to accredit, or not, the journalists who presented themselves for entry into the UN General Assembly sessions. It was a job that I found so beyond my sphere of copy girl that I never dreamed it would be offered to me. I remember doing my best to not show my surprise, probably in vain, and then, coloring slightly, I accepted. I felt about ten feet tall.

There was a nucleus of young reporters in the press section which made up a small circle of its own. There was John Kenton, who later was the best man at our wedding, Ann Burke who was to become Ann Rosenthal when she married Abe Rosenthal—who even then was visibly on his way to becoming something of a star turn in reporting UN proceedings and in doing brilliant incisive interviews with controversial personalities such as Andrei Gromyko.

The Press Section which included the Press Bar was the heart of the affair. It was cozier than the Delegates Lounge, more relaxed. Off the record was the operative mode. One could see: Mrs. Roosevelt in a corner reading the day's newspaper; Wellington Koo, of the China dynasty, doing *The Times* crossword puzzle; or a pair of South American delegates plotting vote strategy on their own. There was a conviviality about the Press Bar, an air of the marketplace about it which made it instantly attractive. During the General Assembly, the press sections of both Lake Success and Flushing Meadows were the cobblestones of history in the making.

When I had time, I said prayers of thanks to the ghosts of my private pantheon, such as Ernie Pyle, for being able to watch reporting history being made and being a part of the making of it. I celebrated my nineteenth birthday in the Press Bar at Lake Success with a champagne glass of Ginger Ale because alcohol went to my head.

A steady procession of the heroes of my life streamed through the Press Accreditation Office. Edward R. Murrow and William Shirer actually walked in together. I had become used to the great and the mighty, at least on the outside, but inside I was still astounded at having a coffee with Mrs. Roosevelt or hearing Jan Masaryk, the prime minister of Czechoslovakia and son of the country's founder, call me the Press Czarina.

A disconcertingly informal person, Ambassador Masaryk had offered me a lift into the city one rainy night. He was a handsome yet touching figure. One sensed the discomfort of being the son of a great name behind the bluff, charming exterior. I knew little about him then, aside from what everyone knew. I didn't know that he was involved in a long-time relationship with author Marcia Davenport or anything else, for that matter, about his private life. On the first ride back to the city with him the car drew up for a red light next to one of the new, luxurious art cinemas on the East Side. He looked out the window and after a second, said, "Would you like to see a movie? I would love to see that."

I was startled. The movie in question was Madonna of the Seven Moons, I think with Stewart Granger. Before I could say much of anything, he was giving instructions to the driver in Czech, who eased the car closer to the curb and we were out on the sidewalk. "I won't tell anyone if you don't tell anyone," he said laughing in complicity. And we went to the movies.

Jan Masaryk was a tender tragic figure walking a tight rope in 1947. The Czech Communist Party, a particularly thuggish lot, would usurp power in February 1948. Still Foreign Minister, Masaryk committed suicide by throwing himself out the window of his residence in Hradčany Castle. He hadn't been able to alter events but neither could he live with them. I was immensely privileged in having grazed his path.

India became independent in mid-August and Partition followed, bringing with it "unrest," which claimed a terrifying toll in lost lives.

Pakistanis suddenly appeared in the press section, something new on the world's stage. A curious woman called Marcelle Hitchmann turned up as the correspondent for the *Pakistan Times*. She was small, dark, intense and fascinating. Of Greek and Italian parentage, she was born in Egypt. She attended the Sorbonne just before the war, spent the war in Cairo and was part of a riveting group of European-Egyptians who were very much in evidence at Lake Success. They seemed to have come into the world speaking a half dozen languages with a marked accent that I gathered was peculiar to the Middle East. I became very friendly with Marcelle, who was by way of being a mentor without ever seeming to give lessons. She suggested books, films, exhibits, people. She was in her late 30s. Since I lived so far uptown she frequently offered me an alcove in her East 70s small flat which I accepted with relish.

Slowly, very slowly, I was moving on.

The 1947 General Assembly hall was a large auditorium accommodating the 52 national delegations, the accredited press and a restricted amount of the general public. Big though it was, it proved totally inadequate for the number of journalists who were accredited to cover it. They came from all over the world, from papers or agencies or radio and TV networks (though there were just a few of the latter in 1947), all demanding space and attention. I realized uncomfortably that I had serious power in my hands and was very nervous about it.

It didn't take long for bubbles to appear on the surface. I had delivered accreditation to Pierre Courtade, the editor of the French Communist newspaper *Humanité*. To enter the United States one had to declare not being now or ever been a member of the Communist Party. However, Communist parties were legal throughout the rest of the world and in power in a growing number of member countries. This singular Gordian knot was unraveled by the creation of a UN visa admitting the foreigner into the United States only as far as a twenty-mile radius of New York. Extraterritoriality. Courtade, an amusing and particularly handsome ideologue, was released from jail in a flurry of flashbulbs.

This was not a decision accepted by everyone. There were diehards in the woodwork who had been miffed by the sudden appearance of Reds on the Long Island Railroad, who engineered further arrests of foreign press people. One was an Indian journalist who had been around Lake Success for months with all his papers in order, or so he thought, who was summarily deported. He was back within a few weeks and began a saga-like law suit that went on for years against the State Department. He had eager pro bono lawyers, civil liberties lawyers eager to defend him and I think the whole affair amused him. He sent me a red sari apologizing for the trouble he had caused me.

But then there was Nikos Kyriazides, a Greek national, who worked for a left wing Cyprus newspaper. No one was amused by his case.

Cyprus was a British colony then, therefore it enjoyed a free press. Being a member of the Communist Party in Greece, however, was punishable by death. This was a conundrum typical of the times because there was no Communist Party in Greece, a fortress of right wing power then. The Communist Party was outlawed. Which is why the Greek journalist worked for a British Cyprus paper. Greece was in the wake of a devastating civil war in 1947, an ugly episode in which no one was taking prisoners. The British and the CIA, not always in synch, were pitted against General Markos, the Communist leader, in covert mountain combat, as well as dirty tricks, in their support of rigid conservative rule.

George Polk, a young American journalist working for CBS, was murdered by Greek government forces, though they not only denied it, they mounted a murky case blaming the insurgent Communists. Greece was part of what Churchill had called the soft underbelly of Europe and it was on its way to being a casualty of the encroaching Cold War.

At 35 George Polk was one of its first victims. Kyriazides's case had to be substantiated instantly. I had been the accrediting officer who had established his status. Norman Ho, a 28-year-old Anglo-Chinese colleague from the Secretariat Press Office, and I went into Manhattan to lodge a formal objection on behalf of the United Nations to the authorities holding him at Ellis Island, awaiting deportation. We demanded, and received, his release.

I don't remember now why we thought we had the authority to question his arrest or even how we knew what channels to go through. But it worked. He was released the next day. And he continued on for his Cyprus newspaper for several years 'til Greece elected itself a mildly democratic government and the civil war petered out.

No one wins a civil war. Greece has taken decades to learn to live with itself in what may pass for harmony.

Norman Ho and I, many years later, looked back in disbelief that we had actually saved his life.

The mayhem in Flushing Meadows as to which journalists got seats in the assembly hall to watch the vote for the birth of Israel was indescribable. There were rows of extra tables with typewriters for journalists but not half enough. I had the discretionary authority to give passes to the Assembly Hall to the major newspapers and agencies which made the minor ones holler in indignation. Newsmen from deepest Yemen, the newest member of United Nations, and the outer fringes of Moldavia stamped their feet when I tried to explain priorities. They were right, in a way. Their readers were as deserving as Londoners or Swedes. It was tetchy to tell them otherwise.

There was a closed circuit television screen that piped the proceedings of the General Assembly into the cavernous press hall but the sound was wonky, the seats uncomfortable and scarce, and no one was happy being kept out of the main hall where the blood was being spilt. And sometimes there were pyrotechnics. Not much can compete in the annals of international diplomacy with the debate between Andrei Vischisnky, the firebrand Soviet hit man known as the Butcher of the Ukraine, Ambassador of its delegation, and Sir Hartley Shawcross the British delegate with the hanky at his sleeve and his establishment arrogance launched into a duo performance wherein egos locked for hours in an unannounced debate that did in the Russian interpreter who actually fainted in his booth from exhaustion. They had screamed insults, bartered crowns in a marathon clash of egos that left the assembly bewildered and upset with a chill reminder that these were only men, after all, pretending to be gods and as such, perilously fragile.

This was a time of marathon speeches by all the Arab countries, their delegates resplendent in a variety of desert robes, many of them fingering worry beads as they spoke Arabic into the mikes. Most of them, I noticed, favored Argyle socks.

The support for Israel was often couched in eloquence as, though there had to be an element of solemnity in their words. It was not just any country; some thought it not a country at all but, rather, a patch of expiation for their own particular shortcomings.

Curiously, the few young Israelis around the press section did not much care for these sentiments. Nor did they like Jewish jokes about the subject. They were disconcerting. Frequently fair haired and strongly built, these Sabras looked nothing at all like their European cousins. Unless one meant Germans. They did look sort of German, one had to concede. I put it to one journalist from a Hebrew paper and he barely smiled.

"We are Sabras," he said. "We don't come from ghettoes and we know how to fight. You're thinking about Jews, that's different."

I was alone when he said this to me, no one shared my shock of disbelief. I told Marcelle Hitchmann, who was Egyptian-born and who had been to Palestine any number of times. She shrugged the young man off. "All pioneers think they are supermen," she allowed. "For once the Jews are not different."

The American delegation, thinking back, was something of a sore spot among American newsmen. There was Senator Tom Connelly, a big white-haired Texan wearing a string tie, which might have been at home in the Senate but not in an international forum. He peered around at the conference table in the Security Council or on the floor of the General Assembly hall as if to say, "Who the hell are these furriners and what are they rantin' about? Git me Jimmy Byrnes on the phone!"

I had actually heard him call for Jimmy Byrnes a number of times and wondered what he expected the Secretary of State to do. Off with their heads?

Once in a while, restlessly waiting his turn on a roll call a vote he would announce himself as the *Delegate from Texas*, making every other American cringe.

Very different from Connolly, the Ambassador, Warren Austin, was a senator from Vermont. A portly gentleman, he looked like a Hollywood version of an American statesman. But the principal member of the US delegation was by far Eleanor Roosevelt, unique in her worldwide prestige. And then, among the others on the delegation there was a Chicago lawyer named Adlai Stevenson. He made something of a name for himself in 1952. We at the UN had had a pleasant foretaste of his engaging brilliance ahead of time. His ease with others made up for the Senator from Texas's gross contempt for world government.

It has gotten somewhat lost in the snowdrifts of the Cold War, but the Soviet Union and its satellites were vociferous supporters of the creation of the State of Israel at the time. Though they would have preferred a State of Palestine to go with it. A charming Jewish member of the Polish delegation, who defected a few years later, muttered that a Jewish State might come in handy later on "when guilt goes out of fashion". I blinked when he said that but have never forgotten the chill in his voice at the time.

The vote was tight. But the motion was passed. The State of Israel was born.

The Jewish Agency winked at my not-so-discreet preference for Jewish journalists in the queue for seats in the General Assembly and they invited me to their celebration. I stood next to Moshe Sharett who cut the huge birthday cake and gave me the second slice; the first going to his wife.

"Not bad for a girl from Incarnation," I told him confidentially, but he only laughed and confided that he spoke Hebrew with a Turkish accent.

Israel was born but the fairies leaning over its cradle were nervous and unsettled. The first gift that came was a war, one of many more that were to follow.

All during 1947 I acquired new friends. One was a beautiful Polish-Russian girl called Irene Melup. She was a little older than I, worked in the Economic and Social division. Tall, with lush dark eyes and hair, she spoke with a rich accent but her English was perfect. No wonder, for she had gone to Bryn Mawr. Her sister was a "whisperer"—that is, a simultaneous Russian-English interpreter and also worked at the UN. She spoke without an accent. They were the daughters of rich émigré Russians who had settled in Warsaw after the revolution, prospered there and managed to come to the United States just in time. Irene brought a set of friends whom I still look back on fondly. They were much like her, Russian-Polish, Jewish multilingual, and we've crossed paths on and off ever since. One became a civil servant in Washington with the CIA, the other would have liked to follow but was rejected. Instead he became a multi-millionaire. Irene remained at United Nations but drifted out of my life as gracefully as she had drifted in.

In the weeks leading up to the vote on Israel, lobbying by the Arab countries was at its peak. The receptions they held, each in turn, were lavish. I was invited regularly, in lieu of Mary Ronay still on her Havana beach, and I discovered what lavish meant. The Waldorf, the Rainbow Room, the Plaza, for starters. The buffets were lobster and caviar laden. Celebrities circulated among the diplomats including the likes of Zaza Gabor or Douglas Fairbanks, Jr. or Nobel laureates like John Steinbeck, whom I looked at in awe. I would have liked to tell him that I had typed out the first chapter of *Tortilla Flat* when I was fourteen and kept it in my wallet, creased and nearly illegible even then.

Irene and her retinue joined me at the buffet tables along with the other "young" press crowd and, occasionally, my friend Ann. We were all of an age, the age when night clubs appear glamorous and, indeed, are. To go to El Morocco implied a whiff of style. I knew it then and had a knack for it. I think I was born with a taste for piano bars. It was certainly well-served in those years. Bobby Short playing Cole Porter at the Ritz Carlton or any number of husky voices at the Blue Angel were worth their weight in college credits. What a fine way to end one's adolescence.

The General Assembly of 1947 voted to hold its next session in September, 1948, in Paris. I sat in my blessed little cubbyhole office and wondered what would happen to me. The conference in Havana was by now over and Mary Ronay, suntanned but grumpy as ever, made it clear she wanted her chair back. I had no claim on it and, for the first time, was a little concerned about my job. It had all come so easily.

Most of my friends, especially the older ones, advised me to go back to college and forget about stopgap jobs. But I thought of next year in Paris. The prospect of leaving these beloved corridors, their babel of languages, the intrigues, the plays of influence, the charm of imagining I was actually living history, was too much. I decided that college could wait; I would get another temporary contract.

"You will not become a reporter by hanging around here," one lovely New York journalist warned me sternly. "Worse, you're liable to marry one. And you're not even twenty."

She scared me, but I was saved by Ted Berkman, who hired me as a public relations assistant to his small staff of what was the forerunner to UNICEF. It was the body that paved the way for UNICEF's creation. He was the director of information.

It is hard to believe now, but not everyone went lyrical at the notion of empowering a UN body to oversee the welfare of children. The United States, for instance. The American super power, as it emerged, would have preferred to keep the reins of largesse in its own hands. It took painful time for me to realize that the east-west joust extended to the hapless leftover victims, the children. UNICEF took a lot of fighting for.

But before that, while I was still in my little office watching all the other press people talk about *Next Year in Paris*, I pretended an air of unconcern. Daniel Schorr, then a young correspondent for the Dutch News Agency and something of a beau, talked casually about looking forward to it. I assumed a self-important air and said, "Yes, I would like to go, too. Because I could have a UN scholarship to an International school in Paris but… you can't get a passage on an ocean liner for love or money…"

I said all this off the top of my head, a place I still talk from occasionally, having no serious plans to go anywhere at all, let alone a school in Paris. Dan looked at me and said, "If you're serious, I can get you a passage on the New Amsterdam."

I stared at him for a second and then, as though someone else had taken possession of my life, I answered, "Yes, I'm serious."

He was perched on the corner of my desk. He reached over, pulled the telephone closer, dialed a number and, as though from far away, I heard him talk easily about a friend who needed a passage for France next June.

I can still see myself in that tiny space where a procession of extraordinary people had passed through and where Dan Schorr was now changing the course of my life while I looked on, barely able to breathe.

"There you are," he said mildly. "I'll take you to the Ritz bar as soon as you arrive."

He did.

When I got a minute I called Ann and told her. She gasped. "You just decided like that? You didn't think it over? My God… Well, that's wonderful!"

I breathed a sigh of relief. If Ann didn't warn me off or think I had gone mental, I must have been right.

Then Ted Berkman's offer of a job on his staff was confirmed. I was off on the way to the rest of my life.

There was no rush to tell my parents that I would be going to Paris in six months, there was time enough to ease them into a frame of mind that might accept it without total warfare.

For the first time in my life I decided to save money. I had to pay for this trip, pay for the months I would spend in Paris, for a little travel, for a year away… on my own. I had never been on my own. The prospect was daunting. I had never really saved, made a budget, or balanced a checkbook. I had never seriously concerned myself with money. My father's daughter!

While I was trying to make sense of the plans one side of my brain had made without consulting the other side, I happened to read a press release on the work done in the field of foreign scholarships for worthy students the United Nations had undertaken. I read on and indeed, there were scholarships for a school of international studies in Paris.

I found the office that dealt with the program, buried deep in entrails of Lake Success. It was headed by a dusty little man with European spectacles and an accent that reminded me of the lending library on upper Broadway where I had first read Erich Maria Remarque. He didn't look as though he was swamped with applicants. When he described the scholarship, I understood why.

As opposed to American universities, European ones were all but free. Tuition was something on the order of $75 a year. That is what the scholarship consisted of, nothing more.

Nevertheless, I took it because it gave me the legitimacy for the trip that I needed not only for my parents' sake, but for myself. I needed the scholarship just as I needed a passport.

The dusty man behind the desk filled out the forms and started what he called "veels in motion."

"We have time," I told him, "It is only January."

He gave me a long look and mumbled something that sounded like "Nah," a whole dictionary of a word, typical of a certain Europe.

I would come to know it well.

Dolores de Soto, Ann Barret and Juan Palà at
the Cité Universitaire - Paris 1949

Juan Palà and Dolores de Soto - Paris 1949

The « voodoo » mask

Christopher Palà - Ca 1954

Juan and Dolores Palà - London Ca 1956

Dolores - 1958

Chris, Dolores, Suzy and Juan Palà - 1960

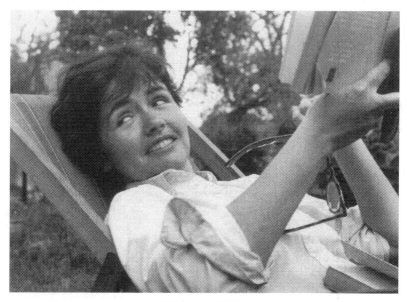

Dolores - 1965

Barbara Grosset

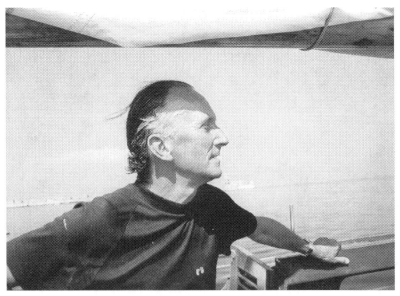

Raymond Grosset

Suzy - 1973

Juan and Dolores - Mallorca

Prix Bourdelle - 1983

Juan - Paris 1984

Juan, Suzy and Chris - Combs-la-Ville

Suzy and Pascal Loir - 2006

Robin Loir - Ca 1990

Thomas Loir - 1994

Juan and Thomas - Combs-la-Ville 1994

Dolores and Susie Ovadia - Combs-la-Ville

50th wedding anniversary - Combs-la-Ville June 1999

Isabelle and Sasha Palà - Washington Ca 2008

Kathleen Grosset and Thierry Mignon - 2007

Adrian Lees

PART 2

By a River Called Yesterday

Chapter 1

When Karina first asked me to this memoir, quite out of the blue, I was surprised because I had started it myself and had written the first chapters describing a New York childhood at a time that has evolved as a period piece because of the immense changes it brought. The world around us so altered the post-war city and its lifelines that I, like so many, drifted into uncharted lanes. I meant to trace all this quietly, though, almost as a secret. Yet a secret squarely put down on paper to make it permanent, sharable, real. A secret that was no longer one.

What Karina was asking me to do was to tell the rest of the tale, to describe the colors and scents of the voyage. It seemed a challenge, a presumptuous one at that.

I was, and still am, doubtful that my story holds any special meaning or sheds light on much more than a certain time in certain places, specific happenstances. Not any more than any other time or place.

Yet, perhaps not. Perhaps the twentieth century post-war was a key moment, riddled with dangerous alternatives, succumbing to some, avoiding others. It was a time when taking sides was, in my mind, an imperative. It was no time for mildness or fence-sitting. If I grew to dislike fence-sitters it was not just me, it was in the air. I had strong feelings about everything, including having strong feelings. It was the weather of the times.

Which was why falling in love with Juan Palà was so easy. Especially since it was made difficult by almost everything and everyone around, including Juan Palà himself.

Not that he was reluctant. It was he, after all, who asked me to dance. But before we get to that point, we should perhaps look at who we were. Once we were dancing he said, in French, "What is your name?" He was looking at me with amused brown eyes, pleased with himself, I thought.

I knew he was Spanish just from having seen him around the Collège d'Espagne, the Spanish pavilion just down the path a little from the American House at the Cité Universitaire on the rim of Paris's Left Bank, an international setting amid tall trees wherein houses built in the styles of the countries they represented were reserved for foreign students in Paris.

It was a campus of magical charm in my eyes, where the One World my twenty-year-old heart cheered for seemed already a reality.

I exaggerated, of course. I still do. But it did have a spark to it then that went with the post-war sense of hope and determination. The foreign students were the personification of the One World buzz.

If nothing else, we all had gone abroad to get to Paris. It took some time to come to terms with the fact that Parisians might have been just as pleased if we had stayed home.

But that didn't matter in the long run. Parisians were not the most vital part of Paris, though they went berserk if one suggested it. Paris was a center, a symbol, a café table, a way of living, a way of loving life.

There was a moment of magic in the immediate post-war similar to other such moments like the Hemingway '20s or La Belle Époque. These are not eternal and they differ from each other, too, but in its own way Paris becomes a character in the play you are living, the play you are creating or which is creating you. I was lucky to have arrived then, to have been twenty then, not ten years earlier or later.

For once I was on time.

When Juan Palà asked me to dance to a scratchy rendition of Stardust at the Franco British Pavilion, which looked like an English stately home, he burst out laughing when I told him my name, pronouncing it, as I do, as though it were English: Dolores De Soto. Then, astonishing me further, he said, "And apparently you are Canadian."

Despite Stardust I stood still and remember even now my astonishment. I am actually half Canadian. I spent my childhood summers in Nova Scotia.

Secretly, I would have liked to have had Canadian nationality just then because Canada did everything right, from entering the war the moment Great Britain did to accepting refugees after it without the quibbles other countries made, especially my own. Canada was vast and generous. No one disliked you on sight as happened to me in Paris once I gave my nationality. Though proud of being an American in the tough-minded way New Yorkers have in their pride—as though the rest of the nation really was Out There in the vague direction of beyond Jersey City—being Canadian would be restful, peaceable, one less hurdle toward acceptance in this strange world of Europe that so confused me.

I looked up at this surprising young man's attractive eyes and his elegantly arched nose, with a tingle of interest and replied, "I am half Canadian. I spent summers there as a child. My mother is Canadian."

I knew from experience that the question of my Spanish name, of course, would have to be dealt with. So, before he could find a polite way of prodding I said, "My father is Colombian. Which makes me a hundred percent New Yorker, to answer the question you are probably too polite to ask."

And he let his smile change gears for a second, then said, "I would have asked eventually but, you are right, I am too polite." He seemed to savor the notion, I thought, wondering then what polite actually meant.

"And you are Spanish, I assume?" The music had stopped but he kept hold of my right hand as though ready for it to start again. We were standing at the side of a smallish dance floor and for a second I felt totally alone, held by a knot of odd conversation with an aquiline nose and sharp brown eyes that appeared to be deciphering a strange script.

"I am Catalan," he corrected. I only vaguely knew what Catalan was but nodded, hoping I would not have to expand on the subject.

"Madrid?" I asked, romantically remembering gallant Spain's capital and its Last Train, catching an echo of the ever present Hemingway who had done it all first. But there was a faint frown now and I held my breath.

"Barcelona? Oh, of course…" I heard my quick cover-up voice say, not really remembering Barcelona and my lexicon of the Civil War, seeing only las Sierras and Ingrid Bergman's worried lines to Gary Cooper, "Where do you put the noses?" in her first kiss.

My shelves of books on the Spanish Civil War deserted me now and the kiss seemed to cover me like a great warm shawl and the conversation danced itself out over the next hour and the one after that, as the young man from the wrong city talked to me, not about Nova Scotia, but about Picasso and Miró and the Romanesque chapels in the Pyrenees whose frescos, he assured me, were breathtaking.

I quite believed him.

That was on February 13, 1949. It was a Saturday and it was supposed to celebrate St. Valentine's Day.

It did.

Chapter 2

My slippery fingers are worse than my slippery memory. But I do remember those first days probably more clearly than I remember the cloudy years of, say, the late '50s when everything was upside down or the mid-1980s when things went so fast I am not sure I can recall one voice from another. Memory is a study in changing attitudes, it would seem. But those months in early 1949 were ground breaking.

The slender young man would pop up at my ground floor window in the American House courtyard with unpredictable frequency. He would amble by for a chat or to invite me to a vernissage at a Paris art gallery or to just to go for a walk. Once he came by with a shirt asking me if I would be an angel and iron it for him. My heart sank. I did not have an iron, I began to tell him, feeling freakish, someone he would never come to understand. We did not have an iron in the house, I thought of telling him but stopped. If I began to describe my peculiar background he would run away and the mere thought of that horrified me.

"Stay there," I mumbled, "I will have it ready in a few minutes." He was framed in my ground floor window, slender and graceful as a dancer and I bolted out my door into the corridor and grabbed a neighbor whom I knew to have an iron and begged her to do what had to be done to the shirt. She knew that there was someone new in my life so she darted to the window, examined the tall young man leaning against a neighboring tree, and gave me a wide smile.

"What does he look like without it?" she murmured, making me blush.

At that time I was in the middle of preparations to go to Prague for a week's visit with two American students, young men whom I scarcely knew. All we had in common was a desire to see Prague then, one year on after the Communist takeover that cost my revered Jan Masaryk his life.

Czechoslovakia was the most willing of the Communist bloc countries to give American students visas, at that time, anyway. It was the one country I wanted desperately to see.

The 1930s and '40s had seen Europe burn itself to the ground in the name of racial purity, ideological justice. Its victims were strewn all over Europe. I had come to see for myself what it meant, who the players were.

Prague was a symbol of immense importance to me then and I was distracted by the brown eyes and beautiful hands that illustrated the young artist's concern for me. "Communist countries are not where young American girls go shopping," he said with a frown.

"I will be fine," I assured him with the bravado of my age. And I was.

At the same time Juan's younger brother, Oriol, had just escaped from Spain over the Pyrenees. He was an expert skier and mountain climber as well as a very active member of the Catalan nationalist group outlawed by Franco. He had climbed to the top of la Sagrada Familia, Barcelona's landmark church with particularly high steeples, and hung a Catalan flag from them. It caused a sensation because no one expected it in those bleak Franco years and it took the police long clumsy hours to cut it down.

Two years later he was caught, jailed and then, thanks to their father's generous bribing of a string of prison officials, Oriol was released for Christmas of 1948. He skied over the mountains and remained in Perpignan 'til the French government gave him permission to leave.

The French were less and less generous with Spanish refugees at that point though they bent over backwards to accommodate those from the Iron Curtain countries.

Oriol did not get a permit to come to Paris, but he got one to go to Rouen. He took the train in Perpignan in that crowded month of February but got off in Paris. They played it by ear after that. Friends of friends helped out, money changed hands. He has been in Paris ever since, is a French citizen, the most ardently Catalan of French citizens in town.

Our lives were changing in those days. My new young man took a place no one else had done. He seemed to be at the window whenever I wished him to be. I had no time to wonder whether or not he would pass by. He would pop up in those early days with a suggestion for this or that museum, gallery show, concert at another of the houses at the Cité.

He had not kissed me but I was not in any way inclined to take him as another one of my many platonic friendships with handsome young men.

I was surely the world's champion best friend, which suited me admirably up to then. Now, however, I was quite sure I did not want to be his best friend.

It never occurred to me that his reticence might be simply because he was shy.

Sensitive, brilliant, a mentor in a new world of art and its politics, and of the Spanish Civil War as fought on the ground, of the poetry of Lorca and Machado which he could quote, of the dark half-world of Antonin Artaud and Paris life in the arts and of its new theater, he complemented what I knew already of Paris life. I knew Sartre's world and the left's role but I knew nothing of his realm of art and poetry and the Europe of a new cultural horizon.

But mostly I liked his hands and his aquiline nose and the way he mispronounced things in three languages. He charmed me but he didn't seem to notice it.

Finally, one night as he stood at the door to the courtyard of the American House, I reached up and kissed him. He looked surprised, embarrassed, pleased. He said goodnight but I saw something new and promising in his eyes.

We began from there. I had fallen in love. For good.

And as it turned out, so had he.

Chapter 3

From those February days through to the end of November we plunged into what was for me a new dimension. He became my gentle lover, patient, passionate and, for me, wondrous.

He had, and has still, a romantic nature that is not always reconcilable with the world around us. He was often jarred by my outspokenness, my boyish use of language. We had a problem, I soon realized, between new world and old world. I shocked him inadvertently. Referring to Evita Peron, one day, I used the word prostitute. I saw his eyes change focus, and I was sorry because I did not know quite how to deal with him. More than anything else in the world I wanted to learn. I wanted him to understand me. This was the first time I had ever desperately needed the support, the concern of someone else. I understood, with great difficulty, that loving someone is incomparably more complex than I had ever thought.

In time he got used to what he referred to as my Americanness but I remained wary of fair wispy women ever since. I never liked the flicker of interest in his eyes when one was around. A fact which made him grin, a little pleased with himself. He has seldom been jealous of me but I have been jealous of him from the first day.

The beginnings of a relationship appear to be cast in concrete.

We took an Easter trip to the south of France and I was astounded that anyone could dismiss the beauty of the Riviera the way he did. Later, when he took me to the Costa Brava, I understood why.

My lovely friend Ann came to join me in Europe unexpectedly then, and we travelled to Spain, all three of us that summer. A decade later the Costa Brava, indeed all of Spain, would become the tourism playground of the western world but in 1949 we were the only foreigners to be seen. And we were very much seen, as it turned out.

Ann was tall and slender, the typical American beauty of the screen. Her bathing suit was not two piece—we knew enough not to do that— but there was an opening between top and bottom, a sort of lozenge that showed the belly button. On the second morning we found an open letter under our hotel room doors spelling out that Spain was a Catholic country and expected its tourists to behave accordingly. Between laughter and tears we huddled in towels when not in the water, after that. Our suntans suffered but the *natives* were mollified.

We had taken two rooms in a small hotel at Calella, a beauty spot favored by the Barcelona artsy upper class. Juan had a small following of admirers among such people for his audacious first paintings. A small following of admirers but a larger following of detractors. Modern art was, in influential Barcelona circles, a very mixed concept. It was Communism tainted by Picasso, it was foreign, it was hedonistic, etc. etc. As were the young upstarts who would have been better advised to paint seascapes of the Costa Brava instead of dark, brooding, near unfathomable women, as he did, showing off his cleverness with color and space, light and shadow as though he were sticking his tongue out at society ... what was he doing in Calella with two over exposed American girls? And who was sleeping with whom in those two rooms overlooking the sea?

We sensed our unpopularity, and we were uncomfortable. The Guardia Civil were not toy soldiers. All the mean little laissez-passers we had to apply for to be able to stay in a town or to take another train to Barcelona... all those small unnerving procedures that had to be followed made me angry and defiant.

In Madrid I deliberately lost my travel permit. An angry hotel keeper took us both to the nearest police station, carrying our bags as though ready to confiscate them if the occasion permitted. The policeman just replaced the lost permit with a second and asked me to be more careful in the future. He disappointed the hotel keeper but I could see the immense relief in Juan's face and I never played games with authority in Spain again.

His brother, after all, was an escaped criminal living in Paris where he lived, too. The Franco police were not above punishing the family for an errant brother's sins. Spain was different, the travel posters would claim in the 1960s.

It was. Very different.

I had come to Europe to go to college. The year's course I took at the Ecole des Hautes Etudes Internationales finished well despite my very wonky written French and my inability to hide what I thought about such subjects as colonialism, then a burning issue with Indochina fighting its way out of French rule.

The professor I had for that subject was probably amused by me because he allowed me to attend a few excellent classes at Science Po, which was something of an honor. I was in Gabriel Marcel's class which was well beyond my academic level and frequently beyond my still fragile French to cope with a philosopher's lexicon. It was the most stimulating educational experience I ever had because the great professor engaged his students in not only an examination of texts but on the world the texts dealt with. A portly man, probably then in his sixties, he would invite students back to his apartment not far from the school off the Blvd. Saint-Germain. I remember being awed by the paintings on the walls, by the heavy rugs and heavier furniture, the dainty tea cups his wife provided, and the formality of his professorial informality. The conversations were theoretically casual but they were nothing of the sort. I had never studied philosophy and was the only American among the students, therefore at a disadvantage in terms of experience. My knowledge of war was theoretical, my losses were, to Europeans, equally so.

I was careful not to show anger when a German student, who had been stationed in Paris in the war years, played innocent victim of Hitler's rise. I made an impatient sound, inadvertently. The professor picked up on it and quietly asked me to explain but I did not have the words then to do it cogently. Worse, the half-dozen French students in the room for the most part were unimpressed by my American anger about German barbarism. We did not suffer it first hand, did we? Our faraway sacrifices made them snicker, which made me even angrier. I glared at the German mutely.

The incident passed. Gabriel Marcel retrieved the moment with an impatient French shrug. He had little sympathy for the German and he liked my quick, if over simplified, gut reaction. But he did not press the point.

Perhaps he felt that pain is not measurable over teacups after classes.

I was unimpressed with the students at Science Po and nothing much has altered my view of them in later years. Except for the happy few, they tend to be the ironclad middle class that rules most of Europe and particularly France with such flagrant inauspiciousness and has done with a few notable lapses, since forever and a day.

In that winter of 1949, Juan joined in with my friends on various occasions. These included an American photographer, Marty Dain, who lived at la Cité who was one of my army of platonic buddies. Marty and I had done a lot of exploring together. Lectures, rallies, political meetings and a range of foreign films which seemed like an education in itself. Georges Charpak, a burly young scientist who had been in Dachau, not because he was Jewish which the Germans did not know but because he was a Communist Resistant, was another. He was Marty's roommate at the Swiss house in the Cité Universitaire. Georges was extremely attractive, a would-be suitor and a good friend. I knew his family and was extremely impressed by his mother, a beautiful woman who wore her long hair in braids around her head, Russian style, and who had been a Resistant as well. She, too, was a member of the Communist Party.

This was something of a handful for a young American girl to assimilate in one gulp. George's family had emigrated from darkest Ukraine but, when asked, just said Russia, which was not quite the same thing.

On the other hand, no one but me would have picked that out, Georges mentioned one day. Most people didn't know where the Ukraine was, he observed.

Not all Americans are color-blind, I told him archly.

He was to win the Nobel Prize for Physics in later life. He and his family remained militant 'til the end. We stayed friends all the way through.

Chapter 4

I suppose it is only the very young who can juggle turnabouts in life with the ease I managed so blithely then. From my circle of politically minded friends, Juan brought me in to his realm of Catalan intellectuals then living at the Spanish House but who were no longer students. They seemed to be a circle within a circle, to my eyes, each with other realms but all converging on the arts. Picasso then was at the pinnacle of his post-war years with young Francoise at his side and two small children scampering over the Riviera sands into the lenses of Robert Capa or David Duncan.

All of Juan's friends had a Picasso connection, it seemed to me. Jaume Sunyer was the son of Joaquim Sunyer, a fellow painter and old buddy, Jordi Anguera was the nephew of Sabartes, Picasso's secretary-com-bulldog, Josep Palau, the poète maudit of the group, wrote massively on the Master, as he did on Antonin Artaud, the really star-crossed contemporary French poet who was living out his last painful days desperate for drugs of all nature in a Paris suburb.

Palau, a startling figure with huge dark eyes often hollow in a bearded face, was born to be a poète maudit. His dramatic gesture of self-exile— he actually had a French mother so that leaving Spain legally was not a problem—was convincing enough that he became something of a icon of Spanish martyrdom in this still nervous post-war period.

Palau decided he was in love with my friend Ann. Though they had never exchanged more than a Bonjour or Bonsoir, he having no English and Ann apparently incapable of absorbing more than two words of French at a time, this was something of a surprise. His dark intense expression rather alarmed Ann and whenever we were all in a group together she edged unusually close to Juan, to his amusement. Palau, who knew famous people and talked about them vividly, told convoluted stories to these relatively unpracticed young men about mature French women who, in the middle of lovemaking, would pull away and say, "Shave your beard instantly or get out of my bed," leaving his audience rapt.

College boy nonsense, I thought at the time, yet, with his burning hollow eyes and flair for knife point drama, he convinced them. He knew women they only dreamed of, he assured them. Real women whose knowledge of sex was the core of French romanticism.

Even at twenty I thought Palau was a dreamer more than a philanderer. Juan was taken in, however. No one could make up these tales, he cautioned me. Just look at his eyes when he describes that apartment in the Palais Royal, next door to where Jean Cocteau lives, he added for good measure. Palau kept his audience enthralled which, I thought at the time, said more about them than it did about him. And Cocteau was famously kind in receiving young aspiring foreign writers. Several friends of mine had been to his delightful flat in the Palais Royal, near Colette's, where he had served them tea or hot chocolate. He would have done the same for Palau who had a bit of a reputation. From that to his sensual women was quite a leap, but then, his fantasy was boundless and he was still young.

Spain and its untried creators had only just emerged from a long night of darkness that began in 1936. It would be another decade before the sun would get further than the beaches. No one on the international political exchange seemed to mind, however. They were all too busy containing Communism. A whole generation of young Spaniards paid the price of that isolation.

If I had gravitated to Saint-Germain-des-Prés and the Café de Flore, particularly, it was because of what I had read about Sartre and de Beauvoir's lives during the war years, first off.

But more importantly, it was around the corner from my school. I took to those streets as I had done to the others in the Village at home, and found myself moved by their sinews, the grace of their houses, and the tempo of their lives. The Flore was not fashionable as it is now but I am not sure that is quite true: there were people who assured me in 1948 that the Flore was for real in the '30s, not after the war. Every generation has its holy places, its shrines. Mine have remained mine ever since, though I bow to the presence of ladies with hats today gaping at current self-styled philosophers more comfortable on television sets than in bookstores. They do irritate me.

Juan was more of a Montparnasse type. Montparnasse was where the painters gathered. There were art schools scattered here and there and buildings with high windowed studios. There was also the tradition of the earlier part of the century. Modigliani's ghost haunted the half-dozen streets around Vavin while young painters chased its echoes.

I had taken to café life with immense pleasure. The Select and the Dome were both favorites. The Catalan crowd had discovered another site just up the block called l'Hôtel des Etats Unis and that year its terrace was a center for much international conversation. Along with the Catalans were a handful of Irish poets and French dramatists, including a few greats like Adamov who was later to literally drink himself to death. Self-destruction was as much a part of the late; '40s as it was in the 1920s. I looked on, saddened at the waste yet touched by the despair.

I remember thinking that I had been lucky in falling in love with complexities of a more governable nature and held on to Juan's artist's hands 'til he looked at me askance.

Falling in love is a maze of contradictions at the best of times. In our case it bore a touch of grand opera. A penniless painter and a young New Yorker who thought she could do it all? I grow faint now imagining all the disasters we could have stumbled into.

But the time came for me to return to New York because I had no money left and had exhausted all the job possibilities available to me in Paris, where I was without a work permit. Paris was full of better qualified, eager candidates jousting for the same jobs.

I was going back to New York braced for what I thought would be a short separation. It was to last a year.

A very rough year, at that.

All of our differences rose to the surface during our time apart. And we could not settle them in bed as we had done so effectively when we were together. And therein lay a principal difference between us. He saw nothing wrong with seeing other girls. An army of Swedes had descended upon the Left Bank even while I was still there. With their long blonde hair, they showed admirable Scandinavian unconcern for middle class morality in terms of faithfulness, a matter which so tortured my still Roman Catholic unquiet heart. I could no more hop into bed with an attractive chum than I could vote Republican. I did not only lust after my silky Spaniard, I loved him. Love was responsibility, it was a gift to be cherished.

Of course, he did not actually say, "Go ahead, I don't mind if you go off with Steve Davids"—he did not even hint at such good fellowship. I knew, however, that though I would have liked nothing better than to explore my newfound physical dimension with the extremely attractive Steve, it would have broken an essential thread that held me to Juan.

I could not afford that. He was my anchor, loving him was my strength. I would give all these secret things to him, not to Steve whose attraction was only horny deep. I loved Juan Palà; I did not love anyone else.

These are the strengths of the very young. I can only thank the Lord's specially appointed angel who took care of foolish virgins and airy artists for being kind to us as we spread our wings and flew straight into the sun.

In New York the first thing that happened to me was a Life Magazine photographer snapped my picture as I was leaving the Museum of Modern Art where I had gone to ask advice about which galleries might be interested in Juan's work. I wore a slightly worried look and was carrying one of his paintings. All the other girls photographed in the story were models with hat boxes. I was flattered, bemused. My mother, that unpleasant woman, was livid because the caption read that I had a Spanish painter fiancé and I was trying to sell his works. She felt disgraced because everyone she knew saw the picture. It was never clear which word she detested most, Spanish or painter.

Her dreams for me of a nice doctor in Scarsdale were dashed forever.

Everyone at the American House in the Cité Universitaire saw the picture, too, including a girl called Mabs who knew nothing about me but would soon learn. I had known nothing about her, either, 'til a caring buddy thought it best to tell me. A few frantic transatlantic phone calls, plus the good offices of my buddy, put paid to that little problem. But I was jostled. I could live with casual sex and all those Swedes but not with a replacement. He should have known better, I thought. When he said, "It doesn't matter," I could not believe him. What does matter, then?

It was a question never really answered.

A year later Juan arrived in New York. I saw him at the rail of the ship, *Liberté*, which was on its maiden voyage. It had been the old *Europa*, a German liner before the war and was, indeed, the spoils of war.

He moved into the sweet flat I had found for him on the third floor of a Brooklyn Heights townhouse whose windows looked out on New York harbor. The quiet street was lined with trees. He saw the skyline wherever he looked and instantly decided that New York was a friendly place, after all. That was November.

In June we were married. June 30, 1951.

Chapter 5

One of the tenets of The Great American Dream is get-rich-quick summer jobs for college students. Most of my friends had done stints at serving on tables in resort town restaurants and had saved respectable amounts of cash for the ensuing winter. What with my odd swinging off to Nova Scotia and then my unexpected job at the United Nations, I never did. I had had after school jobs mostly in New York department stores, addressing envelopes or other such dim duties, but I had never waited on tables. Friends now well into their twenties suggested to Juan and me that a couple of months in Nantucket would set us up for the following winter and introduce him to one of America's great beauty spots.

If waiting on tables as a stopgap job is commonplace in American life, it is a bit of a shock to a European. In France, or Europe in general, waiters are waiters and young men de bonne famille did not become waiters in summer. Or so it was then. But our newly arrived resident was a good sport and he did not even squirm. Neither of us wondered how his nascent English would take to a, say, Double Scotch on the Rocks, for instance, or a couple of home fries to go, or a Chocolate Cabinet—that being the obscure local name for a milk shake in Rhode Island. No one foresaw the language barrier.

We went to Nantucket then, a fabled island whose New England charm was windswept and whale haunted, with small grey houses lining the harbor and a sense of steely peace.

I haven't mentioned the fact that I had suffered from terrible bouts of hay fever before going to Europe. At that time allergies were thought of by Europeans as another fussy American eccentricity. "Real guys didn't sneeze" was the attitude. Even my sainted father-in-law scoffed mildly at the thought of grown men avoiding spring blossoms.

As it turned out, once back in The States my problem reappeared. I was allergic to almost everything that managed to grow on Nantucket's sandy soil. Golden rod proliferated.

My sneezes, coughs, and runny nose resounded across the island. Not a great success at being a waitress—I tended to over heap the plates of any one who struck me as needy and blushed when I took a tip—I was soon fired.

But Juan was an instant success. He was hired as a French waiter in a chowder parlor and I sat unobtrusively at the counter whispering quick translations of the orders as they came. His pleasant smile and slightly ruffled demeanor went over well with the customers and his tips were respectable.

When not slinging lobsters, he painted a series of seascapes which he hoped might sell and did a series of interesting portraits of me. He also did a painting of a little blonde girl, square and sturdy in a violet dress, eating a huge piece of watermelon. The painting in itself is strong, the way the girl is firmly planted on the ground, the colors of the fruit against black lines were arresting. It was also full of a humor he did not guess at.

Little colored girls ate watermelon, the observers noted, not little white girls. Juan was baffled at the painting's reception. He knew nothing of the symbol of watermelon, he knew very little about the South. The black-white question, seemingly immutable at the time, was disagreeably mysterious to him. I had black friends in New York, but not many. I had had more in Paris, where the ease with which we met was not matched in New York. If people thought he was striking a blow for racial equality with his painting, he was pleased but disturbed, too, because he disliked dishonesty as much as he disliked discrimination. He was asked to show a couple of paintings in the local Nantucket Art Show. He refused to show that one.

Predictably, he did not make friends among the organizers who thought him snobbish. Or uppity, the perfect word for the circumstances.

Hay fever did me in and I was remiss in all manner of ways. At one point I thought vaguely about periods. Could I be late? I was always a little vague about dates then and was actually irregular. So I ignored it all and kept on swimming and sneezing and explaining how to make a banana split. July and August rolled by. We went back to Brooklyn Heights in early September. My breasts were a bit rounder than before... but no. Finally I went to see a doctor I had known in Fire Island the year before when I had been visiting with an old UN friend, the great I.F. Stone and his extremely hospitable family in their house aptly called Grand Central Station. And then the Korean War broke out.

He was the only doctor I knew aside from my mother's. He told me quite joyously that I was pregnant and could expect the baby around mid-April.

I could hardly bring myself to believe him.

Between laughter and tears? At least that. Between different sets of wonderment, more precisely. The enchantment of a baby, on the one hand, and the responsibility on the other? I was 23 and fully believed that we could do anything we set out to do. The image of a baby flooded me.

When I got back to the apartment Juan was working on a large canvas of one of his dark brooding women at their windows. I smiled at him in complicity of the most sublime order. He looked at me oddly. I told him, visualizing for the first time, how much a baby would be more than just a sweet extension of ourselves.

I went cold all over.

He stared at me for a long moment in resounding silence. After a bit, he nodded his head and managed a smile. I came down from my cloud and we looked out the window at the passing of an ocean liner. It was heading for Europe.

Real life had begun before I knew it.

Most of my friends, Ann being the notable exception, suggested having an abortion. One even called her own doctor to help me arrange it. I could not do that. My Catholicism, ever a conundrum, was less in question than a simple gut reaction against killing a baby that was both mine and his. Under other circumstances, perhaps. But not his, not mine. The thought of a tiny replica of Juan dazzled me.

Of course, I knew absolutely nothing about babies. I had never held an infant newly born, I had never looked at one carefully. No one I knew had a baby—though in the next year or two almost everyone I knew, except Ann, had one. They appeared to come in bunches that year. My friends prepared layettes, cribs, names for theirs. Some moved to Scarsdale or its equivalent, making their mothers happy, no doubt. Juan and I decided we would go to Haiti. But that deserves an explanation.

We had a Spanish refugee painter friend in the Village then who was married to a lovely Haitian woman whom we had become very close to. They saw how little prepared we were for the sort of domesticity a baby required, so they suggested we come to Port-au-Prince for a while. They were going back then and they thought it would be wonderful for us to spend some time in their island paradise where life would be so much easier. A maid was available for pennies, and they would help us find a nice house with a terrace and a garden. It was never cold, and they would be there and would help us make friends.

Haiti was not the horror story it would become a few years later. It was a playground for literary types, for painters who had Gauguin in mind, for photographers who liked winsome children. We were in the middle of winter, and New York was icy. Our friends, already back in Port-au-Prince, told us on the phone not to think twice. They would find us accommodations and a proper maternity clinic. Come ahead.

It should be emphasized here that Haiti in the early 1950s was totally different to the wretched place it has become. Four-star hotels dotted the island, it was explored by poets and ethnologists, by painters and film stars. Graham Greene was to set one of his best books in a hotel we would become familiar with. The Oloffson Hotel was an imposing gingerbread palace, a landmark then.

A half-dozen other American women had babies at the same time as I did and the local doctors had practiced or trained in the States or Canada. Haiti was very much on the arts map. No one shrieked out in protest when we launched the idea. Only my mother objected, but she had objected to everything I did for some time now. My father merely looked startled. He knew our friends there, however, so he assumed we would be in good company. He wished us well.

Haiti proved to be a revelation.

A tropical paradise is difficult to describe because the very notion is a cliché. Yet Haiti was just that. At first sight it was stunning. The colors of the hills, les mornes in Creole, varied from deepest green to unexpected purples in the changing of the light, the sea was turquoise, the sand was dark… a local joke was that even the sand was black in Haiti. It was volcanic and had streaks of gold through it, making the beaches look like fashionable aqueous hairdos. And the water was never cold.

People look askance at us now when we talk of having lived a year in Haiti, but at the time everyone thought we had won the lottery. We thought so, too.

But before we were to leave New York that winter of 1951-1952, the best was yet to come. Juan was to have a show in a well-appointed gallery whose owners, a remarkable pair of leftist New Yorkers who had strong notions of what galleries and artists should do together for the greater good, offered him a show. They both liked his work, they both liked us. Milton Blau, who later was to become a playwright calling himself Eric Blau and best known for *Jacques Brel is Alive and Living in Paris*. The other was Alan Stoltman who remained a friend 'til his death some thirty years later.

The paintings Juan was doing for the show were coming along easily as though the air he breathed was touched by grace.

He has never worked easily. There is a giving of himself involved in what he does not always present in artists, which is why he is not prolific. His notion of perfection, especially, is stringent.

It made me nervous to watch him, and I used to go for long aimless walks in Brooklyn Heights or take the subway and roam Manhattan alone 'til I thought he would be finished for the day, to leave him in peace.

I hadn't been able to find even the deadliest of boring jobs, being pregnant and showing so early but, miraculously, I did not feel anxious about money at the time. Someone had put Juan on to a lucrative stopgap source which did more than keep us in funds. He became a banquet waiter at the Hotel St. George in downtown Brooklyn. A landmark site from the turn of the century, there was no lack of weddings to serve on Saturday nights. He only worked weekends but made enough in tips to make us think we were flush. Our savings fund for time out to have a baby mounted cheerfully. Haiti was said to be bone cheap.

We were doing fine.

His show at the AFI Gallery was beautiful, the opening well attended. The NY Times critic came and went in a quarter of an hour but he wrote a review in The Times giving reluctant praise. It would seem he preferred young painters to be American but was fair enough to recognize talent even though it was European. Better still, the critic from Art News not only wrote an enthusiastic review, he bought one of the paintings. That was heartening. Juan was pleased. He had made a point.

We left New York on a snowy January day and landed a few hours later in a haze of sunshine on a tarmac where the terminal was a clever rendition of a Cabane Choucoune, a native thatched house with more than a whiff of Africa about it. That was the trademark of Haiti. There were palm groves dotting the hills, the sky was milky blue to indigo. Our friends were waiting for us at the airport. They drove us up from the flatlands by the Caribbean through the colorful hilly streets from another planet, reaching a breezy colonial dream suburb called Pétionville where they had installed us in a self-contained apartment in a sprawling colonial style white villa, tall royal palms shading it from the sun on a Frenchified grande place. Our astonished host turned out to be someone whom I had known at Lake Success. We stared at each other under the tropical sun and burst out laughing.

Albert Mangonès had been a familiar figure in United Nations corridors. He was an architect, though, and did not choose to stay in New York as a UN consultant forever. His attitude, common among the Haitian elite, was one of the basic conundrums of this benighted paradise. Its elite would return from foreign educations, talk progressive policies but did nothing to change matters, nothing that worked. Even the sincere ones the talented happy few achieved little in terms of real change. It must be the sun, one observer noted wryly.

Yes, well.

Chapter 6

We had the most beautiful baby boy early in the hours of April 3rd after having gone for a ride in a jeep to watch the Rah-Rah, a sort of jamboree, that downtown Port-au-Prince put on for April Fool's Day. It took him 23 hours to appear but he looked absolutely pleased to have arrived and gave a lusty yell to let us know he was here. We called him Christopher, John Christopher, actually, in honor of the Roi Henri Christophe who made this tiny island paradise into an empire that took on Napoleon and won. Let no one say that Haiti does not nurture a sense of its own uniqueness.

On April Fool's Day they were dancing in the streets, carousing, screwing in the bushes, all being Haitian customs for any auspicious occasion.

There was a touch of Carnival all year round. Haiti, in my eyes, had the feeling of a lost continent with people left over from a West African corner that had dislodged itself from the mother continent so long ago no one remembered the way back.

As we settled in we soon discovered that there was a considerable foreign colony, mostly but not exclusively American, with a number of trust fund chaps and their wives, several of whom had babies locally as I did, who lived like their uncles had lived on the Riviera before the war. Sea, sun, cheap maids and lovely gardens, with excellent rum for pennies. There was a sense of this generation's would-be Scott Fitzgeralds among the middle-aged idle playboys on the edge of their legacies. They dotted the hills around Port-au-Prince, drinking rum and talking nonsense. I was surprised at the clusters of society names who lived on, with third wives and new children.

There were a couple of Europeans writing books on voodoo with the generous help of the island's three poets. One of those poets took us to see a Voodoo ceremony up above Port-au-Prince in a scrubby yard. It had already begun when we arrived.

Mauriceau Leroy, the poet, was greeted as he pulled into the enclave by the priest, who was a foreman on a building site downtown. He led us to a lighted area where the mass was already in progress. Two women were writhing on the ground, sweating profusely while the circles of onlookers swayed and chanted. The poet, kindly trying to get me a good view, brought over a wooden chair and motioned me to stand up on it. I looked over in panic toward Juan who was already holding out his arm to steady me. I am a bit clumsy at the best of times. This was not the best of times. The voices of the swaying congregation were unnerving, the limp creatures on the ground were frightening. I would have fled if I could, but I got on the chair and held my breath and watched the madness all around me in the dark night speckled with clumsy lamps.

The music rose, as did the sound of the chants and suddenly my wobbly chair wobbled a lot more as a small wiry old woman clambered up to share it with me. The poet motioned me to hold fast and not be afraid. Juan stood next to me like a barrage. The old woman began to wriggle in tune to the music and, gripping Juan's shoulder and Mauriceau Leroy's hand, I jumped off the chair just in time. The old lady twirled into the air after me, fell straight out on the ground and never lost a beat in her chant. I was sorry I was not one of those people who faint.

Let no one be abused, Voodoo is alive in the core of these people. And that might go a long way in explaining how the country works. Or doesn't work.

Still, Haiti was breathtakingly beautiful then with colors that mesmerized, colors seen nowhere else. The sea was nothing like other seas. The water was warm to swim in.

But the Haitians charmed one into believing that there was a way out, especially those left wing Europe-educated ones whose families had been bleeding the island of its future, of any future, for that matter, for generations.

The gruesome Papa Doc would obliterate their class but put in its place underbred hitmen from the shanty towns who only wanted what the elite had, not what they should have aimed at. Thuggery for the pleasure of thuggery killed Haiti. Envy is a despicable sin. Haiti was to die at its own hand in a few years to come.

It was a fascinating place to be, but it was not as inexpensive as it was supposed to be. We went through what we innocently thought of as considerable savings and there were no Hotel St. George banqueting weekends to pull us through. Juan sold all the paintings likely to be sold in a matter of a few months. He then set about making his version of Voodoo masks, something that does not exist in reality but which sold well in the curio shop on the seafront where the tourists from the cruise ships flocked to find authentic Haitian lore. He did small cut-out sculptures in copper of Haitian figures: girls walking with baskets of fruit on their heads, lithe and long-legged as they were in real life.

The shop was owned by a Viennese Jewish refugee who fetched up with his parents in Port-au-Prince at the outbreak of the war and remained there. He and his aged parents had declared before a Haitian court that they had African forebears in their family history and were thus accorded Haitian citizenship. The one Haitian law that protected blacks was that one, the claim to African ancestry.

The pragmatic Viennese merely shrugged that one off and said all humanity began in Africa. So, nu? The Fischer curio shop was the mecca of Haitian art fanciers who could not afford the prices, or had not the wit, to buy the real paintings from the art center newly founded by a wonderful American, DeWitt Peters, who brought Haitian primitive art to the world's notice just at that time. Mr. Fischer, in the Port, sold minor stuff 'til he found Juan, who made beautiful versions of what he saw in Haiti. What Fischer paid him kept us in rent and baby food but we needed a lot more. Haiti was more stimulating, more sophisticated, less innocent than our friends had described, but it was infinitely more expensive in the long run. As an example: we could buy three lobsters for a dollar but a jar of mayonnaise was three dollars. We had lobster with a little lemon juice instead.

I managed to find a job as a hotel clerk for a month but did not have the proper working papers so risked deportation or a fine for the American hotel owner. His aunt, a nasty little lady from Chicago, kept $25 off my pay as punishment for not having the proper papers. I did not go back for a second month.

A plan to do a picture book with photographer Arthur O'Neil fell through when Arthur could not interest the only publisher he knew.

Only the beautiful baby boy thrived. He gurgled and smiled early as if he were enjoying the sight of the banana tree leaf that opened before our eyes as we ate breakfast on the terrace. Rampant nature and the warmth of the sun. The maid put out his bath water to be warmed by the sun hours before his bath which, I was sure, gave him the extra vitamins and minerals he needed to avoid colds for the rest of his life. That turned out to be vastly inexact but he did grow to be 6"4', which I am sure had something to do with those sun-infused baths.

A baby in warm weather is at perfect ease, unrestricted by snowsuits, mufflers, gloves, or cold. Every day was Sunday for him.

We left the small lodgings in Pétionville for a smart little bungalow in the hills above Port-au-Prince and had a maid to cook for us and help watch the baby. He bloomed. He was bouncy and bright and had my De Soto eyes.

We made friends easily with the remittance-men foreign colony, though they could not have been more removed from us: indigent millionaires in a warm climate where lobsters, rum and labor were dirt cheap, sex casual and unimportant, and the real world at a great remove. Haiti was that, too.

We were totally out of our element and frequently found ourselves in cock-eyed conversation with aging playboys lamenting the Roosevelt years as the end of their world.

We were just about keeping above water, but we had no idea of how we were going to finance our way back to New York.

With the birth of the baby we ran into another kernel of real life we had not thought about: nationality. Of course he was duly put on my American passport and was declared at the US Embassy at birth. The spiky Spanish Consul, whom we had come to know socially since he was about our age and turned up at the same parties among the foreigners, soon asked when we would be registering him as Spanish. He had come up to our house just to find out, he said. Juan said as politely as possible that he would not be registered as Spanish at all.

A second Spanish Civil War almost broke out on the patio, but it was averted by the baby's sudden crying—loud shrieks from an infant wakened by a raised voice. Franco's man quickly took hold of his temper and sat down on a wicker chair, embarrassed and deflated.

Juan went to pour diplomatic drinks. I brought the baby out, who quickly stole the stage. The edgy diplomat retrieved his composure and murmured something like there was no rush ... he had 'til he was 21.

My children speak Spanish as well as Catalan, but neither have ever claimed Spanish nationality. Christopher was 23 when Franco died and democracy began to seep back into Spain in the form of a near miraculous constitutional monarchy which we warmly welcomed. But that was far in the future then.

We sat at the bar of the Hotel Riviera near the sea in Port-au-Prince where a handful of American expatriates had gathered to follow the radio coverage of the Eisenhower-Stevenson elections in 1952. Jerry, the hotel owner, ourselves, and the Moodys were the only ones nervously rooting for Stevenson.

All the others, the society chaps with their trust funds, seemingly terrified by the specter of a Stevenson win bringing egghead intellectuals into power, all noisily counted the States for Eisenhower. In truth, not one of them gave a damn about the General, it was tough minded John Foster Dulles and, tangentially, Sen. Joe McCarthy who were on their minds. The remittance men and their wives were not so much Republican as deeply, mindlessly reactionary.

I had heard phrases like "the scum of the earth" used about strikers in Detroit or "the great unwashed" in talking about New York.

Over their rum and Cokes they seemed to me that night to be harbingers of all that could go wrong with America in the foreseeable future. Picket fence conservatism was not in view here. It was unthinking privilege, and little else.

I wanted nothing more than to go home to New York then. The votes came pouring in over the radio for General Eisenhower as though Republicans were streaming through the airwaves into our sticky night. Jerry, the hotel owner, Juan and me and then, surprisingly, Mr. Moody and his wife, sat glumly at one corner.

Mr. Moody, the contractor who built all the roads in the islands, and his wife, who was a Bacardi rum heiress from Cuba, were solid Democrats. He was one of the richest men in the area and, certainly, one of the nicest, as we soon learned.

"What are you doing here?" he asked me, giving me a smile. I think I might have blushed.

"We don't have the money to leave," I said flatly while he nodded, clearly having expected as much.

"Where do you want to go?" he continued.

"New York. I'm from New York."

He smiled, as though expecting that, too. "I have a plane going to Miami on Saturday. There is room for you and your baby. Not your husband. But I have a banana boat leaving from Cap-Haïtien on the following Wednesday. He can take that to Jacksonville, Florida. How would that do?"

Thus, as yet another state fell to Eisenhower, our local millionaire saved our lives. "That will be fine, Mr. Moody. How can I ever thank you?"

He laughed and said, "You just did."

Juan saw le Roi Christophe's insane Citadel as he flew over the slip of Hispaniola that was Haiti, in another of Mr. Moody's planes. It was a magnificent but crumbling symbol of how not to establish and maintain statehood.

Haiti at the end of 1952 was ripe for a dictator, but not even the feckless leaders that we knew at the time deserved what was to happen under Duvalier. Yet no one did anything much to oust him. People like the Moodys left before they were murdered. The elite as we knew it was decimated, but a society of violence and mindlessness took its place. Never stable, it became palsied with anarchy. Even under the gentle proclamations of its would-be savior priest, it continued to crumble and to wither the ambitions of those who looked as though they might set it right. The countryside was ravaged, what little resources it possessed were devastated, the magical hills, les mornes of Kenscoff, with their purple tones, had been burned for charcoal. The poor had eaten their own landscape.

Haiti was vandalized not by foreigners but by other Haitians who let it happen. For whatever reason, it is Haitians themselves who bear the responsibility. It is surely a unique case in history, as far as I can see. A failed state in the middle of the Western Hemisphere? Not just poor but failed. Destitute. The recent horrendous hurricane that hit it with almost biblical force proceeded to unmoor it even further.

Nothing positive has happened to Haiti in the past sixty years. It makes me livid with indignation to think of that scale of failure. It is a cautionary tale.

Our son tells me he is embarrassed to tell people where he was born, which makes me sad on a number of levels. When we lived there I remember thinking that when he grew up he would be rather pleased to show off his adventurous start in life. It seems I was wrong.

We got back to New York under bright pale blue winter skies and drifts of snow. I had $7 in my wallet after taking the cheapest flight I could find to New York from Miami. My parents did not meet my plane, so my bankroll went on a cab up to Washington Heights. I should have asked Ann and her husband, Bob Barret, to meet me, not my parents. My mother was outraged at our situation and made it clear that Christmas or no, baby or no, we were no longer welcome in her home.

Her home. My father seemed to be invisible. Presumably he knew of no fury like an Irish fury, no disdain like that of a mother for a son-in-law who painted pictures rather than working for a living. She literally put us out.

Friends of Juan's, a Barcelona buddy with whom he had gone to art school and who was now married to a Cuban professor of Spanish at Rutgers, happily took us in. Not so much us, really, but the gurgling little Christopher who began his long career in charming people during that rude winter of early 1953 with ready smiles and clapping hands, enchanting anyone who saw him.

Stopgap jobs from which I was quickly fired followed, including one selling stockings on upper Broadway, for $1 an hour. I worked eight hours, earned $8, was thanked and told not to come back tomorrow, but we celebrated with dinner at the Automat, which welcomed babies with ready high chairs.

I found us a room on 92nd street off Riverside Drive and then a job as a clerk at a big pharmaceutical company. Juan made figurines cutting out copper plate, astonishingly good Spanish dancers with stunning little asses, and then a series of perfectly sculptural bulls, bull fighters or, again, Flamenco dancers with all the taut grace they evoke. In Haiti he had kept us going with his Voodoo masks, inspired by African sculpture, so these dancers were a logical next step.

Years later someone whom we hardly knew invited us to see his collection of African art and showed us, as his prize object, a rare Haitian Voodoo mask. Juan did not flinch as he recognized his own. Nor did he tell the man that there was no such thing as a Haitian Voodoo mask.

His own work moved into a sphere toward which he would turn some ten years later and never leave: sculpture.

I wish we had a Voodoo mask now, just to remember how it all began.

The icy winter of 1953 faded into spring and, totally by chance, I found a job that fit me. Something called the Christian Democratic Union of Central Europe, with offices on East 53rd Street, was looking for an English language editor-cum-secretary-cum-speech writer-cum anything else a small, peculiar organization might need in its dealing with the world of foreign policy in New York. As vague as it could be, it was perfect for me who had no real college degree but, instead, an artist husband and a small child. I spoke French and Spanish, could fake Italian because of Catalan, knew all about the United Nations because I was there from the beginning and was on waving terms with half the staff. On top of that, Konrad Sienkiewicz, the Polish Secretary General who interviewed and hired me, discovered that I was conversant with Pan Slavism and he decided on the spot to put up the salary to $500 a month.

At the time it sounded like opulence. Three months after arriving in New York with $7 in my wallet, we were back on top. Top was relative, of course. It was merely the exact opposite of Bottom.

Chapter 7

At the outset I told Konrad Sieniewicz that I was a good Democrat, a Stevenson Democrat, that I disliked virulent anti-Communists as much as I did Communists and that Senator McCarthy was an American virus as detestable as Stalin was in his. He said, "Fine," and went on to ask me why I had visited Prague when I was a student. My answer seemed agreeable to him and he called in his Czech colleague, a former judge in Brno, Bohmir Bunza, to meet me. We discussed the beauty of Prague rather than the pitfalls of dogma and I was hired on the spot. My life—our lives—had taken a great leap forward. It was one of those chance events that turn everything upside down forever.

The Christian Democratic Union of Central Europe was lodged in a ground floor apartment in an East Side brownstone. It consisted of representatives of exiled parties from Poland, Czechoslovakia, Hungary, Slovenia and Lithuania, all of which were members of the International which grouped CD parties worldwide. The Christian Democrat movement had emerged as one of the major ideologies in world politics after the war. In an ideology prone age, they were representative of a shaky Center in Western Europe and a defeated Center Right in the now Soviet-dominated east, though the Czech and the Polish parties had more radical wings.

I was slightly ill at ease in taking the job, but our recent brush with poverty had made me less observant of nuances than I might have been a few years earlier. On the other hand, I saw nothing particularly defensible in Communist rule or, worse, its brutal takeovers in Europe. Soviet-style democracy was as much a failure as any other kind of leather-booted doctrine. While socialist standards were admirable as goals, they did not appear to function anywhere but in our dreams and, possibly, the British health care system. Scandinavia was successful democracy, not socialism, in that property was owned not by the State but by individuals. A vital distinction, that.

My troubles with my conscience in working for an anti- Communist group was one of those little dichotomies I seem to fall into more easily than other people do, but I lived with it. I had learned to live with a whole range of odd prickles in those early years of being an adult.

Within a short time I became very fond of my Central European bosses, even the Lithuanian one who, in his convoluted English, gave me a horrific glimpse into what hatred of another people can do to a national judgment.

"I have nothing against Germans," he once said, "but I hate the Russians."

My skin crawled. He saw my expression and laughed out loud. "In America you know nothing about what happens!!!" He laughed good-naturedly. I felt anger burn within me.

"Never mind," he said blithely. "You will never have to know. It is too far away."

We became friends, most of us. Our home lives were too close to the office for us not to become friends. Bunza had left two small children in Brno when he escaped in 1948 and was fatherly with me. He liked to play the cello for Juan, with a nod to Casals, and to play marbles with Christy who was walking and talking by then. He, primarily, was most concerned for me because he saw a very young woman with too many responsibilities for her age and not enough time, walking a rocky edge.

It was a very rocky edge then. We had enough money for the roomy apartment which we had found, miraculously, in the lower regions of The Village, a five-room walk up in a renovated Italian tenement on Broome Street. It was bright and sunny. We had a living room, a big kitchen dining room, and three bedrooms, the largest of which became Juan's studio.

He was, I realized so much later, deeply unhappy at that time. His life had been mortgaged to the baby, in his eyes, to domesticity, to his role in a family. Too soon.

Of course he loved the baby and, in reality, had a way with him that I did not have. Perhaps all Mediterranean people are born knowing how to relate to children. Perhaps it is some extra gene that goes with olive oil and red wine. Perhaps being the oldest of five was the reason. Perhaps my being an only child was another. Perhaps it was because I spent ten hours a day either working or on the subway to and from my other life. Whatever.

From the beginning Juan knew what to do with the baby while I stumbled. Perhaps, too, I was born knowing how to find a job, any job, and how to take it without blinking. I was good at that. Even in a mini depression, even without a conforming C.V. that lacked a viable college degree, even with the handicap of having a child—illegal now; at the time any young woman with a child was often automatically disqualified. A personnel chief at Helena Rubenstein looked at me aghast and said, "Of course I cannot hire you. You would favor your child over your job if the question ever arose." She looked at me, indignant that I should waste her time.

The 1950s were a long time ago.

As beautiful and as loved as he was, the baby grew to be a bad eater. I would come home well after 6 pm, having had a day of sometimes delightful but never quiet international chaos to deal with, then a plow into the subway rush hour, which I loathed, to be greeted by a Juan who was clearly impatient to go into his studio and close the door, only to feed a little boy who had not seen me all day and who did not like eating and who needed a bath. He loved the bath, and so did I, but not the meal. He had me against a wall and I actually came to dread it.

Why we never altered the routine, why we did not simply say Juan would feed him before I came home—a system most working mothers resorted to out of sheer common sense—I will never know.

Except that Juan, who had his own notions of roles, thought I should feed him. He made me think so, too.

It was a thorny issue. There were several more. I am not sure why, but no one ever advised us or even hinted that we were going about things all wrong. Not even Ann, who must have seen. No one did anything, and time hung heavily like a weapon over our heads.

Beyond that, though, we had interesting friends and were relatively relaxed. We went to the theater, he went to concerts regularly with an English friend. "I am a Carnegie Hall widow," I would occasionally grumble, but the one thing Juan admired New York for was its affordable concerts. There must have been other advantages, but I can't recall him mentioning them off hand. He did not adjust to New York. He did not like our life there.

Chapter 8

There were highlights, though. There always are. A friend of mine, John Donahue, turned up in Vermont as editor of a local newspaper. I had met him on the ship returning to New York from Paris in late 1949 and we stayed in touch. He found us a cottage to rent on Lake Champlain for August that year, 1953, and we acquired a marvelous vintage car, the last model Chrysler had produced before our entry into the war, 1941. It still had a running board and it drove like a charm. It turned out to give us what seemed like a touch of freedom.

We drove up to Vermont for August and made new friends. By then Christy was two, talked perfectly clearly and made friends with the next door neighbors who had a boat on the lake. He astonished everyone around by taking to Danny's Daddy's Motor Boat, a tongue twister no one else could utter as effortlessly as he could.

In packing the car for our summer trip, Juan stared at a bundle of books I had taken from the library to read on summer afternoons. Staring at them in clear rebuke, he said angrily, "Are you planning to read all month!?"

I was shocked at his reaction because, yes, I had been planning to read all month. Which brought to light another thorny difference in us. I had read all my life. Each of my parents read in the evenings. Reading was one of the major bases of life as I lived it. My parents' living room had a wall-to-wall bookcase. His parents' house had his paintings on the walls and a piano. There were no books.

We had a basic differences whichever way we turned. I read all the library books I had brought with me and he, in turn, read a few, as well.

But we did not mention the incident again. It was, so to speak, buried alive.

Clark McBurney, a poet and essayist as well as publisher of slim volumes of poetry, turned up at the Free Europe Committee working with my Christian Democrats.

The Free Europe Committee, a not terribly well-concealed adjunct of the CIA to support communities of political exiles in a variety of guises, including the Assembly of Captive Nations, a parliament of exiles which was planted in a building across the street from the UN building, that gave voice to exile political communities.

Clark was an unlikely figure in the Free Europe galaxy, which included many unlikely individuals, depending on the year. He had been Tennessee Williams's college roommate, had published some of his lesser plays, and was a published poet and critic himself.

He was to save our marriage, if not our lives. We saw him and his fragile young French wife, Marie José, frequently. He spent time with Juan and looked at his paintings with interest, and they talked ideology and philosophy late into Village evenings. He was a Washington Square café sitter. So were we. With Christy asleep in his baby carriage. We became good friends after working hours. It was a blessed closeness, I thought at the time, because I was nervous about our tomorrows, sometimes even of our todays.

It was, finally, Clark who engineered our move to Europe. A bit deviously, but it worked. Some months earlier a charming Free Europe official had taken me to lunch to sound me out for a possible job in a new office they were thinking of opening in Paris. 1954 had seen new interest in Central Europe for a number of reasons. Phil Abbey thought that they should have someone with press abilities and who knew French in a small office in Paris.

I was still very young and could not pretend to a high salary so, he reasoned, I might do well. And I would be a bargain. No one likes bargains more than a financial advisor. Free Europe was rife with financial advisors, he assured me. They might think that Riga was the capital of Transylvania but that did not matter, they ran the railroad.

"I think they will fall in love with you at first sight once I tell them you will settle for less than $10,000 a year," he said. The sum was so vast I nearly fainted.

Unfortunately, the kind Phil Abbey was to fail in his plan. A nice candidate with a catchy name, Connie Dulles, got the job. Her salary was twice what I would have settled for, at that. So much for idle words.

But my candidacy managed to spring back, and a year later we left Broome Street with the blessings of the Christian Democrats, who wanted me to be able to be happy, and the empathetic Clark McBurney who wanted Juan to be saved, along with our marriage if possible.

He told me later that he could sense Juan's despair more acutely than I imagined. He also sensed the inexperience I showed in dealing with it. He was a wise man as well as a kind one.

I often raised a glass of champagne to his memory in later years, in heartfelt thanks. He did not stay at Free Europe much longer nor did his marriage to Marie José last. I have never been able to thank him properly. It is a pity, for I owe him more than even he imagined.

Chapter 9

This would be the time to explain The Free Europe Committee, Radio Free Europe and even the CDUCE in the context of the very Cold War of the 1950s. At least a glancing description would help.

Although RFE (Radio Free Europe) was owned and operated by an adjunct of the CIA, it was a reputable news agency run by reputable journalists. The headquarters was in Munich, where a sizeable compound was established in the very attractive Englischer Gardens housing the entire operation.

Munich itself was the heart of the Kingdom of Exiles in that icy Cold War. All colors, all countries, all ideologies had a corner to work. The world of political exiles was colorful, tragic, spiteful, grandiose, generous and vicious all in one breath. Exile is a hardship no matter how highly placed the individual might be. It is the erasure of one identity and the forcible acquisition of another. It is a chafing dish for spite, for getting even, for getting back—of old comrades turning on each other for a new vision of the greater good.

In the mid-fifties it was a matter of winning rounds, not the whole match. The whole match was ill-defined in all the world leaders' visions except, perhaps, for Stalin, who knew by the end of the war he had won for a long time to come. Thereafter, satellite countries were led by imposed thuggish strongmen, and by thin-lipped ideologues, icy men who had become inured to mass murder by the bestialities of World War II. Humanity had dropped a notch; the unacceptable became a way of life. Concentration camps became commonplace. Ideology was twisted to fit the needs of the conquest of the moment. Ideology, tragically, got lost in the fray.

Yet it became clear that our damaged post-war man needed a semblance of ideology to survive, be it only the decency of the common good. Imposed from above by a historic bully, Russia, the new ruler of the Soviet Union, began just a little further along on the map, in Berlin. Europe was slashed down the middle. It was not a time of peace, it was something new... a Cold War. And the air tingled with its dangers.

In 1955, then, I joined Connie Dulles and her secretary in the small Paris office. Mademoiselle Groslier, Connie's secretary, a woman in her fussy seventies, had been the private secretary of Royal Tyler, a curious American diplomat and scholar, as well as a member of the Bonaparte family, during his years in pre-war Budapest. She gave the operation a tinge of old European approbation. This whole affair was to free a captive Europe, was it not? So said her presence, much as an endorsement might do a bottle of time-honored cough syrup.

During my two years of being with the Christian Democrats in New York, I had learned to swim in the turbulent seas of exile politics. My sympathies were with the left-leaning clan, the side that looked for a solution, not an armed conflict. There was an irresponsible right wing among the exiles that would have allied itself with any extremist current available to dislodge the Communists from Eastern Europe, but these seldom had democratic pasts on which to draw. Worse, their conduct with the Germans during the war was seldom exemplary. Concentration camp guards had an embarrassing number of Baltic nationals. Regional rivalry had been fearsome throughout history. Communist occupation had not done much to change that, either.

An American had little background in such finesses. Earlier, I had been horrified to learn the depth of Catalan hostility to the rest of Spain except, perhaps, for Andaluz poets. That hostility made me uneasy because I had seen Spain as a unit, a brilliant, gifted whole. Inured though I might have been by this example, however, the genuine hatred I found among these Europeans who lived in each other's pockets—from an American viewpoint—was deplorable. Moreover, I had no doubt that any future peace in the region would be disastrously compromised by what seemed to be eradicable ancestral hatred.

I talked of this to a Slovak diplomat in exile, the son of one of Czechoslovakia's founders, and he hesitated a moment before he said, "There won't be a Czechoslovakia then; it will have fallen apart before. They have nothing in common but geography. You watch."

He was right. The separation between the Czech lands and Slovakia was relatively smooth. But look at what happened to Yugoslavia, the one country that had outsmarted the Soviet Union, the one country of the

Eastern bloc which maintained itself outside Stalinism. The West did nothing to save it when it began to fall apart.

On the contrary, Germany opened the floodgates. It opened the way for Croatia to eclipse itself and the Clinton administration bombed Serbia's bridges, thus ushering in total chaos and demonizing Serbia in the process. It also gave birth to a new little country called Kosovo in the heart of Europe, a brand new Moslem state. That is really thinking ahead, isn't it?

Who would have bet on that in 1956 when the Paris office began to flourish under the name Free Europe Exile Relations? But that was later. First there was 1955 Connie Dulles supervising stipends for now-forgotten representatives of what were little more than local branches of exile communities in Paris.

Connie was a pert young woman whose father was a history professor in Ohio and a first cousin of the Dulles brothers. Like her father, she was a liberal Democrat and not a bloodthirsty anti Communist, as might be surmised. We had known each other in New York and had even gone up to their house in Vermont one weekend, which happened to be the day Juan got his driving license from—I forget why—the State of New Jersey.

Connie was pleasant, cautious, a bit unsure of me, but quite happy to give the newly-created job I seemed to come in the door with a try. She knew I was not after a career and thus was not about to compete, and she knew that she held the financial sword over my head should I suddenly have an attack of ambition, so I was no threat. And I wrote the reports that she labored over, with ease and dispatch.

Stupidly, I had rented a house in the suburbs without really checking out the metro system. The real estate office had told me the metro was a few minutes away and so was the bus stop. The house was big and had a pretty, if somewhat wild, garden for Christy. I thought that it would be a good starting off place.

It was not. The metro was far, the bus further. I had to walk through woods in the still dark early morning to get to the office by nine. I was frequently late. I hated it.

Juan's youngest sister came up to take care of Christy, which should have been a godsend but she had a Spanish idea of meal times so Christy was frequently unfed, still dressed and dropping with fatigue when I got home around 8. American schedules went out the window as far as he was concerned. Tina, my sister in law, could not understand why I was upset at his eating "a little late."

I did not want to admit that I did not look forward to feeding an over tired three-year-old who had an eating problem, after a day that had begun twelve hours earlier... but I should have. I should have set out at the start that I came home too tired and too late to feed him.

My winter of discontent? To this day I don't know how I got through it without committing mayhem. Just in time, we found a flat in Paris and left woodsy Clamart overnight.

The flat on the rue Condorcet was petit bourgeois, expensive and cramped but it was in Paris. I could walk back and forth to the office. It only took about thirty minutes either way.

Someone in the New York office, a self-sufficient young man called Roger Bull, without consulting anyone else, decided to cut my salary in half because he considered me to be "local hire." I was not.

It took all those long winter months to clear it up. Those months coincided with one of the coldest winters in French history. Paris froze. Outdoor pipes burst, leaving frozen puddles of refuse on the sidewalks. Cars skidded, walkers slid.

Juan's brother and his wife and their very tiny baby took refuge in our living room; the pipes in their suburban flat had burst leaving them without heat or water. Caroline Pezzullo, my militant friend from New York, came through needing a roof. She was President of the Young Christian Workers Women's Division and had been at a conference in Rome. She couldn't afford a hotel so she moved into the room with Christy and Tina. A little more and we would have qualified for Shelter status.

Connie eventually wrote a note to Roger Bull saying the Palà family was no longer eating dessert because of the cut in salary. I stared at her.

Then Jim came. Jim McCargar was a tall, very elegant gent straight from Nob Hill via the Navy during the war and a stint in the early, still noble-minded CIA, which disillusioned him and angered them forever.

Jim had sensed the change in the Central European air. He saw the signs in Poland, he read the warnings in Hungary. When he came into our little office, handsome and breathing promise, I felt an instantaneous presentiment that everything was going to snap into place.

I was not quite thinking of the Hungarian Uprising, of course, nor even the Poznań riots. Only a few stargazing exiles imagined that. I only meant the stopgap job which had proved so far to be a dismal millstone was going to vanish and I would come alive again. My dispiriting dreary winter was at last over. The promising spring of 1956 shimmered before us.

The first thing we were to do when my salary was reinstated was to take a cheap flight to London.

Chapter 10

Connie had liked the patroness approach to her job; she was more comfortable with refugees than exiles. Jim instantly changed the tone. A whole new cast of characters appeared on the threshold. The very air tingled.

On the first day of his reign, Jim called me in and looked hard at me—amused, but hard. He said, "What the Hell are you doing here?"

I remember my eyes widening because I was not expecting that. I fumbled for a second and then blurted out, "Juan wants to live in Paris. This is by way of being a job."

He took this in and finally said, "Okay. From today on, you are my Information Officer and we double your salary. And that cost of living allowance gets put back in. Roger Bull indeed." And he shook his head in impatience. Jim changed my life. And Juan's.

Jim McCargar's arrival in Paris signaled a complete weather change. New office premises were found a little further up on the rue de la Paix from RFE. We were at No. 15 on the corner of the rue Daunou, and Harry's bar was just down the street. On the other side of the rue de la Paix there was a small anti-chamber of our premises, l'Ambassade de Champagne, a cosy lounge which I had barely noticed before but which was to become a favorite refuge from then on. On the rue Ste. Anne there was another bolt hole, a restaurant bar that held particular charm, a touch of the secret corner Paris is so good at. Or was it just the right moment, the right place? 1956 was a time for such places, backdrops to a revolution.

With Jim at the helm of a different ship, much more suited to me and what I am good at, and our finally moving into a pleasant place to live, Juan and I seemed to emerge from a cloud of heavy silence onto two differing but brighter paths.

He had not done much work in Clamart or in the flat on the rue Condorcet that followed it. He had no room, really, and not much inducement. Never a prolific worker, he found it difficult to get started and even more difficult to accept the freeze he so often experienced. If he produced anything in that period there is no trace of it now. Worse, he seemed to grow further away from me with every new international crisis I was involved in. He stood further back with each new gunshot. When the Poznań revolt shook Europe he showed no inclination to help me bridge the gap between my presence at home, later and later in the day, and my ever more demanding schedule at work.

Tina soon left us and took a job with friends running a restaurant in St. Germain des Prés. We then began that nightmare of the working mother, the Au Pair syndrome. Charming girls who lived in but went out, who were supposed to save your life but regularly complicated it … a few were capable with Christy, took him to school, and fed him dinner while I worked increasingly erratic schedules and while Juan detached himself more and more from my world. I saw him drift away but had no idea of how to reach out.

An unattractive chapter opened here when we collided with something I had not fully understood. I should have known better.

Women always found Juan attractive, they were to do so for the rest of his life. I was unprepared for his reactions, however. When in that rocky period in the mid-1950s it became obvious that his widening detachment from me and my involvement with the color of change in the world meant his reaching out toward others, I was stunned. It was like a slap in the face. True, my job had grown from just a way of keeping us alive into a fascinating window on our world and I enjoyed it and felt a sense of purpose as my involvement increased—all that was true. But my brilliant rise would never have transpired had it not been my urgent obligation to have a job in the first place.

There is a bit of graffiti going around lately which reads, "What Do Artists Do All Day?" I know what they do: they brood. They are not the happiest of people, they are seldom sure of themselves, they cry inside at the slightest frown from others. Yet they protect themselves like nobody else. They wrap their arms around themselves and rock back and forth gently telling themselves it will all work out. Which is why, in company, they seem different from everyone else. They put on good faces, expressions for outside consumption. They do not abide by everyone else's laws because they are different from those others. So when called upon to behave according to everyone else's scales, they balk. "You are asking me to be someone I am not," is what they are thinking, resentfully. And it is true. I was asking Juan to behave like he asked me to behave.

In those long confused months after we had returned to Paris, he was closed in with his own demons. He fought his demons his way, not mine. If opening the door to our women friends in the afternoon was one of them, what the hell. There was nothing wrong with that, in his mind. And if I judged him with the wrong measuring stick, that was my error. I should have known better.

The upside down logic therein is what makes artists different from everyone else, for they believe it. They believe in the presence of the "duende," a Spanish magical creature similar to the Irish sprite or leprechaun who gives you the magic you need to be an artist. A great cante jondo singer will have duende or not be a great cante jondo singer. Picasso has duende, Matisse is an intelligent painter. The difference is obvious.

I should have known that, of course. I should have made place for it in my heart, he was telling me silently with his eyes. There are things you should not have to put into words.

He was fighting for his own survival, this was part of his armory. I should have known that, too. Or so he thought. All his life Juan has had a certain idea of what an artist is. I have not always understood that.

Nor did he give much thought to my need, in my late twenties, to be told I looked pretty in that white Dior top I had just bought on sale or that a jacket picked up in Rome during a conference looked perfect on the balcony of the Castel San Angelo.

I had to accept the difference he claimed for his own needs, the part of him that had nothing to do—in his eyes—with our life together. Artists are different, he was saying out loud. I should have known that from the start.

The chance encounter that happens between two people that leaves nothing in its wake but a secret smile is a fairy tale. But should something happen like, that, it can make up for a thousand ills. Real life does what it can to heal and the compromises we eventually made served us with adult insights we, or rather I particularly, so badly needed. And, to my amusement now in looking back, it turned out to be a one way track.

On the rare occasion mention is made of a certain European diplomat of those days, Juan makes a face of indignation and injury. Distaste, even. He never saw the startlingly blue eyes or the wicked grin or heard the slightly accented British English I did. Or perhaps he did and realized that there was a not-to-be ignored side of me that favored the Ritz bar or the Crillon and driving around in a vintage Jaguar. The driver of the Jaguar was my revenge. He knew it, of course, but was gallant enough to pretend otherwise. He helped me get over what might have been a foolishly unbridgeable rift.

That is still sweet to remember.

The fire and fury in the streets of Budapest, the brief spellbinding moment when the Communist empire tottered and almost fell, were monumental moments to witness first hand. There was intrigue galore, there was a peak of promise and then, with the Western invasion of the Suez Canal Zone, there was bitter collapse. Not quite as simple as that, of course, but it had been so close. The foundations of Communism in Europe were shaken and eventually rebuilt along different tracks, but the impact was immeasurable. And the bitterness of Hungarians that the West had permitted it to fall apart remains indelible to this day. *Where were you in 1956?*, they will say to you now.

Where indeed. We had entered into a different time zone.

The Free Europe office was now a hectic hive of dedicated young people—only the accountant was over forty.

Tom Donahue was a New York trade unionist who lent brilliance to his concept of workers' rights. He was, and still is, for that matter, tall, and Irishly handsome with a quick wit and New York sharpness that I treasure. We shared a singular moment in history then, we were on the edge of the world looking in and we shared the stench of defeat. We are the same age and from similar corners of New York, a further link between us. (The rest of the staff talked funny, we claimed, they all came from Out There.)

It says something that we have remained close for nearly sixty years. That is what that period did to us. More than any other decade, in my experience, those Cold War years were defining ones. The lines were drawn. We were who we were and we saw that where we were going was not always the quickest way to Heaven, though we did not always agree on where Heaven really was.

Chapter 11

Friendships are made at all times of life, but there is a touch of burnished gold to those who began in one's young years and continue into old age. Susie Ovadia, whom I met on the first day I entered the RFE office, is a startling case in point. She was sitting on the corner of Allan Dreyfus' desk. As Connie introduced us, I was mesmerized by whatever it was she was saying, probably outrageous, by the way she said it and the amazing beauty she seemed to be totally unconcerned with. A shock of black hair loosely cut, eyes like a tiger's, and evident curiosity about me and what I was doing in the fussy little cubicle that Connie and Mademoiselle inhabited at the end of the corridor. I thought she was stunning.

Mademoiselle, an encyclopedia of Who's Who in several orbits and always eager to whisper her knowledge, told me as soon as she could that Susie Benedikt was the daughter of the Benedikt newspaper dynasty in Vienna, and her mother was a Swedish countess—which explained everything, she inferred. I knew enough about Central Europe by then to be instantly impressed though I had never heard of the Benedikt dynasty.

As irreverent as she was beautiful, as insightful as she was irrepressible, as different from me as one could hope for, she has been a pillar in my life ever since.

"We are getting married next month," she had been saying. I muttered something pleasant. "Well," she said with a toss of the black hair, "It's about time. We've been living together for the past two years..."

Everyone talks like that now, but no one did in 1955, and I can see the expression on Mademoiselle's face to this day. I burst out laughing. She still makes me laugh and she is still delightfully outrageous. My life would have been dimmer without her.

Friendships are anchors and I needed them more than most. I needed reassurance, I needed help. For a long stretch of time, living in a world of spinning values, of devastating changes in the way we lived our lives, I needed the anchor that was friendship. Perhaps too many people demanded too much from a still very young lady. The roles I had to play were frequently written for a more mature protagonist. No one, least of all myself, acknowledged how much I played life by ear. The political judgments, the tricky jockeying for position I was faced with in my job—which took so much of my life—was exhausting. I had little time to question it, however, little time to do anything more than fly it on automatic pilot and hope for the best.

I admit to having a taste for automatic pilots. I also enjoyed flying off to Berlin or London or to a conference in the Castel San Angelo in Rome at a moment's notice. I buzzed around Europe writing reports on international conferences of Christian Democrats, Federalist Youth Movements, Agrarian Reformers, Romanian Culture in Exile… I was younger than most of the Youth Movement people, more socialist inclined than those who championed the cause, more Christian in my doubts than the Christian Democrats and all that helped. I knew enough Spanish, French, Catalan and, probably thanks to the cinema, Italian, to ferret through Romanian, so I ended up working with the most rewarding of the exile communities.

I liked hanging out at the Ritz bar or the Crillon as well as my near native Café Flore or the Select in Montparnasse. I liked being able to afford good clothes for a change, bought on the generous cost of living allowances while travelling… I slipped into top gear with ease and hoped it would last forever.

We sent Christy home to my parents one lovely September but did not go to bed that night 'til my mother phoned us from her apartment saying he had arrived safely. After, he was to declare transatlantic flying very tiring. We buzzed around four-star restaurants and once even spent a night at the Martinez in Cannes. We were headily enjoying ourselves.

American policy changed, hardened, grew more tuned to the military than the intellectual currents in government policy. Soon the military had entered our little arena. In something of a palace revolution, Jim McCargar was fired. Bob Grey resigned. We would all have liked to do the same but our personal lives did not permit such gestures. Tom left as soon as he could, however, back to the Labor movement he had taken a leave of absence from. I had no such choice. I had to stay afloat in Paris; it was where our lives had taken root.

After the McCargar years, the American Right got hold of Free Europe and it lost its way. In the hands of insular bureaucrats who judged the

Cold War in terms of inches on a map rather than the scope of ideologies, everything changed course. I hung on because I had to.

By 1963 the office had shrunk to Gene Metz and myself, plus the accountant and one lone Hungarian who was more of a token than anything else. The Free Europe Committee closed its doors in Paris not long after and hung on in London for a bit more.

The world turns and takes you with it. I can only be eternally grateful for having had my odd, somewhat embarrassing job for so long, for having had an American salary which might have been modest in American terms but was opulent in Paris, that permitted us to buy a small but lovely house on the Left Bank and, stretching a little, a thatched cottage in Normandy as well as a 400-year-old house in the last unspoiled village in Mallorca which we kept for the next forty years. None of these houses were expensive but they gave us what we needed as a basis for what was to be a very chancy financial future for the rest of our lives.

As well as a second child. I realized by the end of the 1950s that a second child would make us a family, would make us whole. Juan reluctantly agreed. "A single child had been a touch of madness," he said, grinning. "A second one would be its confirmation." And then he smiled. "Whenever you like…?" he said.

We surprised the obstetrician by consulting after being late for one week. "Eight days," he confirmed, looking very puzzled. That was all we needed.

We argued names 'til she was born on September 22, 1960 and her name is Suzy because on the operating table where I had a Cesarean, I dreamt that someone was banging on my belly singing Oh Susannah at the top of his voice.

Chapter 12

But to go back a little, it was when we moved into the atelier on the rue de la Tombe Issoire in 1956 that Juan's mood changed. This was the studio he needed and this was the atmosphere that afforded him a new start. A big, burly Greek sculptor who had a charming American wife lived in the courtyard opposite us. Costas Coulentianos was his name, and he worked in metal. Sculpture in metal, as opposed to being cast, was a somewhat new school, as opposed to carving in stone or even wood or molding in plaster. Working with metal provided a directness, a symbiosis with the material and the artist that opened new avenues. Juan watched Coulentianos work with increasing interest.

He was encouraged by another artist neighbor, who admired his painting, Sugai, who was already a prominent Japanese figure in Paris at the time. He, his wife, and Juan developed a pleasant friendship, couched in oriental formality that was touching to watch. Sugai admired Juan's painting and, in his creaky French, encouraged him to go further. They had what to me were fascinating conversations, always a little formal, in a very bizarre mixture of French and English covering both their approaches to work. Sugai gave us each a present of a drawing, a very generous gift for a successful artist who sold copiously.

Another Greek couple, Cosma and Ariane Xenakis, lived in an adjacent studio with a child Christy's age. The courtyard was convivial, child friendly. It was there that Juan became increasingly drawn toward metal sculpture.

The first piece he finished, indeed, was the figure which had been the core of his last oil painting. It was as though he had peeled the figure off the canvas and welded it into an iron presence. I forget why but the piece was called Manuela. She was a tall figure, amazingly graceful and she was the first sculpture he was to show at the much prized Salon de la Jeune Sculpture, held in the gardens of the Musée Rodin. Juan had caught the attention of an influential critic who ran the Salon, Denys Chevalier, who was to do a lot to further his career at the time.

Around then Susie and Silvio Ovadia came to the studio and viewed his first few metal pieces with great interest. Susie said to me at the time, "Wonderful. He is hammering out his frustrations. What a lucky man." He was.

Within a year his work had attracted attention and he was invited to show in various prestigious salons, including Réalités Nouvelles and le Salon de Mai.

The dark roads he had encountered in his painting had vanished, and a whole new horizon opened to him with sculpture. He had found his way and quietly went ahead with it. There were early experiments with constructions in metal wire, spheres or large rectangles, each with a world within. One of these wire worlds was in an exhibition at the Museum of Modern Art in Paris and a Figaro photographer snapped a picture of a man as seen through the wire labyrinth. It was published on the paper's first page.

My lovely friend Ruth rang up one morning at 7:30, almost yelling into the phone, "Juan is on the First Page of *Le Figaro*!" forgetting that I am not an early riser and couldn't have cared less at that hour. He was pleased, though, and thanked her, looking like the Cheshire Cat.

He knew he was on his way. For him to be sure of himself, sure of the direction he was taking, was a major change. He had groped during the last years of painting, hesitating in his use of color, his approach to form. As the colors grew less important and the form more incisive, the move into sculpture was inevitable. A whole new spectrum opened up before him.

Just around the time that Suzy was born, he was a happy man.

At the office, the world of political turmoil continued at an alarming pace. The chaos of Central Europe was intensified by the West's failure to defy the Soviet Union over Hungary. No frontal attacks were indulged in on either side so that a permanent sense of possible disaster was created that was to last for another decade. It is easy to look back and cry coward now, but no one in his right mind wanted a showdown at that point. It was up to a sensible Center to keep things quiet. Unsolved, but quiet. It was time to think of alternative ways to live together in a world of total opposites.

The Fifties were at an end.

We gave a New Year's Eve party in our house on the rue de l'Aude in 1960 which started out small but grew to be something memorable that went on 'til dawn. To our surprise afterward, we counted among the guests eight prominent psychoanalysts, five Irish poets and a drift of journalists, painters, actors and a couple of unclassifiable Paris characters who made up the population of the Flore or Select, depending on the season. It occurred to me that night that though Paris was an uncomfortable place to live at the moment, what with the Algerian war being played out on its streets in unnerving guerrilla incidents, we were now a part of it and that had its charms.

Moreover, we had just won the American elections and had John F. Kennedy to show for it. We had a President we were proud of. I had worked briefly on the campaign, though Americans living abroad were still not able to vote, and felt a part of his victory. It was a fine time to begin a new decade, I thought. But neither I nor anyone else around me had the slightest inkling that it would be the decade that would knock us all for a giant loop.

The sixties were upon us.

Chapter 13

We had a new house, amazingly almost totally paid for at the start, a beautiful new baby and Juan was launched in a medium he seemed to enjoy. He liked banging away at metal, we noticed, considerably more than he did searching for the perfect grey. For an exuberant Spaniard who reveled in cante jondo, he had a remarkable *retenue* when it came to color. I once bought a smart red suit at Jaeger's in London and he blinked when he saw me turn up in it at the airport. "It is red," was all he said, giving me a peck on the cheek. "Very red."

His sculptures did not distract by color, they cut into space and stood absolutely still. He who was all movement and grace in his body, brought stillness, stasis even, into his world. There has always been an intriguing contradiction in Juan Palà. It is perhaps most visible in his work.

The little house on the rue de l'Aude was perfect for us. A block from the enchanting Parc Montsouris, it had a dining room and kitchen on the ground floor, a pocket sized patio, which I called The Garden, that led to the atelier, which was smallish but adequate. Adequate for the time being, that is. Juan could not do big pieces there but for the moment no one had commissioned any so it was not a problem. The studio was his haven, his domain. It took another twenty years for him to realize he had outgrown it.

On the house's first floor, we made a living room out of the two small rooms we found. There were two fireplaces and three windows that gave height to the room and let whatever sun Paris provided flood the space. It was a room perfect for parties and we did not hesitate to give them. My children and my friends' children grew up passing peanut trays to willing guests. Up another flight were two smallish bedrooms and finally, a few years later, we built a fourth level for our bedroom which turned out to be the quietest bedroom I have ever had in France, including the countrified Combs-la-Ville that was alive with local traffic by dawn each day.

The rue de l'Aude was muffled, cosseted. It ended in a flight of stone steps. It was out of a Jean Gabin movie. Taxis frequently told me it did not exist. Sometimes I thought they might be right and I only made it up.

We moved in during the summer of 1959 when my friend Neely Wheeler kindly camped out with me while Juan was in Spain with Christy for the summer and I didn't fancy staying there alone. We lived in that house 'til the summer of 1981, when we went off to a Normandy exile while Juan built a house on the rue de la Butte-aux-Cailles on the other side of the Parc Montsouris, a lifetime later.

Or so it seems now.

Our lives blossomed in the '60s. It was as though the little house opened doors we had not guessed at. The world around us sizzled. East-West politics as seen from the rue de la Paix had veered into a causeway of sneaky turnabouts. No armed battles but lots of murky skirmishes. Exiles whom I had known as pillars of their communities in those early '60s were caught red-handed spying for their Communist governments. Cultural battles waged, different from the previous decades' warfares. Less lethal, perhaps, but murkier. Personal honor on an individual level came into play and was frequently found lacking. There was a battle for men's imaginations as well as their souls. Books like *The Captive Mind* drew the lines of battle and warned of the no man's land at the goal post. Or Egon Hostovský's underestimated *The Midnight Patient*, which showed the no-win future ahead of the blistered present.

The early '60s brought the horrors of Vietnam into the foreground, too. Honor in battle had become a definition lost from sight. Napalm and Agent Orange disgraced us. Israel had fired the Middle East into a further ideological furnace with everyone losing and all sides failing. East and West were further divided by increasingly arcane definitions of freedom, loyalty and especially honor. The grace of our new young President, his language, his baggage of renewal, was tipped by the Bay of Pigs misadventure which was to color the Cuba policy the US was to carry out 'til today, three generations later. The '60s led us to Chile and Pinochet, the death of Allende, the US role in the grim brimstone of Latin American policy. The '60s brought protest, but they provided the scene the protest was aimed at with bloodied accuracy.

At the beginning of the new decade though, the party was just beginning. We were delighted to have suitable premises. It is hard to imagine how we juggled our social scene between our Paris intellectual crowd, mostly from among the arts, and the others who mostly came through the office. In the post-Free Europe times there were some friends who overlapped. But suddenly there were more Americans through an unexpected source, an American women's club: American Wives of Europeans.

I am an unlikely candidate for a woman's club under any circumstances. I am not a club person. At that point in my life I also thought I liked men more than women. I was unlikely to deliberately go out and seek to exclude men from any social circle I might be interested in. I had a man's job, I lived in a circle more open to men than women, and I had the wrong kind of small talk. My beloved friend Ann was my unique confidante. It is not for nothing that I grew up as an only child of older parents in New York, after all.

Yet when I saw the ad in the personals column of the NY *Herald Tribune* asking for American Wives of Europeans to get in touch with Phyllis Michaux to talk things over, I did not hesitate a second. I was looking for other children like mine. I wanted other little boys for Christy to play cowboys with in English. I wanted other English-speaking children to come to visit him so that he would not grow up thinking his parents were Martians, which he tended to do already. I called Phyllis, arranged to meet with her in Harry's Bar, our office hangout just a block away, and took a giant step in my curious life as an American abroad.

Unfortunately, however, none of the other children he eventually met spoke English at home. But I was to make friendships that would last the rest of my life. And our children would, too, though they spoke French together to the end.

There was Barbara Grosset, to begin with. Barbara, the beautiful, the fey, the gifted for happiness. Barbara who was married at least as happily as I, if less dramatically. She was the wife of Raymond Grosset, the ground breaking director of Rapho Photograph Agency who knew many of the same people in the press world that we did as well as photographers whom I had admired for years. And who lived off la Place Vendôme, so they knew the Ambassade du Champagne as well.

Barbara became my instant friend. We had Irish Americanness in common, Catholic educations, love for New York, foreign in-laws, foreign languages, foreign concepts, foreign everything to adapt to... and both welcomed a breath of the Hudson's air. Barbara grew up on the New Jersey side of the George Washington Bridge, I on the Manhattan side. We became instant friends. I loved her, her husband Raymond, and her children. She died before we got old, while we looked on helplessly. Raymond, who was seventeen years older, outlived her graciously and her little boy Mark died unforgivably before he was fifty, leaving us all in shock. Kathy and Jessica, her daughters, thank heaven, are vivid parts of our lives still, but Barbara, who was so vital to mine, died in 1986. It wouldn't have seemed conceivable then when we first met. But when is early death ever conceivable?

The Free Europe years were fading, then, in the mid-1960s and a wider stage was set. The mood was for change. Noisy change. We were all set.

Chapter 14

Ever since Christopher was born I wanted to be the kind of mummy that takes her children to the park every day. I did not, however, yearn for the part of that image that shows the hubby in Scarsdale complete with station wagon and an Irish setter. I would have fled Scarsdale even if it had been outside Paris. But I did yearn for a bench in the Parc Montsouris near the sand pile. I was too late for Christy but just in time for Suzy, who was two-and-a-half when I was finally fired from Free Europe and its gainful employment. Not unexpectedly, either. But what was unexpected was that my mother was with us, too.

My story with my mother is too long and rocky to go into here but despite all that had gone before, when my father died sadly in January of 1963, I brought my mother to live with us in Paris. I am to this day unsure of how that decision was made or why. She had a life full of friends that I knew nothing about in New York and held a two-day wake for my father, which I found grotesque, wherein she entertained streams of people I had never heard of, let alone met, most of whom had not known my father, either.

I was amazed to learn Mother had a full secret life of her own in which roleplaying apparently was a major part. I didn't know that about her either. One of her roles was the helpless widow with the affluent daughter in Paris. Etcetera.

So, when my father died she just about walked out of her Washington Heights persona and became the leftover widow in the Paris park who pined for her wrested home, alienated among the French speakers and held captive by her selfish daughter. I don't think she pretended it was for her money, though I am sure she was tempted to.

It took me some time to realize what a hideous mistake I had made in thinking she wanted to come to Paris to be with us.

She enjoyed playing roles, however, and went on to spend the rest of the decade, not in Paris but in the more amenable West of Ireland where she ended up living comfortably in a modern hotel, well cared-for by the staff, among a coterie of admirers, 'til the eve of 1970 when she died peacefully with both a doctor and a priest in attendance.

The '60s sprung my mother, too. She had a magnificent funeral.

My severance pay from Free Europe unexpectedly bought us, not comfort nor even time, but two more houses. The thatched cottage an hour and a half from Paris which we restored ourselves, was the first.

We fell in love with Normandy. We all but dreamed of William the Conqueror sailing forth to capture England for the rest of time. A few miles from our thatched roof lay Dives from which small port the great king sailed. And his mother's house still stands on the coast just a few miles up the road. In 1966 we went to a commemoration of the 900th anniversary of 1066 and all that, in one of the abbeys which had blessed its passage. History is at your fingertips occasionally. Normandy is particularly good at history and I fell hopelessly in love with it.

That particular abbey, le Bec Helbuin, was more fanciful than others, however, because it also houses within its Gothic walls a Museum of the Automobile. Medieval bell towers plus racing flivver and rumble seats, all to the sound of the carillon chimes of medieval bells.

That was house number two.

Unexpectedly, someone I had met on a ship coming back from a home leave visit to New York in the winter of 1962, and who lived in Mallorca, called up one evening when we were having dinner with friends and said, "There is a nice house for sale here for $2,000, why don't you come down and see it...?"

Juan was on the phone with this somewhat confusing well-wisher. All we could hear was his side of the conversation, which was pretty arcane. "How many rooms? Five? Six? What do you mean, we can build a kitchen? Oh, there is a patio? Umm. You can take a tramway to the beach? A tramway? A village with a tramway?"

At the dining room table we were in fits of laughter. "Buy it," our friends cried out.

"We will all come down and visit you," said one.

"Buy it and come back to the table," I added.

So he did. That was early 1964. It was house number three.

Coincidentally, Juan flew down to Barcelona to see his ailing father shortly after that conversation and mentioned the house in Mallorca to a gathering of relatives in his parents' house. When he told them it was in a Mallorcan mountain village six kilometers from the sea and was going for $2,000, everyone told him to buy it even if there was no house, the land would be worth that. And that if he didn't buy it, they would. It must have been the last real estate bargain in Spain.

A three-story stone house built at the foot of a 400-year-old church in a village voted most beautiful in Spain, it was by way of being miraculous. We restored it without turning it into a suburban cottage, keeping its original whitewashed walls, but we built a big kitchen-cum-dining-room and, above it, an equally big bathroom with a pool-like tub with beautiful Moorish tiling around it, complete with potted plants to set off the tub. It was the village sensation. In the patch of land in front of the house—it was built on a recess in the cobbled street—we put up a lovely wooden wall so that we acquired a patio in which we planted a lemon tree, a palm and a mass of bougainvillea that hung over the wall. The house was on a street with steps. Nestled by the baroque church, it was where all the tourists took pictures. A mixed blessing.

This was the corner of Mallorca which has attracted artists and writers since the 1930s when Robert Graves settled there. He chose it on the recommendation of Gertrude Stein, though most people have forgotten that. It has been a mecca for "names" ever since. The coastline is roughly etched into the island's mountain, weaving among coves and grottos stunning wherever you looked. It is one of the world's great beauty spots.

We kept it for about forty years.

The tramway the chap on the telephone went on about is a 1930s landmark. It goes from the town of Sóller to the Port of Sóller meandering through olive trees or citrus groves or honking geese in someone's backyard. Like most things in Mallorca, it is a national treasure.

It was when we bought this house that our London friends, Frank and Crokie Allen, who marveled at our mobility despite the lack of a steady income, dubbed us Palà Poverty Properties.

These precious houses proved to be the only clever thing we ever managed to do financially.

That was the background. What was more to the fore in our lives then was the Peace Movement, on one hand, and my new choppy career as a writer-translator. Somewhat by chance I slipped into the world of translating film scripts.

Translation is a knack. It is also, in my mind, not something you learn, it is a knack you come equipped with. I was never able to learn to drive a car, mind you, but I have been able to translate from Italian, a language I guess at rather than really speak. That is what I mean by a knack.

Something has to make up for a lifetime of running after buses, I suppose.

Helen Scott, an old friend from my early days at United Nations, was the unlikely source of this jump. Helen was a small, fat, pugnacious American Communist. She grew up in Paris, the daughter of a Russian-American Jewish newspaperman in pre-war Paris. A militant teenager by the outbreak of the war, Helen was already a member of the Jeunesses Communistes. She remained a militant 'til there was nothing left of the ideology to adhere to.

During the war the Free French sent her to Brazzaville, in the Congo to organize a communications system. She was totally bilingual. Somehow she was on the staff of one of the US Justices at the Nuremberg trials. How she did all this while being a vocal member of the Communist Party is beyond me, and she never really explained it. She fetched up at the UN secretariat in the immediate post-war, which is where I met her.

She was extremely kind to me then and was generous with her time and her patience. Helen was fond of me in the motherly way childless older women have toward the very young who visibly admire them, as I did her. She was generous with her experience, which is generosity of a special kind, and I am still grateful to her for that. When Juan came to New York she was one of the first to make him feel welcome.

After we came to Paris in 1955 we lost touch, but only because of geography. Then one day Juan and I were sitting at the Flore and I saw her walking down the boulevard. I was astonished because she had been one of the first to be deprived of a passport by the McCarthy era State Department. She was one of his earliest victims, along with Paul Robeson. I called out to her and she stared. I blurted out, "They finally gave you a passport?" Heads turned at the café terrace.

"Are you two still married?" She countered. And we burst out laughing.

Helen's life, so politically oriented up to then, had undergone a sea change when she was hired by the French Film Board in New York to help promote the Nouvelle Vague. Helen, the union organizer, Helen the martyr to the cause, pushing French movies!

She was assigned to be Francois Truffaut's interpreter when he visited the US to promote his first film. The rest is history. It was symbiosis at first sight. There are all kinds of loves in this world and they found one which had nothing to do with sex or obligation. It was pure, it was heartwarming, and it was funny. Laughter and indulgence, a perfect match.

Helen became the English language mentor of all the New Wave films in addition to being Truffaut's closest associate and confidante.

She was a monument in the Paris film scene. Her militancy changed shoulders. Because she could not deal with the failure of Communism, she turned her back on it. The world of la Nouvelle Vague was open to her and she leapt into it on both feet.

Helen was the first to give me a tricky film script to translate, one of Truffaut's more literary ventures taken from a Henry James story as well as a somewhat obscure Joseph Conrad tale. The result was odd and the language was difficult to render. I went over her initial translation and, together, we turned it into something quite different. It was challenging; I enjoyed it.

That was the beginning, the first of hundreds I was to translate for the next 25 years.

Another friend, Judy Mullen, did much the same for me. Between those two initial sources I built up a reputation, if that is the word, with several directors whose scripts I worked on regularly with varying degrees of pleasure. To drop a few names: Costa Gavras, Alain Resnais, Danièle Delorme and Yves Robert, who had a production company, or Jacques Perrin who eventually became head of the Film Board that attributes subsidies to films in progress.

I had no desire to become another François Truffaut's English alter ego, like Helen, or to be part of the making of movies, like Judy. I looked on what I was doing as a painless way of making a living and I came away from it with the net impression that I, who has an aversion to cars, would rather be a racing driver than a serious filmmaker.

The egos involved in the movie industry are comparable to hot air balloons and are just as inflammable.

But, in their kindness, Helen and Judy Mullen kept us afloat for a good long time and I can't imagine what else I could have invented to take their place. Because my subsequent career in letters got off to a very slow start.

The sixties came in to our lives with a roll of drums. The first being the birth of Suzanne Gabrielle Laura Palà, Suzy, in September 1960, a splendid way of opening a decade. I was still working, we had our own house in the 14th arrondissement at the tail end of Montparnasse, we were doing fine. But it was not all smooth-running.

My father's death shattered me. It was our first experience in the loss of a parent. My father had not been ill, just a little more frail. The last time I had been in New York, he refused to go to the theater because he said he could no longer hear well.

He grew dangerously ill over Christmas 1962. My mother phoned me on January 2nd saying he was ill and I should come home immediately. She could not deal with it. I was not sure I would know how to deal with it any better but I wanted to be with him, inept or otherwise.

I called my friend Tom Donahue, who by then was back in New York after his stint with Free Europe in Paris. An odd distinction to belabor him with, I felt he was the only one I could count on who knew the ways of real life and death and who would not begrudge me the kind of help I needed.

I reached New York in time to try to get my father checked into a hospital—a nightmare experience of being turned down by bored admissions clerks in several hospitals before finally being accepted in one, I think some five hours later.

I had no experience with death and did not know how to face it. When he asked, at one point, "Am I going to die?" he was calm. It was more a point of interest to him than one of panic.

I said, "No, you are going to get better and you will come to Paris with me for the winter."

He smiled and nodded his head. "Isn't that supposed to be Napoli?" he asked, his voice soft. It took a second for that to click but I laughed out loud when it did. Vedere Napoli e morire? He looked pleased that he could still make me laugh.

The emergency hall of the big city hospital soon doused the smile, however, and it was all I could do not to break into screams. After over an hour's wait in a crowded public room he was negligently placed on a wheeled bed amid what struck me as being a parking lot of recumbent emergency cases. He was quiet for the most part, patiently waiting for someone to diagnose him. He had a weak heart, we knew that, but we did not know anything more. During the hours I spent with him, no one in charge gave me any firm information except that I would have to leave because we were already past visiting hours.

I stood next to his wheeled bed asking a variety of uniformed personnel if he was going to be given a room before dinner or was he not going to have any dinner at all? The question perplexed them or annoyed them, therefore perplexing me. *Why was he being shunted around like left luggage,* I asked one unhelpful orderly.

"Left luggage?" he repeated, as though parroting a foreign tongue. "Where do you think you are, lady, the Waldorf Astoria?"

I would have liked to have punched him. I heard my father's admonition. "Dolores... don't. Don't."

Then someone else took me by the arm and said, "Visiting time over. Time to go, lady." Whereupon I was physically urged toward the exit. I wanted to insist, to resist, but I could not. They led me to the door, pushed me through. I heard my father call out Dolores, as I was marched to the exit.

Someone at his side said, "Tomorrow, Pops. She will be back tomorrow."

He cried out, more frightened still by that. I was firmly led out the several doors with his voice ringing in my head, clearly terrified: "Dolores, Dolores."

Finally out on the unfamiliar street, I realized that though it was January, I was awash in perspiration.

A cab finally appeared. His radio was blaring out ill-tempered music. I asked the driver if he would lower it, that I was feeling a little upset. He said he would feel upset if he lowered it.

I was astonished, but it was too late to go cab driver shopping in a strange neighborhood so I just sat back and pretended nothing of this was happening, that this was not New York, not my father, not me.

A few hours later the phone rang in the living room. The doctor's voice at the other end was strained, as though in deep discomfort. "I don't know what happened. He just died."

I didn't know what happened either. My poor Daddy had long since stopped trying to understand what had happened, I thought, in that ice cold moment. He was finally freed from having to attempt to understand. The word release came into my mind. I wondered what he would have made of it. He probably would have smiled at the word release.

In the West of Ireland, the colorful English spoken includes the word keening. In the years that followed I thought of that often. That is what is done over the dead, or was done in the more demonstrative past.

Now we are just discreetly silent in the midst of death.

Mother spent the rest of her life pampered by distant relatives who became close friends. She spent it speaking English and eating the kind of food she enjoyed, as opposed to what she had found in Paris. Most importantly, she did not have to cook it, for she lived in a hotel aptly named The Welcome Inn.

She had one of the most rewarding Declining Years I know of. The Queen of The Tall Tale had a very happy end. She even saw her daughter's picture all over the literary pages of the British press when *In Search Of Mihailo* came out as a publishing wunderkind that made me at least appear to be rich. She liked that.

I had at last done something she could be proud of.

Amen.

These were the years when the real world encroached and I became actively involved in the Paris branch of the American peace movement. It was odd how I fell into an American expatriate flow literally by chance. During the Free Europe years most of our friends were European. The '60s brought the American Abroad dimension into it.

Being a permanent foreigner is something of a strain on the identity button. Especially in a place where the natives are given to asking when you are going home.

Other Americans were more than welcome in my life at that point. Surely the most rewarding, if not awe-inspiring, among them was Maria Jolas, certainly the most fabled. She was by then a legend. At the heart of the literary 1920s in Paris, she and her husband Eugene, along with Eliot Paul, were the creators of *Transition*, the literary magazine that was the beacon of twentieth century literature. Not only American or English but international as well and its work, through translation, opened the doors to a wider multi-lingual world of letters, the arts and, of course, the noisy newcomer, cinema.

Chapter 15

I had wanted to write fiction ever since I can remember. At NYU my creative writing prof encouraged me and once in a while in later years I would come upon a badly typed short story I had submitted then, with good marks but notes about bad typing.

Now I had the time and the impetus to try my hand at a novel. There had been a need at the back of my head to explain what it had been like to be young, American, anxious to be part of the new post-war world in Europe, to believe in the peace to come, to fall in love ... all the things I had grazed in my eighteen months in Europe at the end of the 1940s.

That brave new world we sought then did not happen, but I wanted to explore the moment when it was still possible for the very young to believe it would.

That was the idea. It was not the love story I had lived with Juan, it was the love story that I might have lived with someone else. I had grazed a half-dozen young people in those student days headed for chaos while they followed what they thought were their stars.

At that time my house was full of the presence of Christy, Suzy, Mother and Juan in his studio, so I took myself back to the Flore where I had started in 1948, and wrote *In Search of Mihailo*. It was not about a Spanish painter, it was about a Yugoslav Orthodox theology student whom I did not know.

It took me through the winter and spring to write it to my satisfaction. At the same time I was working on movie scripts and translating a novel by a friend, a fascinating French writer of complicated thrillers who was also in charge of a reputable collection at one of the major paperback publishers. They had an impressive stable of writers, though, and he was well placed in publishing.

His name was Stéphane Jourat and he was married to an American painter we had known when we first came to Paris, Mimi. They had three little boys. Stéphane changed my life just as his own was dramatically falling apart, as Mimi went off to California for what she said would be a short visit home but, once there, filed for divorce. Stéphane was shocked and distraught but, in the end, helpless. He left Paris, his world, his job and his friends, making it clear he did not want to be contacted. We felt bereft but after a few fruitless attempts, we gave up the search. He had simply walked away from his life. But he published *In Search of Mihailo* in French before going. It was no longer just a manuscript. It was a book.

Previously it had gone out to a half-dozen publishers in London and as many in New York. Everyone had something nice to say about it but all declined reluctantly, claiming that it did not have enough reader appeal to take a chance on, or words to that effect. It would not fly in Topeka, they were saying.

As it turned out, they were wrong.

Another friend, an Oxford don, said one day while he was having dinner with us in Paris, "Would you like me to show your manuscript to Iris Murdoch?"

Even Juan looked up. Iris Murdoch? She was the woman writer I admired most at the time. I loved her style, her temporality, her sidelong glances at religion, her Irish Englishness. I looked at Henri Tajfel, my illustrious friend, and said, "Yes, please."

So he did.

And she wrote me back an eleven-page letter telling me she enjoyed the book enormously, that she knew the Paris of the end of the 1940s even down to the bars I mentioned and she loved my characters. But… she reminded me that there are rules to the novel and that I had violated one of the foremost: I had revealed on page 40 what had happened to *Mihailo*, so the rest of the book was a static story of why it happened. Whereas suspense is a rule of fiction and I had broken it. She was right.

It took me another 18 months to rewrite *Mihailo*. By then, Stéphane had talked his bosses at Fleuve Noir into doing a collection of works by women and to start it off he suggested a handful of published writers like Monica Dickens, and one unpublished one… me. By then we were into April, 1968.

The principal snag, however, was that Stéphane preferred the first version… the brooding static story. It was more like a French novel in that form, closer to what was then being toyed with as the Nouveau Roman.

I had not meant it to be anything resembling the Nouveau Roman and felt he was making a terrible mistake. However, from there to refusing to let him publish it was a long ride.

Our good counsel, Frank Allen, in London said, "No one in the English-speaking publishing world will read it in French... they will just look at the cover. Publish and be damned." So I did.

And at the end of 1968 a very young publishing house, Allison and Busby, bought *Mihailo* and made a commercial hit with it that I still cannot get over. It is one of those quirks of luck, fate, chance or divine intervention that makes life worth living and publishing a high-risk industry.

Iris Murdoch said, "No," when I put that to her. "It is because it is a good book," she said firmly, but her eyes told me otherwise.

Juan got the first of what was to be a series of state commissions to do large scale sculptures in a program called The One Percent. This entailed that one percent of the budget of every public building being built would be given over to a new work of art. It was a pet project of Andre Malraux's and he will no doubt have gone to Artists' Heaven because of it. It saved the lives of countless French artists, including Spanish Juan Palà. He was to do about a dozen such works over the next fifteen years.

I had tried all avenues open to me at the time, circumvented by my being a foreign national living in France and thus without the right to work for a French employer, but without much success at finding another job. Toward the end of the 1960s I was ready to declare defeat when an Israeli friend turned up with a new venture and needed someone exactly like me to work with... who knew the ins and outs of international organizations in Paris, arcane at best, plus a working knowledge of several popular languages.

He was Etan Shafir and had been head of Bonds for Israel in France for some years where my very dear friend Ruth Froma had worked. Etan had come up with a small foundation project that interested Baron Edmond de Rothschild who eventually housed it in small but elegant offices on the Faubourg Saint-Honoré that included a pavilion, promptly dubbed le chateau, at the rear where Etan and his charming, patient wife lived.

The Middle East Peace Institute was exactly the sort of institution I was good at. It meant well, it worked among a grass roots target area and its purpose was to fund what have now become known as start-ups among the Arab population. It was minor key, its subsidies were without strings, it was well meaning and it was a reflection of its times. The fact that it would be short-lived would not come as a surprise, but it was worth trying. The late sixties was a time suitable for last ditch attempts at good will even on a shoestring budget.

Unfortunately, however, the budget was inadequate and I could only afford to work half-time. We managed to do a lot between nine and lunch time, nevertheless.

I also wrote speeches for le Baron Edmond, who liked them immensely when he read them in the office. He carefully put them away in his pocket for the banquet in question where he proceeded to speak off the top of his head. Whenever I had occasion to see him he would all but tap me on the cheek in thanks for my speeches and never once let on that he did not give them.

He was a much-admired gentleman.

It was at the MEPI office on the Faubourg Saint-Honoré that May '68 caught us. May '68 was the heady parenthesis in our lives, in the life of Parisians and over the globe in many other equally unlikely cities that changed everything or changed nothing, depending on where you sat. We lived it headily like everyone we knew and we remember it as one does a corner of treasured time. It is too important and would be too long to go into here. Perhaps someplace else at another time.

Juan, the children and I left for Mallorca after school laboriously broke up in late June. Suzy had gone through wracking whooping cough which coincided with the end of May, in every sense of the word. We spent a still nervy summer trying to get over it, wondering what kind of autumn we were going back to.

I was to return to Paris in September and the new year would begin for MEPI. It would be business as usual. Or would it?

The May events had shaken up all things French far more thoroughly than was realized. It had put into question things that had seemed rock-like before. I turned forty on August 1, 1968. Let no one say that forty is just another birthday. It is not.

I had started out particularly young. I was very young at the UN in Lake Success, very young turning up in Paris, much younger than all the others wherever I had worked… along with Tom Donahue at Free Europe who was a couple of weeks younger still. And suddenly that particular jewel in my crown was no longer there.

One is not young at forty. Moreover, I was, for the first time in my adult life, unsure of what I was doing. I was unsure of the solidity of my household… unsure that I was right in imposing a Spartan lifestyle on our two children. Suzy was too small to notice, but Christy was visibly put off by having less money than his friends.

I seemed to have gotten lost in the shuffle and, for the first time ever, I questioned the whole picture. The summer was spectacular that year, probably because the Paris events had shaken up most of Europe, even the weather, and everyone seemed energized by the tingle left in the air.

We celebrated my birthday at the dining room table that included my mother-in-law, recently widowed, two nephews from Barcelona, Juan, our two children and myself. The children had placed pretty packages in the middle of the table and suddenly one of them said, "Where is Daddy's?" Even his mother looked aghast.

Juan had neglected to get me a present. I looked at his very diplomatic mother who was stiffly attempting to brush off the situation. She said, soothingly, he just forgot. Dear God, that was all I needed to hear.

For reasons no one can quite fathom, Juan has been incapable of choosing a present for me for as long as I've known him. Either he ignores the occasion and looks blank or, very occasionally, he produces a superb portrait he has managed to hide while working on it so the surprise effect is enormous. He has some mysterious masculine ailment about presents. On that particular occasion I found it unforgivable.

Before I broke into tears, or worse, he rose up from the table and bolted from the dining room. Concepcion, our marvelous Fornalutx maid, who had concocted a superb dinner, and a couple of friends who had just dropped in to wish me well and stayed, managed to cover up his absence 'til he returned from the fastest shopping trip to Sóller on record where he had picked up a Mallorcan suede handbag all done up in colorful wrapping. He thus saved the day. Other friends dribbled down to the house and an impromptu party marked the occasion. Champagne mollified whatever anger that clung to the wreckage.

The bag and its tinselly wrapping was still in the drawer where I had put it on that August 1, 1968 when we sold the house in 1997.

But, all told, I was deeply hurt by that neglect. It was one stone too many. We finished the summer, were in Barcelona on the way back to Paris, having closed up the Fornalutx house 'til next year when, while sitting in a Barcelona tramway together, I looked over at Juan and said, "I am not going home."

He stared at me, taken aback. "Where are you going?" he asked, as though spellbound.

It took me just a few seconds to answer. "Geneva."

His eyes widened further and he echoed, astonished, "Geneva? Why?" Why indeed.

A few weeks before we had been to a party at Robert Goulet's house, the French Canadian writer who had introduced us to Mallorca. There had been a fair amount of new people in the village that summer, including a couple I was chatting with idly on the terrace. The man was a journalist. We compared notes. He had just spent two years in Geneva working for one of the international organizations on a short term contract. He said, "You should look into it. If you really want a job you can always find something in Geneva. Short term contracts, especially. Career stuff is harder but for a year at a time, it is no problem."

I remember listening to him while sipping champagne, thinking of Geneva and what I recalled of it. Pretty city, international, easy to live in, child friendly. Hmm.

I had known several itinerant writers who had spent pleasant time there, some who had even settled in. And Georges and Dominique Charpak were there, breaking atoms. I filed it away at the back of my head that night on the terrace.

A few weeks later on the Barcelona tramway it became my new reality.

I believe that Juan actually thought I was leaving him then. He seemed shocked but very quiet 'til I managed to say something coherent. I am not sure even now that I knew exactly what I meant myself. Did I mean to leave him? Break it all up, divide our lives, walk away from all I had been committed to? Injure those so thoroughly dependent children? Probably. But probably not. Not really. A little but not all the way.

His eyes, so stricken, so dismayed, stopped me. I might have meant it at first but not firmly enough to actually carry it out. There, on the tramway we muddled through the hot, sticky afternoon looking for a way to change everything we knew, to make it better.

As it turned out, it was not all that difficult to break up a way of living and invent a new one. I went back to Mallorca and reopened the house in Fornalutx with Suzy, who was not quite eight years old and still very pliable, though when she held my hand crossing a street I noticed that her grip was tighter than it had been.

Juan returned to Paris with Chris. Much aided by friends, he found a boarding lycée in Grenoble for that school year. Christy was at that awful adolescent age when everything we did would be seen as disastrous. At seventeen nothing was going to please him anyway. He was an exemplary teenager, a textbook case. Somehow, Juan managed to get him settled into a state boarding school in the Alps with easy access to Geneva for long weekends and holidays.

I eventually went on a scouting trip for four days. My particular guardian angel must have been wide awake, for the ILO was celebrating its fiftieth anniversary and needed an extra English language press officer. I applied and, with the help of the US delegation and Tom Donahue's intercession, I was proposed for the job and got it. The salary was fair which means it seemed sumptuous to me at that point. And it was tax free.

I still had to go to the West of Ireland to see that my mother would be all right during those eight months I would not be able to check on her as I did regularly ever since she moved there. Ireland is an out of the way destination from Mallorca, so I went via London, which had cheap Dublin flights. I usually stayed over with friends and took another cheap flight to Dublin the next day, which is what I did then. Except that one of our dearest friends in Mallorca, the poet Charles Plumb, somewhat tediously insisted I see a young publisher who was just starting out a new publishing house with an Oxford friend, Margaret Busby, and who was looking for writers.

Clive Allison was 26, a blond cherub, Margaret Busby was 24, a black silent doll. Reluctantly, I called Clive. Amiably he suggested meeting at a local pub, The George. Of course. When I saw the pair of them waiting for me at The George I could have clobbered dear Charles. These cherubic infants of the New Age were not even going to make it to page twelve of my novel, not in this seriously Swinging London post-'68 climate. I nearly bolted.

But, we got along pleasantly and talked mostly of Paris and the new face of France.

I left them the manuscript.

It had turned out to be a pleasant meeting, but I was all set to forget it. So, off Suzy and I went to Ireland. On the day before we were to leave for Geneva a letter for me came to The Welcome Inn from Clive Allison in London. My first reaction was one of irritation since I assumed it to be a rejection. I read it out loud to Mama and to my two cousins, Maura and Kathleen Collins, who had adopted her. "We read your manuscript with interest and pleasure and we would like very much to publish it...."

I looked up in absolute astonishment.

It had actually happened. *Mihailo* would be published in English. The French text had not really counted for me. It had to be in English. In English it was my book.

I had done it.

There are years that go by without leaving more traces than notes on a calendar and there are others that storm through, changing everything in sight. The months between November 1968 and July 1969 were like a hurricane. I landed a job at the ILO without a hitch, Juan and I found an apartment equally easily, though outrageously expensive in accordance with Geneva's bizarre temporary housing situation. A city of international organizations, it is also a city of landlords who can do what they want on the furnished apartment market. Prices are double those of Paris but since there is no way of avoiding the situation, one learns to lean back and enjoy. We took a large, roomy, over-furnished, vastly overpriced flat on the rue de Lausanne just a block away from the ILO headquarters in the lakeside park and next door to a pleasant school for little girls, perfect for Suzy who had just turned eight.

Suzy might have suffered from the ructions of that period, not going back to Paris on time for her 2ⁿᵈ grade class at the école publique—not going back to Paris at all, for that matter. But she took it all nicely and gazed out at Geneva with its park and lake and the presence of squirrels with equanimity and pleasure. She even liked being the new girl at the little Catholic school and had new friends within days. There was talk of snow in the air and she looked forward to a whole new panorama in life. We got her a sled for Christmas and the weather was gracious enough to deliver snow just in time. Suzy would have a Geneva accent by the time we left in July and had learned to ice skate like a dream.

Predictably, Christopher hated his boarding school in the mountains near Grenoble. He and another boy decided to run away. They managed this with a maximum of fuss on the part of the school, the parents and, of course, succeeded in getting themselves expelled. There was a touch of nightmare in this gesture for they were literally in danger of freezing to death during the night they spent on the Alpine road heading toward the Côte d'Azur. They did not, however. They merely got themselves expelled from the school instead.

Kind friends helped us get him accepted into a lycée in Annemasse, just outside Geneva on the French side, and all slipped back into its sulky place, but not without a horrific fright and a sense of helplessness I wish on no parent. Not even him.

The ILO was the first international organization to have been created in the twentieth century, predating the League of Nations. Its implantation in the sleepy Swiss town on Lake Geneva was due to its founder, Albert Thomas, who favored it. Subsequently the League of Nations and most of the other international governing bodies joined it there. Geneva turned into a small Swiss city with an uncommonly cosmopolitan population, nestled in the Alps with so much to offer in the way of sheer enjoyment of the surroundings that one sounds like a travel agent when describing it. International restaurants, visiting theater companies and concerts, ski slopes literally up the road a piece, skating rinks within walking distance of wherever you are, and jobs for an interesting transient population. Everyone speaks several languages with a few notable exceptions.

I had a friend, an American woman of great distinction, married to a German-Swiss publisher, a gracious hostess to a highly select set, yet she spoke nothing but New York English. Her dinners were not only fashionable but the food was excellent and imaginative. I finally got the nerve to ask her how she described chopped liver to her local charcuterie and she merely looked down her nose and said, "I pointed." Of course.

I settled in shakily with the two children and a very demanding job doing what I had learned to do at the UN in the late '40s. It would have been a little bit easier on me if Switzerland had not been the world capital of the clock. Suzy's school let out at 6 p.m. punctually. I had to be in front of the door to collect her at 6 p.m. on the dot. It was a ten-minute run from the ILO on the lakefront to her school a few blocks down on the rue de Lausanne. But ten minutes past 6 was not 6 p.m. and those ten minutes drove me berserk. I managed, however, with the help of an angelic colleague who watched me juggle for the first few days and then offered his help.

Joe Haden was an ILO staffer from before the war. He was a labor expert who had lived all over the world and had come out with a baggage of kindness and comradeship that I have seldom seen equaled. He helped me with the rigid pick-up and drop-off schedules, he helped me make the super markets before they closed … minutes before. He helped me through that winter in unspoken ways I will never forget.

Joe was particularly touching when it came to dealing with the problem of my difficult seventeen-year-old boy who proved so fractious. He had had a son, he told me at length, who was of a similar disposition. Christy reminded him of his boy and my situation reminded him of his own. Joe's son survived adolescence and went on to California where he was part of the NASA training program. He died of a sudden heart attack at the age of 28, his adolescence not that long past.

"When something like that happens to you, nothing is ever the same again," he said to me one late afternoon, just before he was to run out and fetch Suzy for me because I had a press release to finish. That was all he said. I loved him very much for that.

Meanwhile, Juan had rented our house on the rue de l'Aude in Paris to a delightful Australian scientist and his family, so our finances were beginning to rise above the water level. He was doing his first One Percent sculpture and had determined to make it a noteworthy piece. It was that. A stainless steel construction about seven feet high and an oval shape made of clusters of small pieces soldered into a whole, it was a stunning work. He wanted to do something he could not do otherwise because he could not afford the cost of making it. That cut in to his budget, perhaps, but it was worthwhile and he was pleased with the outcome.

He was staying at friends' places, house jumping, so to speak, and coming up to Geneva whenever he could. It was a new arrangement for us, a kind of lopsided honeymoon. Few of the people I worked with at the ILO knew who the attractive guy was who would, very occasionally, turn up at the gate to fetch me and I only told a few. After the fiasco of my birthday, he did his best to provide a dash of romance into being the dark stranger at the gate.

And it worked.

I made friendships that have lasted 'til now during that upside-down year and it is pleasant to look back so many years later to realize how genuine they were.

The American head of the press division, John Western, gave a small informal party at his house for the staff. I went with Suzy. An international press crowd is always a pleasure for me. There is a touch of class reunion to it. Though in this case I did not know any of them before, we had inevitable friends in common. There was a sort of comradely scent in the air.

I heard a female voice with an American accent I instantly placed as New York in the next room. I scurried off to find out who. She turned out to be Judy Tomero, a New Yorker from Far Rockaway who had just married Rafael Tomero, a Spanish translator who happened to be the cousin of Maria Zambrano, Spain's great woman philosopher who lived in exile just on the other side of the French border.

When I told Judy that I had had a Spanish husband for the past eighteen years she took my hand and squeezed it. "Tell me," she said, and I promised we would be friends forever. And we have been, until a few months ago when Judy died on a summer visit to Mallorca with Rafael, going back on her promise to me to come and see us once more before I left the house in Combs forever. But that is another story.

Our stay in Geneva was punctuated with such friendships. It was a move that did not last long in time but was immensely long-lasting for its coloring of the rest of our lives.

I wish I knew who the chap was that I had met on that terrace in Fornalutx, the one who recommended Geneva for a quick job if I was broke. I would like to at least thank him for the tip.

Tony Curnow, a New Zealander newsman, was another colleague who remained a friend to this day and who was immensely helpful when both children came down with the chickenpox during the General Assembly of the ILO which was attended by countless heads of state including The Pope and Haile Selassie who had been there fifty years earlier.

I don't know how we got through the five days of chicken pox. Especially Christy, who was seventeen and therefore harder hit than Suzy. Joe Haden did the shopping, I remember, since he was not part of the news staff, along with a Cameroonian radio chief for whom I occasionally did interviews with Spanish labor people on the sly... he did not have a budget for them but both he and I enjoyed snarking the Franco regime representatives of a labor movement that had lost the Civil War thirty years before. These were slightly off the cuff and I was never sure where he broadcast them to, but it was a treat for me to disarm my Franquista subjects with my American accent and then snap them in two with an unexpected political snare. Fortunately, none of them complained officially so we got away with it.

The little pleasures of life are the sweetest in the long run.

Of all the friendships we made in that Geneva period, the most long-lasting was with Isa and Jacques Vichniac. Isa was the *Le Monde* correspondent in Geneva; Jacques was a freelance interpreter, but principally he was a poet. The two of them had been iconic Resistance figures during the war. They lived in a ground floor apartment that was on the order of Grand Central Station, the house on Fire Island where I had come for one day and stayed four belonging to I.F. Stone on the weekend that the Korean War broke out.

The Vichniac house was like that, elastic and welcoming. They became my friends, but in time they also became the surrogate parents of our son. Christy was to find in them exactly what he needed in relating to the world of adults and we have been in their debt ever since.

They were, on top of all the rest, among the most endearing and amusing people I have ever known. They gave my Geneva experience yet another dimension.

I would have stayed on at least another year had it been up to me. But once the fiftieth anniversary program was over, the ILO did not need the several extra press officers it had acquired for the occasion. Another job possibility turned up, however, and though somewhat hesitantly, I was ready to take it on.

It was with the IOS, a somewhat shady financial money market concocted by an American financial wizard, Bernie Cornfeld. I forget how but I knew his number two person, a woman called Gladys Solomon who was his chief of staff. She had been around Paris in the '50s when Cornfeld came up with his financial idea of how to make a pyramid of money turn you and your neighbors into millionaires all on the legal up and up.

They had a building opposite the ILO on the lake front, they had a staff of international lawyers and in that year, 1969, they were on top of the world. Gladys Solomon offered to hire me to run a sort of start-up scheme that would involve the wives or grown children of their salesmen in the field—the field being anything from Ireland to Indonesia passing through Zanzibar. They were grassroots enterprises that would make people self-supporting in an unhealthy economic area. The IOS personnel, or rather their relatives, would appoint a local head of the small enterprise and watch over the funding. It was more or less what MEPI proposed to do in the Occupied Territories in Israel.

When Gladys offered me the job we were having a makeshift dinner I had put together on the rue de Lausanne because she wanted to see us at home. There was something uncomfortable in that notion just as there was something uncomfortable in the whole premise of the IOS. On the other hand, it was a job I could do. It paid more than the ILO and another year in Geneva was not disagreeable. Especially if I made a decent salary and could afford more help. And Juan would have been free to spend less time in Paris and more with us. It might even mean finding a studio for him in Geneva... It opened doors.

I sounded out friends like Joe Haden who assured me that there was probably nothing seriously wrong with the IOS, otherwise the Swiss would have been on to them by now. He surmised that the Swiss would not allow them on a main Geneva street if the premises were not kosher.

What the hell.

Chapter 16

My brief association with Bernie Cornfeld and his money-making machine was amusing, well-paid and, thank heaven, inconclusive.

Knowing as little as I did about money and its investment, I was hesitant to actually invest in the project, especially since the fabulous fortune I was supposed to be making through the stream of sales *Mihailo* had made even before it came out in the bookstores, had yet to materialize into cash. Just as well.

After second and third thoughts about it and about not going home to Paris, I backed out. Just like that. And I went home to the rue de l'Aude. We all went home.

Another miracle took place when the extremely understanding directress of one of Paris's best schools, l'Ecole Bilingue, agreed to accept Christy for his final year. In essence, he had gotten himself thrown out of the French school system by failing at the Lycée in Annemasse, which he did roundly.

Mme. Manuel knew all there was to know about fractious teenaged boys and she also knew that not having the Bac, the French high school diploma that was so much more, he would have been in deep trouble. I think she saw my disarray and empathized. She, too, had a difficult son. She looked at me sympathetically and said she would take him in Terminale, the last year of the French lycée system. "But I am doing it for you," she added with a smile. "He had better shine."

He did.

He actually liked the school and he got remarkably high marks on his Baccalauréat exams. It was the only time in his life he did that. But it was a welcome relief. Christy was happy. Hallelujah!

Suzy had always been happy. As recompense we decided to send her to the Rudolf Steiner school which was just a block away. We were more or less in funds again, we could manage the high fees. Why send her to the run down, overcrowded, dingy public school just because she was an easy child, after all? Steiner offered imaginative learning in an atmosphere totally different from the rigid French system that showed no signs of melting despite the promises of May '68. Steiner encouraged languages, taught her German, and the arts and, importantly, most of the children in the small class were, like her, foreign. She blossomed and remained at Steiner 'til she was seventeen. A bit too long, perhaps, but it gave her a baggage she was to call on the rest of her life.

We were all back home on the rue de l'Aude and we were living happily ever after. It was a fruitful time for all of us.

The 1960s had been chaotic but the '70s were to be more deeply subversive. All the protests just beginning to emerge that had been ignited in the bonfires of 1968 became open warfare during the 1970s. Peace movement action abounded. New voices were heard. It was to be prime time for a dissident. The Vietnam War was in everyone's living room. Burning children became a yardstick with which to measure national interest or national ignominy. The peace movement in Paris took up much of my time.

Juan had a series of public commissions which permitted him to make monument-sized sculptures, otherwise unaffordable. He had had a show in Brussels in late 1969 which was a serious push for him. Work produces work in his case. He opened one furrow, pursued one direction and in so doing lighted the way toward new ones. He has always worked like that and I have always found it fascinating to watch it happen. The year of upside-downness we had just bumbled through had proved to hold a number of springboards for us both.

Ann Barret, during this time, had been living out the last years of her husband Bob's life in the tiny Chesapeake Bay village of Toddville. Bob was a southern gentleman, including an almost indecipherable accent spoken in a low voice that made communication a process of stealth and discovery. He was handsome and courtly, a gentleman of the old school everyone talked of but no one knew. He had points in common with my father. Not only just alcohol but courtly manners unexpected in our times and place. He was an anachronism with a sense of humor. He lived in his own small yet wide world with odd windows of his own design. Fortunately, he liked me. If he had not, Ann would have to have dismissed me from her world. One more narrow escape. I would have been orphaned without her.

When we had first met at NYU she was working at NAM, National Association of Manufacturers, for a man whom she described as something out of a southern novel. He was from one of those families that Tennessee Williams might have borrowed from for a quirk or two, Mayflower stock mixed with Cavaliers, shameful descendants of slave owners who voted Democrat and favored rights for everyone... all with good manners. My slogans elicited a nod from him but he would have a faraway shading in his eyes, as though he was seeing another country, not the one I meant, and in turn, he tried to let me see another light. His South was long since gone, just as his notion of land and country was of another age. Dialogue was odd but there was a gentle entente between us or, perhaps, between Bob and the world which made him into a near unique presence in my life.

Ann had fallen in love with a magic spell and they lived happily ever after. His sense of the ridiculous was as sharply gothic as her New Yorker's nose for the present. They had a unique marriage, cut off from the realities most people lived with, in a universe they very kindly shared with us.

I had been to visit them twice in their timeless hamlet not far from Washington yet anchored firmly in the middle of the nineteenth century... from lack of indoor plumbing to the familiarity with their early American furniture to which they clung, not because it had market value but because it was Aunt Carrie's and it was nice to remember Aunt Carrie and the way she had with shortbread.

Ann and Bob retired to Toddville in 1955 when he was about fifty, well short of retirement. They retired because they could and very much wanted to. They had met when Ann, still under twenty, came to work for him at NAM. He had been happily married to a Greek-American former ballet dancer for many years. Childless by choice, they had what everyone, including themselves, took to be a happy marriage. What transpired with Ann was beyond that marriage and had no intrinsic reason for happening at all. It was just one of those things.

She said that they were discreet and through the several years that it went on she had never imagined that it would ever end in marriage. Bob had found himself in that less than enviable position of being in love with two women, despite himself. But he was married to Dorothy and nothing would sever that particular truth.

One day Dorothy found out. Their perfect marriage had been defiled, she said. She left. She took a plane to California. The plane crashed. All on board were killed.

It was a gothic tale out of one of the southern novels they so prized. Ann, still in Europe at the time, waited for what she called a decent interval before returning to New York. It was then that I got to know Bob, because I went back to New York before she did.

He and I were a pair of grass widows, so to speak. I found him fascinating in his otherness, his place in a society he saw from the outside because he lived within a South no longer real, somewhat colored by his formative years in the '30s, moral to the extreme yet Dionysian as well.

He and I would walk through Central Park as though it were his garden and, in a way, it was. He had never lived in New York further than within walking distance of his office or the park and he was familiar with small corners of it no one else seemed to ferret out. He was a secret person with a wealth of lore in his head and a strong need of being alone. I enjoyed him but was perplexed. I could see Ann embarking on an unsure adventure with him like no other in our circles. But I soon realized that that was precisely what she wanted and that Bob was large enough to carry her through. He was, indeed. They were perfectly suited and they enjoyed their curious self-banishment to Chesapeake Bay.

He died at 64, which, as they say in Ireland, was no age. And Ann was left very much alone. It was not only her husband she lost, it was her whole way of life. He had taken her life with him. She had to make another one on her own.

So she came to Paris and stayed with us. She was entering a new life on her own while I was getting back into one that had almost slipped away. I was delighted to have her at hand.

Returning to Paris after the momentous year in Geneva and the welcome change in circumstances, through *In Search of Mihailo*, the sudden emergence of Dolores the Writer, had left me slightly shaky. Also, I hated being forty. Ann's willing ear, her indulgent yet sturdy heart, were godsends for me. I needed her to hold on to. She stayed 'til Easter and then flew to Chicago where Lorraine, her sister, lived.

She proceeded to make a new life for herself at the University of Chicago Press and, on another level, with a scientist called Ted who was tall and fair like Bob but a physicist with no penchant for literature and a total indifference to the world of William Faulkner. They got along well for years and she assured me that in life no one is replaced, new ones just drift in for the time it takes.

I forgot to tell her that when she left Paris early on Easter Sunday, it snowed.

The time it takes?

Ann was my pillar when my mother died. Her anger at my mother's outrageous behavior toward us during our marriage remained sharp. If I came to terms with it, Ann did not. When Ann died, just short of the new century, I cried not only for her but for what had been most of my life. She was my memory, my magic box of secrets.

I have never stopped missing her.

Paris had rarely seemed as attractive to me as it did then. A Barcelona doctor had shamed me into doing a strict diet involving diuretics which knocked off fifteen kilos in a short time. Though I had not got used to being forty and even now dislike the sound of the word, I was in great spirits. With encouragement from Clive Allison in London I started work on *Trumpet for a Walled City*, a novel set in New York and Paris. Totally different from the mood of *Mihailo*, it was a wry tale of what we do to each other, all in the name of love.

I enjoyed writing *Trumpet*. I was enamored of the male character and each of the others were real people to me. I saw their eyes flicker, I heard their hesitations, I felt their remorse and I laughed with them. It is a delicious thing to plunge into a world of your own creation, to unravel knots as stubborn as your own and just as perilous. It is an immense kick to be funny in someone else's head, to flirt with someone else's eyes.

I was careful to keep Iris Murdoch's words in mind as I structured the new book. Or as it structured itself, for once again, my characters played themselves all over the pages and made up their own minds. Eileen, particularly. Several male friends cornered me on Eileen. Yes, she did it all wrong, I answered. But that is what people do. And if it turned out all right at the end it is more to the luck of the Irish than either of the two protagonists.

People in love are seldom rational, I answered Ted Berkman, my friend and mentor. They trip over their own definitions, they pratfall when they should glide. It is grace that allows them to pick themselves up at the end, grace alone. That is what falling in love is all about, my characters are telling us.

The first few years of the 1970s were rich for me in terms of friendship, in terms of work and also, for a change, in terms of harmony, a word I am not often given to in describing my own life. I was deep into the peace movement, I felt energized on all levels, money was not a hassle; in a sense I felt free.

I was going up the Champs Elysées one day when I passed the Air France office. As though guided by a willful imp, I went in and bought myself a ticket, round trip, to New York. For the following week. I went home and called Allen Stoltman and his wife, Evelyn, gallery owners and old friends, who made a point of telling me how great New York was and how spacious their apartment was compared to our little house in Paris.

"I am coming on Wednesday, can I stay with you?" They were too stunned to say no.

I stood at their tall windows on 7th Avenue between 55th and 56th Streets and looked down on Broadway, on Times Square to my left, the tops of the trees in Central Park on my right, the honking horns, the muted sirens like whispers of Gershwin in my ears and I cried a little, to myself. Strictly to myself. I would only admit to myself that missing New York is like a hollow within me, like an unsolved riddle, an absence. I am the last person to have left New York, I loved it so. This was the first visit in seven years. That was criminal.

I walked all over the city. I did what I did when I was cutting classes in high school, walked from one end to the other, or almost. I gobbled up the Village, not without a tug at the heart for its changes. What was currently called the East Village remained for me the Lower East Side and I did not like it then any more than I did when I was fourteen. I found no charm in poverty, in run down tenements and uncollected garbage. My actor friends, Silvia Gassel and Joel Friedman, lived on East 11th Street and 1st Avenue in a middle income project, which was handsome. They were on the tenth floor with a wraparound terrace providing a stunning view. Neither of them had grown fond of the neighborhood either and were quick to tell me they thought I was in for a shock when I saw Washington Heights.

New York changes the way Paris does not, I realized. Avenues A and B had been gentrified through such public housing as theirs and the restoring of patches of 1920s buildings, thus making it trendy with little theaters, restaurants and pubs. Tompkins Square was super trendy but I still saw it as a stone's throw from the Bowery and totally lacking in charm, despite Auden's whispered voice. Wonderful lofts in those streets now housed the well-to-do, the painters with Madison Avenue galleries, and the uninhibited rich. New York had turned its derelict past into a smart set present. I frowned, not quite understanding the process.

Washington Heights, as Joel and Sylvia predicted, jostled me. I knew it had gone somewhat Cuban in the early 1960s while my parents still lived there but I did not know just how far. And it was not just Cuban. In the usual pattern of demography in New York, anywhere on Manhattan does for the first stop in an immigrant's life, but after a few prospering decades the immigrant, by then with a family, moves to the outer boroughs in search of green spaces, better public schools and an easy subway ride. Queens is the first choice, or New Jersey hard by the George Washington Bridge. And so it was even now.

Washington Heights, so European, so Viennese in the war years, was now saffron-scented, rumba-echoing Caribbean. As I stood on the corner of 175th Street and Broadway outside what had been one of the great movie house palaces of the country, Loew's 175th Street, I was amazed to see that the billboard announced that it was the temple of Rev. Ike, an African American preacher.

When I was a child there was a huge organ in the theater played by a tall balding man who thumped it rousingly while the audience sang out the words of all the popular songs on the screen, songs I still remember the words of. Wild Oscar used to be seen in the neighborhood walking a pair of superb Afghans who were as sleek as he was. He was an icon. I guess the Reverend Ike is another icon in this very different age. The two images collided in my mind.

The theater's space, with its roomy orchestra and its ornate balcony where a boy might steal a kiss at an opportune moment, where Errol Flynn plunged a sword into Basil Rathbone's cold heart, or where Barbara Stanwyck just walked down a street.

That was all gone.

Yes, Washington Heights had changed. A whole chunk of it had been pulled out to make room for a new entrance to the George Washington Bridge. There was a cross-town overhead super highway where my friend Vera O'Neill used to live, and my dentist would have been surprised to see his whole block turned into a middle income housing project like the one Joel and Sylvia lived in downtown.

Broadway, where I grew up, looked like another country. Wares from the stores were displayed out on the street. As I walked down I dodged colorful luggage, the latest in baby strollers, bins of pineapples and avocados in front of what had been a kosher butcher. There was a faint whiff of arroz con pollo, which I fancy, emanating from several eateries. The Jewish deli on the corner of 177th Street now offered Comidas Criollas.

I wondered what my father, Francisco de Soto del Castillo, would have thought of all this: the outdoor market look, the whiff of spicy food, the snatches of slurred Caribbean Spanish heard from the passers-by? He would have been astonished, for one thing, at the numbers. And the total absence of discretion. No one here had ever heard of When In Rome, clearly.

Discretion, as he understood it, was not an option, it was an obligation. But this was another time and there were no quick answers. What was at play here now was something that went well beyond a changing neighborhood. It was another attitude toward immigration, integration. It was another attitude toward who and what makes a nation.

I could see other children skating on Fort Washington Avenue, other bikers on the hills going down toward the river, their voices calling out game plays. The parks were unchanged, the ridges that marked the terrain of the American Revolution were still there. Fort Tryon still smelled of well-tended flower beds and its medieval herb garden as I remembered it. The Cloister bells still sounded from the tower and I could see the bench my father favored for its sweeping view of the Hudson.

He loved this park, this view, these scents. That was what remained. That and the results of the first revolution.

It would take care of itself. As everyone knows, the past is another country.

I set part of *Trumpet for a Walled City* in Washington Heights. It was the least I could do.

When I think of the '70s I think of the Peace Movement, Watergate, the death of Franquismo on one level, and on a gentler scale I think of London, our lives in Mallorca, and the immense importance of friendship.

The latter might well have something to do with my status as an only child distant from any immediate family. My beloved cousin Mono was a unique presence in my childhood, and though I became very fond of his sister Margot and her family, that came much later. My distant cousins in Ireland were immensely important to my mother's life and therefore to mine, but they referred to us as friends rather than relations and I was forced to follow suit. Perhaps they had enough cousins in Castlebar and the question of choice that friendship implied was more important than the distant ancestors we shared. I, of course, was only too happy to share an ancestor.

But the importance of friendship was reflected in the importance both London and Mallorca took on in our lives.

We made our first trip to London in the early spring of 1956. My salary had been readjusted once Jim McCargar stepped in. We arrived there on the earliest low-cost airline in town, Skyways of London, which meant a bus to Beauvais and then a small plane over the Channel to Kent where we took another bus into London, deposited at Russell Square. The English bus, called a coach, was a delight because it went through towns, passing churches, squares and shopfronts with that careful lettering which epitomizes English townscapes perhaps more than anything else. I found England, as seen through the Skyways bus windows, to instantly fit into the picture that English literature had drawn in my mind. I fell in love with the English countryside even before London. It was everything my imagination had promised. Few places can claim that.

Juan had been brought up to believe that if it was English it had to be grounded in fairness, it had to be honest and it had to be tolerant. I had no such illusions. His father, who spoke English well and who actually looked English with blue eyes, light hair and a penchant for Savile Row elegance via his Barcelona tailor, worked with the Quakers during the Spanish Civil War. He was general manager of their operation in Spain, based in Barcelona, consisting of feeding the population then half-starved by the war. His father brought Juan, the eldest and the favorite, to the office with him, thus giving Juan a grounding in English plus his quite serious admiration for the English people and what he saw as what they stood for. He, unlike me, did not have an Irish mother or Michael Collins in his family tree.

I had a serious dichotomy with regard to the English. Their class system, their mindless self-satisfaction irritated me, yet the ghosts of Dickens, Richard the Third, Shakespeare and the Globe, the Brownings and Graham Greene were there haunting their streets. That quieted my mixed feelings and I moved along with my copy of the *New Statesman*, hopelessly in love with it. And I had a newcomer in my pocket, to prove its perennity: John Le Carré.

I felt toward England the way a Graham Greene-lover feels once he has been betrayed and looks back. The love is there but it is imperfect. Yet there, nevertheless. And, complex though it might be, London has never fallen short of my expectations.

Along with New York and Paris, I literally love London.

Later on we brought Christy with us and when he was seven, we left him for a few weeks with the Allens. He was immensely fond of both of them, of their amazing Georgian house in Epping Forest and its stream of teenagers, plus Frank and Crokie's friends, many of whom were impressive like Norman Lewis and his wife Leslie, or the beautiful model who was so quintessentially English that she rose when they played "God Save the Queen" on the radio. And there was the budding actor, Derek Jacobi, a school mate of Mark's. Even a seven-year-old felt the attraction. Everyone at the Allen house spoke well, mainly, I thought, because Frank inspired one to speak well. His own diction and delivery was so immensely pleasing that one's slouching speech cleared up in his presence.

At that time, beginning with 1956, my job brought me to London more frequently than I had ever expected. I used to stay with them and use my cost of living allowance to take us out to good restaurants, theaters and proper pub crawls in taxis. They introduced me to the quintessentially English custom of clubs. Frank was an active member of the Savage club as well as the Sherlock Holmes, as well as a frequent visitor to the Holmes pub in the Strand. He gave Juan a club tie on the strict condition that he not wear it in London for he was not a member. Juan thought that was hilarious.

I went along on Sherlock Holmes Walks, a practice that would only be possible in London where eccentricity is in a class of its own. These were organized walks through various dank corners of London which had been the scenes of such and such novel or story. We examined the streets in great detail. At one point I happened to be in London for two successive such pilgrimages. There we were, a dozen or so adults following a lecturer who carefully pointed out streets, alleys, houses, steps, windows and streetlamps that had played significant roles in this or that story and were vital to their characterization. I found myself walking next to a concentrating middle-aged gentleman who wore a long heavy winter coat against the weather. He looked like a cabinet minister but was, Frank told me, an editor at *The Times*. On the second evening he turned to me and told me gently he was most impressed by my interest in Victorian London and would I, by any chance, care to join the Victorian Society, of which he was chairman, for a visit to Victorian Manchester next month?

Frank glanced at me but turned away before I was undone by the hilarity in his eyes. I declined the invitation with the proper regret, to which the gentleman said, "Perhaps next year." And we continued toward Baker Street in pleasant silence.

I was seriously tempted to join the White Hart Society, however, which was devoted to the cause of Richard III, maligned by a young Shakespeare then currying favor with the usurping Tudors in making a monster out of a loving and reluctant king. Josephine Tey's rousing novel, *Daughter of Time*, had ignited my never very far from the surface sense of injustice at his wretched place in history. I should have joined but I did not. Such delicious whimsy was difficult to manage from Paris.

London, far more than anywhere else, fired my sense of whimsy. I thrived on those streets yet I was not sure that I would have wanted to live there. It would have been a more encroaching place, in my case, than Paris was. I could be an American in Paris without the slightest hesitation. My identity was not encroached upon. In London, however, I would have been drawn into English life. The New Yorker would not have stood up for long in London—they seldom do. Whereas, being an American in Paris was practically a nationality in itself.

No, there was too much of London to resist. When, in the early 1960s my boss at Free Europe offered me a job in the newly created Portman Square office I declined. It took a lot of stamina to do that but I don't regret it. Or at least, not very much. Identity is the only baggage we leave this world with, after all.

Which brings us to Mallorca. We had visited Barcelona every summer not only to be with Juan's parents but also to give the children a sense of Spain. Even Franco's Spain, it being the only one available.

But Mallorca turned out to be special. It carried with it a whole new chapter in our lives, an enormous enrichment. It was by way of being a gift from heaven for we did not seek it out and we almost didn't take it up.

A house in Spain meant more than the promise of sun and easy gazpacho. It meant bringing the children into the orbit of Juan's heritage, his very essential Spanishness. That might appear to be obvious but it was not in reality. We were an English-speaking household that celebrated Thanksgiving in the middle of Paris's 14th Arrondissement. The children spoke English before French, though French was the language they went to school in. Several of our analyst friends assured us we were burdening them with too much baggage.

The scientist who discovered dyslexia, when diagnosing Christy with that disorder, glared at me and said "Madame, be happy your son does not stutter." My punishment for imposing a multiplicity of languages, countries, even dwellings on a little boy. That was Dr. Ajuriaguerra, one of the most revered psychiatrists of his time. Note that while Juan and I were sitting side by side facing him at the time, in a consultation organized by André Green, a close friend who had diagnosed the child's dysfunction in the first place, and who reassured me that it could be corrected, the eminent specialist only spoke to me, not to Juan.

I tried to laugh off his incipient misogyny and to put it down to a bunch of other things, but I was wary of how much Spain I wanted to introduce into their lives, nevertheless.

They both loved their grandparents. Christy particularly was close to his cousins and aunts in Barcelona because he had had contact with them each summer. Suzy, who was only three, was amenable to everything. But the prospect of a house in Mallorca was irresistible to me, most of all. I love islands, I feel at home on them. I was born on one, after all. Mallorca seemed nothing short of miraculous.

Of course we knew that this was the sacred turf of the eminent British poet and novelist, Robert Graves, and that he lived there more or less surrounded by a court.

I had read his book *Good-bye to All That* with absolute enchantment when I was quite young and took him to be my kind of rebel. I was, of course, totally wrong. His good-bye was more like an au revoir. When we met we did not click, not because of a difference in how to view class warfare but rather because I did not engage in his fanciful fun and games.

I had read *The White Goddess* and had been overwhelmed. I disliked his Lord Jesus, however, and should have guessed then that he would present the kind of problem I often encountered with contemporary British writers. Their erudition enchanted me, their "sufficience" angered me. There are writers like that in all societies, of course, but the British are more insufferable than others. Graves, outside his books, struck me as passably obnoxious, yet when his friends in Spain talked of him he seemed kind, human and protective of the island he so treasured. I was mildly apprehensive of meeting him, but his island sounded like heaven.

So, when Juan came back from Mallorca that May 6, 1964, the customs man at Orly asked if he had bought anything in Spain. He grinned at the man and said, "Yes, I bought a house for my wife."

We then began our Palà Poverty Properties scheme that permitted us to spend long summers away by renting out our Paris house to a wonderful New York teacher called Freddie Friedman who had recently lost her husband. She financed her children's summers abroad by letting out her own house on a Long Island beach and escorting a couple of her young daughter's schoolmates for a summer in Paris, in mine.

I never knew how many youngsters she had in tow but there was a pile of sleeping bags stored in the cellar and we got nice Christmas cards from girls we never met but who had fond memories of our house which they fervently hoped to see again soon. It was an arrangement made in heaven.

Mallorca proved to be high on the list of the most beautiful places I have ever seen. We found ourselves in a medieval village on a mountainside high over the Mediterranean with other yet more rugged peaks surrounding it. The narrow streets of baked stone houses with red tile roofs was, by then, classified and nothing outrageous could be done to spoil it. Though, over the years, the greedy islanders and their friends the promoters did their best. The Germans were masterful at this pillage, turning whole mountainsides into hideous developments like birdcages when seen from the sea.

The sea, of course, was everywhere. High ridges of red rock dipped down into the blue depths wherever one looked and the first thing we yearned for was a boat. It took a few years but it was the first thing *In Search of Mihailo* bought us, aside from a new lease on life.

The sea was at the perfect temperature for long swims, it was tempting and taunting, and it changed colors and courses from town to town. The Nova Scotia child in me took to those coves like a minnow come home. Nova Scotia was beautiful but Mallorca was graced by the gods. Indeed, there was more than one eccentric in the circles that Robert Graves's presence on the island attracted who believed wholeheartedly that after the Great Destruction there would be only a few select places saved on earth to go on and recreate it and Deya would be one of them. Why not?

Deya was down the coast from our Fornalutx. Close enough to go see friends and eat at a couple of pleasant restaurants or to swim at its Cala but far enough to avoid its many personal feuds.

Like all such communities, it was fun, but it was more fun still, I thought, to look in from the outside, at a distance. When we first arrived in 1964 there was as much a gulf between the proper Englishness of Fornalutx, with a certain late Lady Shepherd who had arrived in the '20s, as its patron saint and a few elderly Britishers who raised toasts to the Queen at dinner parties, and us as there was between the Deya crowd which I bridled at instinctively. We were, in point of fact, far more at home in Deya than in Fornalutx but I chose to ignore it.

Chapter 17

We have been blessed throughout life with strokes of luck no one would have ever predicted. The house in Fornalutx was perhaps foremost among them. A few years before, we had been offered the chance of buying a small house in Cadaqués, one of the most beautiful villages on the Costa Brava and next door to that great Spanish monument, Salvador Dali. I took an instant dislike to the snobbery I found at every turn of its beautiful streets, every curve of its exquisite grottos, every sigh of its name-dropping clientele at the local cafés or the pecking order of the beach.

Cadaqués is a perfect lesson in what twentieth century tourism managed to do with villages all along the Mediterranean that attracted artists, because after the artists came the hordes. Select hordes, of course, but no less trying. There were writers, painters, poets, sculptors, photographers, dancers, singers, musicians, publishers and they all basked in the sun shared with Dali and Marcel Duchamp, on either side of the bay, and compared last night's dinner parties. Who was talking to whom at the local "in" café, who was seen leaving whose house when all the lights were out?

I disliked it on sight. Juan took a few days. I find snobs amusing, generally, but not for more than an evening at a time. By the end of that summer we dropped all notions of buying a house on the Costa Brava.

If anything, we feared, Mallorca might be worse. How many times had we run into Brits or Americans or anyone else for that matter, say to us at a party or at a café table, "Oh I love Spain, I just came back from Deya." And Juan muttered that the one place in Spain he wanted to avoid was Mallorca.

Never say never.

Fornalutx was tiny and its colors looked as though someone had painted it and it had suddenly come alive by magic. A mountain range rose slowly out of the sea, rough and stony, dotted with almond and olive trees and terraced orange groves. Stone houses ranging from shepherds huts to graceful mansions with red tiled roofs dotted the slopes and the sea took your breath away on all sides. The blue of Mallorcan waters is distinct and if someone tells you that it is your imagination, ignore him. It is the essence of all blues. It does not take long to see why all the eccentrics drawn to Mallorca's rocky coast feel so at home there.

It began with George Sand and Chopin. The French lady writer took her tubercular lover and her two naughty children and settled in a monastery that let furnished cells and proceeded to terrify the locals. Not so much because they were immoral but rather because the great composer was coughing his lungs out in their midst while Sand romped around in trousers a good century before Ava Gardiner, and her children dressed up in sheets at night to frighten the monks in their cells.

A monastery is a monastery. Perhaps Mme. Sand did not check it out before arrival. It did nothing for nineteenth century tourism, of course. It is a wonder that Mallorca ever let anyone off the passing boats after that episode. But Mallorcans are exceedingly accommodating. To the island's great cost, at that.

Graves settled in during the 1920s but in Deya just up the road a bit from Valldemossa and, peripherally, Palma, the capital. It was a period of seeking out sun and sand, so others followed. Fornalutx appears to have attracted literary school masters, mostly British.

Then came John Polimeni, the very British son of a Sicilian businessman father and Alsatian mother, London-born and -bred, a product of St. Paul's, a veteran of both wars and a great lover of music. He was one of the founders of Glyndebourne. John, or Poli, as everyone called him, was encyclopedic on music but particularly on opera. He bought one house in the village for himself in the early '30s but then, genuinely fearing that the villagers would starve during those harsh depression years, he bought four more. He restored them not only tastefully but painstakingly in the style of their original incarnations. Unlike the Germans, who were beginning to buy houses in Mallorca and who turned them into German sanitized sleeping units as fast as they could, or his fellow Brits who gussied them up with WELCOME mats and chintz curtains, Poli restored their charm. His houses, which he would rent to his choicest friends only, were delights with whitewashed nooks and crannies and furniture that looked as though it was made to measure. He would vet not only his tenants but, unobtrusively, other foreigners who found their way to the village and he would give charming lessons on how to treat the villagers, what not to say to the obtrusive Guardia Civil policemen who garnished the quaint streets, how to treat the maids and gardeners—not to mention the plumbers and others of their sort—plus the etiquette in what to pay the maid, the rules of shopping at both village shops and sitting at both village cafés without playing favorite, thus duly respecting their ancestral feuds.

He was the self-appointed arbiter of good taste and the regent of the valley. We met him in 1964 but by then he was a legend. He had brought to Fornalutx a host of musicians and music lovers. Glyndebourne South, as some called it, and they had settled in under his tutelage. They were, of course, gay for the most part. They were all well installed as part of the local foreign hierarchy when we arrived. As newcomers, of course, we required instruction. Poli was quick to realize that I might be salvageable despite the drawback of my nationality. A Spanish foreigner like Juan was by way of being a plus—there were few Spanish summer people on the ground. I could sense that we would have been more welcome if I had not been American and if we did not live in France. Nothing much good could come from artsy types who lived in Paris.

We had to climb a serious social hill before the Brits, who were the landed gentry of the valley, took us in. Perhaps it was because the children were beautiful or because we spoke a brand of English at home, but by the end of the first month, we had more or less passed muster. At least with the Polimeni side of the café.

Fornalutx had a second Polly, though. She was a clear offshoot of the first English generation and it would be several summers before she invited us for drinks on her terrace. Her name was Polly Dixon-Clegg. She had been installed in Fornalutx since the '20s, a widow from Bournemouth whose husband had died from lingering WWI war wounds. She was the dowager duchess.

Our first summer there was confusing because of living with hammers and chisels underfoot, the second was more complex still because I caught hepatitis almost upon arrival. Frank and Crokie Allen had come down to see us, thank heaven, and it was Frank who picked up on the symptoms because the local doctor was about to give me streptomycin which would have damaged my liver forever. Someone in the valley had come down with mild typhoid which was very hushed up because it was so bad for tourism but which went away after a course of streptomycin. The local doctor thought I had probably drunk from the same well. Frank arrived just in time. I changed doctors.

But it did nothing for my idea of How To Enjoy Your Summer Holiday. I thought back fondly on boring Normandy, where we didn't know anyone and had only the countryside to count on and no debilitating diseases in the grass.

The third summer set the tone for what seemed to be the rest of our lives and I now look back indulgently on the awkward first act. A time we can only think of as the best years of our lives.

We soon discovered that spending summers in the same place involved a delightful sense of continuity that was something like living in episodes. At the beginning of each new July we caught up on, and savored, what had gone on since the previous September—though, as the years went by, many of us saw each other during the winters, too. A sort of club grew from the summers along with deep friendships and commitments. Our coast of Mallorca was a republic of its own in many ways. As in all collectives there were sour apples, unchartered jealousies, petty willfulness. When, for instance, after years of financial havoc, we suddenly became solvent with a bang thanks to *Mihailo*, everyone who knew us was joyful for us. Except in Mallorca where a couple of our buddies pouted. Only among the literary aspirants who dotted the landscape did people sniff petulantly.

I laugh at the reaction now, but at the time I was hurt. There was a counterpart to that attitude and it was no less off-kilter. We suddenly became popular with the arbiters of good taste who had ignored us before *Mihailo*.

The Sóller valley is on the island's rough-edged coast. Its villages are on peaks and before the automobile the villagers were often at daggers drawn. The not so distant past is reflected in its present. Fornalutx was, when we first arrived, still in its Dark Ages. Every foreign owned house had a maid who cared for it while it was empty, and that person formed a faithful family servant relationship with its owner. All the owners, except us, were foreigners. Juan was not only Spanish but he was Catalan, as well.

Mallorca is, historically, a conquest of Catalonia's, a very long time ago. It was at the time of the Conquest, in the Middle Ages, a rock full of vines, olive trees, opulent citrus groves and an indeterminate pirate population. King Jaime invaded it and fought off the Moors, who had invaded it earlier and planted the olive trees and dug the irrigation trenches that survive 'til now. King Jaime made it Catalan, which evolved into being Spanish. The local language is called Mallorcan, which it should not be because it is actually Catalan with a rustic accent. No end of complications arise from all this.

Most non-Spaniards are unaware of the ill feeling between Catalans and the rest of Spain or the ill feeling of Mallorcans to Catalans. My Catalan, in any case, was totally oblivious to the fact that he was considered, locally, to be an invader. The Enemy.

The three main Balearic Islands are totally different in character though they share much of a single past. Menorca was British for a while thanks to the eighteenth century British relationship to The Sea. Mallorca has always been crafty with a finger up to judge the prevailing winds. Ibiza is small and dark and proud. Twenty minutes after Franco rebelled against the duly-elected Republic in 1936, Mallorca declared defeat and adhered to the new rule. To say they have a conservative streak would be the geopolitical understatement of the year.

The Sóller valley, producing much of the island's citrus fruit, pursued the rules of commerce and went one step further by establishing grocery stores throughout France and Belgium to sell them. Half of Sóller lives in funny places around the French countryside. We once noticed a Spanish sounding name in Deauville over the door of the fanciest grocery store in town. We enquired and a somewhat sniffy owner replied that yes, her father was from Sóller. She had manifestly lost the Mallorcan affability on the way.

Now, while most Barcelona schoolchildren know that there is clutch of islands out there called the Baleares, of which Mallorca was the biggest but Ibiza the sexiest—all were a mecca for the sunburned Brits and the flaky Germans—they knew little else. A nice spot to sail to on a weekend but little more. Catalans who went anywhere for the summer went to the Costa Brava for the simple reason that it was the most beautiful place on the Mediterranean and you could get there in a couple of hours with the whole family fitting in the car.

So, armed with this folklore, when after a summer of very strange behavior on the part of the workmen and the town hall officials, sometimes verging on the surly, the penny dropped. The villagers were not sure about us.

They liked foreigners to be foreign. We understood what they were saying, which was unheard of. Also, Catalans were The Historic Enemy, the conquerors.

Here was another one buying up a house at a bargain price from a local smuggler who had been caught and needed to pay a fine by yesterday, poor kid. The house had been put into his poor mother's name but the Palma judge had it in for him and was just about to land him in jail, had not a buyer been found with cash on the line. The smuggler really was headed for jail when Juan arrived.

Juan, of course, knew none of this. He particularly did not know that Catalans were The Historic Enemy in the island. He had been innocently delighting in the quaint turns of phrase the people used in daily speech. He was bemused by their antiquated proverbs and funny ways of pronouncing words. He was busy being charmed. It never crossed his mind that they were not.

Mallorcans are born knowing how to screw foreigners. They do it with a servile smile and an assurance that no one understands what they are saying in their secret language. We broke the cardinal rules without knowing it.

For the next forty years I marveled at the difference between the majestic beauty of the island and the character of its inhabitants. All the Balearic Islands are beautiful, most Mediterranean islands are, but few as seriously as Mallorca.

We made ourselves at home and pretended all our neighbors were as happy as we were.

As luck would have it my birthday is on August 1st, so that celebrating it was our major social effort of the summer. We had all sorts of ways of doing that. A party at the house which dribbled down to a local restaurant was my favorite. We had made friends in Deya early on so there was a Deya contingent, and another from Sóller and then another one of friends of friends. They were very open-house events. In 1968, quite by chance, my beloved buddy from Hungarian Revolution days in Paris, turned up a little further down the coast, to my undying delight. Robert Gabor and his wife Elizabeth bought a house and some land in Sa Canonge, a dream of a hamlet down the coast toward Palma. Vivi and Andy, their children, became part of our lives then. And forever after.

Mallorca brought us magic even in unlikely ways. It enlarged our family as the children grew. The case in point being Karina Ovadia who initiated this whole memoir venture. Karina shared her adolescence with Suzy, as they were born the same year, and she was a vivid part of our Mallorcan life.

On her head be their memoirs.

Friends were as much a part of Mallorca as the sun, the sea and the mountains. We shared, we learned, we laughed with and embraced an enriching variety of people who came with the house, so to speak. But it was not one community, it was many.

And they were fixtures in our lives from then on. One day we were driving up from Sóller while the sun was hot and high in the sky when Juan stopped the car, leaned out the window and said to a chap on foot laden with painting gear, folding easel, canvas, boxes of paints and brushes. "Can I give you a lift?" Juan asked.

Freddy Gore turned around and said with a tired smile, "You already have." And that was the beginning of a close, warm and almost unique relationship that went on 'til Freddy's death some forty years later. Freddy and Connie and the children, Charlie, Georgina and the irrepressible Geraldine.

Fredrick Gore, the son of one of Britain's great post Impressionists, was among the interesting innovators of his generation. He was a master colorist and infused a startling sense of pictorial vigor into his work. His colors flew off the canvas and commanded your attention to the line and the drawing. Freddy was also the Vice Chancellor of St. Martin's Art School in London and he saw in Juan's work a statement on sculpture that commanded attention. He was a major early supporter. He was also to write an introduction to the catalogue of the Prix Bourdelle for Sculpture, France's only national prize for sculpture, that Juan was awarded in 1983, almost twenty years later.

That first summer I was particularly amused because one day I had been sitting in the patio when I heard people going down the steps outside our wall and I heard a little voice pipe up: "That's where Suzy Palà lives." It startled me because the Suzy Palà in question was three-and-a-half years old and I was not aware that she had a social life of her own. That was Geraldine who might have been six. There was definitely a Children's Republic of Fornalutx here which we didn't know about. The Gores had been coming to the village long before us and rented one of Polimeni's houses up the village steeps to the top. The view was spectacular over the red tile housetops through the citrus groves and patches of olive trees.

So, of course, was the climb up. And a couple of curved steps even higher was another Brit whom we came to love.

John Hands was tall and militarily handsome with an imprimatur of the British Army about him that might have put me off. I am, after all, both American and Irish-American. An overdrive of Britishness ignites all manner of genes in me. John was different. I adored him. His years during the war and after it were out of a Lawrence Durrell novel. Like many prototypes, John was nothing of the British colonel he seemed.

His grandfather came from a Jewish banking family in Germany who were the first to introduce checkbooks into the British banking system. John's mother was Irish and had been a beautiful dancer in music hall. John went to a proper public school and then Sandhurst, from which he tumbled straight into WWII where he had a career to nourish a dozen movies, mining and then demining the desert. He ended up a colonel.

John was married to a small chubby younger woman called Faye with whom he had two daughters and, at last, a son. His first wife, who died early of cancer, had given him two daughters, Patricia and Olivia, who made up the pack of beautiful girls in residence at the top of the village with their tall Grenadier father in charge, flanked by young Daniel, the heir apparent. But John was much more than that.

He had happened on Mallorca in the thirties when he was very young. He and a few chums had chartered a boat and were roaming around the Mediterranean when they called in at the Port of Sóller and looked up Polimeni and his houses. John bought one, at the top of the village, looking over the world.

The Spanish Civil War soon erupted, followed shortly by the Second World War.

John's war was hair-raising and his survival verged on the miraculous. Indeed, he came out not only alive but with a lovely American wife whom he had met while on leave in Jerusalem, and their first small daughter, Patricia, residing at Shepherd's Hotel in Cairo, like the protagonists of a half-dozen movies in which Peter Lorre and Humphrey Bogart light cigarettes for Lauren Bacall. He was still in his twenties.

Sometime later with his young family now installed in Surrey, he remembered his house in the Mallorcan clouds and they all went down to see about it. John's wife died soon after, leaving him with a second daughter. He met Faye later on, married her, started another family and resumed summers in Mallorca. The dashing young wartime officer evolved into the colonel in the Reserves, the pater familias of a batch of very English beauties and one of our most esteemed chums. We were as different as one can imagine but we had enormous fun together from the beginning. He tolerated my politics like the British gentleman he was, though I always had a sneaking suspicion he voted Labor on the sly.

His wife was something else. When she left him after seeing him through a heart attack, but only just, he turned to us during the long summer vacations as a sort of surrogate family. That was during the years we had a boat, and John was an expert sailor, so it all fitted in gently and those summers were particularly rich.

Fornalutx and Deya, then, were different planets joined together by shopping for groceries in Sóller. Deya people swam in the exquisite Cala or any one of half-dozen adjacent ones. All of them involved long climbs down and up. Juan loved these little excursions consisting of negotiating rocky paths with sheer drops into the gorgeous blue sea. This New York child did not join in. I was reminded of the hoots of laughter from the other kids at the sight of my rubber beach shoes at the lake in Digby. My asphalt trained soles rebelled at the touch of mud even at the age of ten. Now my entire frame trembled at the sight of terrain more appropriate for a mountain goat.

Suzy and Chris clambered up and down with their father, clearly at home with his genes. The scenery, however, once one got either up or down, was almost worth it and even I realized we were in the midst of glory. Just a tad hard to get to.

One of our most precious friends, who sympathized with my city kid ways, was Jimmy d'Aulignac. He was from Barcelona, the elegant Barcelona still anchored in the past. I saw something pre-war in him right from the start.

His father was a French businessman who had spent most of his adult life in England because he had British nationality since he was born on a British ship. From the stories Jimmy told of his father, beginning with a shipboard birth, he must have been another persona from a novel. He married a Viennese woman in London and had a happy but childless marriage for many years. When his Austrian wife died he went to Barcelona where he remarried and had three children, of whom Jimmy was the youngest. His father was 74 when he was born and lived 'til Jimmy was a teenager. They lived in a fine villa in Sarrià, one of Barcelona's most elegant fringes, and Jimmy and his sister Suzy were brought up in a climate of international ease. Their brother had died tragically in early childhood.

Suzy was a beauty. Rich and social as well as brilliant, by all accounts. I often looked at her full-size portrait done by Prim, one of Barcelona's prominent portrait painters.

The pre-war Europe had long since vanished, of course, but it took a little longer for the news to reach Barcelona. The Jimmys of Paris and London's post-war had vanished by then. Only in Spain was there a scent of yesterday still lingering on the air.

I told him that one day but he only smiled, very slowly and blew some smoke my way. "Anthony Powell?" he offered. Jimmy was extremely well-read. He had been at school in Scotland during the Spanish war and in Barcelona during the '40s he went to the English School, which somehow still survived.

His father had managed to shield his children from mid-century havoc from the grave. Jimmy got a degree from Barcelona University in modern languages. Well he might.

When we first met him and his German wife Frauke we were at a party in Fornalutx, in a biggish garden where I was busy keeping my little Scottish Terrier from peeing on people's feet, something he thought was allowed. Jimmy had been watching him, amused. He walked over and introduced himself and when I told him my name he smiled. "Oh, I have heard lots about you, but no one told me about a Scottie."

Juan could easily have had mixed feelings about Jimmy at first. He has little time for society figures and even less for what might be called society, particularly if they came from Barcelona. Yet Jimmy was above and beyond such pigeon holes. Nor was he really a snob. There was a touch of surrender mixed with another of self-mockery about him. He did not take himself seriously and managed to avoid judging others. He liked good books, he liked good poetry, he listened to music and to his friends' conversation … all with a sense, in my eyes, of gentle detachment. No, he did not judge; he simply observed. Jimmy was a visitor.

I asked him why he never wrote. Everyone else in Mallorca wrote, when they did not paint, and he was a master story teller, so? He laughed lightly and said, "I read. And I cultivate my garden." He did indeed have a remarkable garden in a place where the sun scorched the hardiest of blooms.

That year a newcomer, Tony Johnson, gave me a birthday party on the terrace of his extravagantly beautiful house in Deya. Jimmy said he would think of something to go with such auspicious surroundings. He was not overly impressed with Tony's recent arrival in Deya, which had something of a Marine Landing about it.

When the evening came, he and Frauke came up the white steps with another chap in tow, all smiles. Jimmy said, "This is Alastair Reid, he is my present to you. And he came willingly."

Whereupon Alastair gave me a jolly kiss on the cheek while saying to Juan in Spanish, "With your permission."

Alastair Reid, poet, writer, translator of such impossible poets as Borges and Neruda, chronicler of Spain in the New Yorker with his regular Letter from Spain, was one of my heroes. I had had no idea that he lived part of the year in Mallorca or that Jimmy and he had been friends for decades.

He was a precious gift then and forever after and has become a friend of Christy's over the years, for good measure.

In those early years up through the late '70s Jimmy worked, predictably, for an advertising agency. Then one sad day it sold out to an American firm. A Chicago efficiency expert came in and the first to be fired was Jimmy.

He had had the use of the office Mercedes as well as the office plane. We were toying with a weekend in Tangiers for just the four of us when the blow fell. "Wouldn't you know," was all he said, "Just before Tangiers."

If I speak less of Frauke it is because there is too much to say about her than a memoir like this calls for. We remained friends all the way through. And Juan and I were among the few who remained so, in the lean days that followed.

After the demise of the advertising job when it became clear that it would not be replaced by anything similar, family friends gave Jimmy a sinecure job as manager of a Barcelona cinema. Time passed.

Jimmy lost the house in Deya, which he had been renting for over thirty years. The landlord suddenly claimed he needed the house for a nephew who was getting married. Jimmy tried to fight it but failed. Losing his garden was a blow. The meanness of his landlord after all those years was uncalled for, but sadly predictable. He lingered on in Barcelona in failing health for a time. He was not old, possibly in his fifties.

When I last spoke with him it was on the phone and I asked if he was all right for money. He hesitated for a fraction of a second then said, "Yes, I'm all right now."

Later that day, the only one we were spending in Barcelona, we happened to visit a gallery on the Paseig de Gràcia. The first thing I saw upon walking in was Prim's portrait of Suzy d'Aulignac. The family jewels up for sale. They would see Jimmy out.

And that, surely, put a final note to someone who remains for me a silhouette at a table or at the bar in a Barcelona café on a quiet street and with an interesting clientele.

Jimmy prized good conversation; he liked listening to ideas well-put. I have missed him ever since.

I should explain who Tony Johnson was.

One summer we heard a new buzz from Deya that left the minor key folk of Fornalutx intrigued. We have had our share of millionaires, of course, but nothing quite as bizarre as the chap who had Deya all atwitter. His name was Tony Johnson, he was from the north of England, it was said with a frown, and had just retired with a million pounds. He had come down to Deya to invest in houses and thus make friends.

The outrage matched the degree of nobility of the listener. Graves, it would seem, was furious that carpetbaggers would invade his temple. The Mallorcan rich were irritated but waited, because money is money. The rest of the foreigners varied. As long as he stayed in Deya, we in Fornalutx opined, who much cared?

One day we were visiting with George McDowell, a New Yorker in Deya for many years who had seen a number of would-be Gettys come and go and was indifferent to one more when, from an adjoining terrace, I heard my name called and a smiling stranger say "I know your publishers in London and I am so happy to meet you..."

I took his outstretched hand and was unsure what to say.

"I'm Tony Johnson," he added. And so began a pleasant relationship with a quietly extravagant chap who did things with a slightly comical low-key flourish. I do not usually take to men who throw money around obtrusively, who sport beautiful girls on their arms effortlessly and who invade the stratosphere as though it were there for conquest. Tony Johnson did all these things but on such a quiet note that it was difficult to object to him.

Not everyone agreed with me. Particularly his fellow Brits. Perhaps he showed off with them and not with us. John Hands, who only tolerated him because we asked him to, suffered him but little. John would not include Tony's drink when he paid a round at the local café terrace, which made the waiter's day. Squabbles among the foreigners were heaven to the locals, of course.

Tony was soon at home in Deya where he had installed himself in a fashionable villa with a view worth the gold he paid for it. He only used a few of the rooms and furnished it sparsely. He invited us to stay overnight several times and I was amused to see he used nylon sheets.

Young women fell over themselves for him, something that mildly surprised me. Of average height, neither fat nor thin, neither handsome nor ugly, he was pleasant. No sex object, to my eyes, he attracted amazingly lovely women including one called Monika, who was there with her little boy in the Cala one day when she went over to him, sat down next to him on the rocks and said conversationally, "I would like to spend the night with you."

True, sex was in the air. It was the raunchy extravagant free sex world of Woodstock and the post May '68. In that climate of protest and spiritual anarchy, couples like Juan and me were looked upon as an anachronism. This amused us, but once in a while I felt a shard of hostility among these suddenly liberated women, usually German but also English, exploring a class agenda.

I never gave it that much thought but occasionally wondered whether there might not have been a kind of envy in there, mixed among the slogans of the day.

We became good friends. Tony gave us sound advice on how to invest and stood by my side helping me open an account at a Jersey bank. He stayed with us on the rue de l'Aude before buying a flat of his own in Paris and Juan went with him to the notary to negotiate the purchase since he had little French. He became a friend. As rich friends go, he was pleasant company.

But his arrival heralded a change in Deya, whether he knew it or not. Richard Bransten was the next millionaire to take a Deya farm and renovate it. After which came a clutch of rock singers. I ran out of interest at that point. Those years had brought vast change everywhere, of course. Mallorca was no exception but it did not change colors overnight. The cast changed but there was a hard center that preserved all the essential ingredients. No one has yet cried out in dismay at the sight of a summer millionaire: "Hey, Ma, there goes the neighborhood."

My dear George McDowell is still having breakfast at the café every morning and so are a few other old-timers. They are bemused elder statesmen at this point, like veterans of forgotten dynasties.

But Mallorca has a rich and varied heart with a past that includes princes and pirates. It has ample space for everyone. I wonder now if Tony Johnson ever guessed at the effect he might have had when he arrived with his ready checkbook. Probably not; he was not the first to do it. I'm sure he got a fine return on his initial investment. And the local museums in Deya are all devoted to Robert Graves along with a couple of other foreign artists little-known beyond these shores.

In the long run, that's what counts: memory.

Chapter 18

When things go well, I've noticed, they go well all across the board. I picked up the phone one day and called Philip Spitzer, my agent, and said, "I'm coming to New York, what do you say?"

I heard his laugh and he answered, surprised. "Three cheers!"

And so I began to come home. Alone. Like some sort of rendezvous between me and me. Deep inside, I had never reconciled myself to being abroad forever. I looked upon my life in Paris as a stroke of luck but I was seriously conflicted about no longer being a part of New York. Few people understood this, apart from Ann, and I seldom discussed it with anyone but Juan. He, of course, felt guilty. Justifiably so, it must be admitted. It was a no-win situation so we made jokes about it, leaving it at that. We needed a new calendar that would accommodate winter in Paris, summer in Fornalutx, spring and autumn in New York.

Not to mention a new bank balance.

Since it was a problem that would never be solved, the best solution was for me to make quick little trips on my own and hope my friends with extra beds would not get tired of me. Since most of them often dossed down with us on visits to Paris, it was not a problem. The first few of those '70s trips landed me in the middle of Manhattan in an apartment out of a movie set. It was the perfect way to go home.

Philip Spitzer set me up to see several editors. *Mihailo* had come out to good reviews except for the NY Times where a staff reviewer gave it a half-dozen unkind lines which, of course, devastated me but which everyone, including Philip, told me to ignore. Everyone knew the reviewer hated books about Paris, said one writer friend. No, said another, he hates books period. That sort of comfort helped. A little.

Mihailo made the cover of *Publisher's Weekly*, they reminded me, pay no attention. It was hard to convince myself that it did not matter and, naturally, I never went along with their reading. But all the other reviews were at least good and the book was serialized in *McCall's*. It had been serialized in France, too, and in England in *Women's Own*. All of this had happened recently at the time of the first trip, so much of my time was diverted to lunches with editors for which I was grateful and yet detached. I have a truancy streak which I cannot always explain to others.

But I was comfortable with the very helpful Kitty Benedict at Harper and Row who teased me about my spelling and prodded me about the next book in embarrassing detail. The second book was still mainly in my head. I was vague when I talked about it. She raised an eyebrow but waited for me to commit myself.

"I will have a first draft soon," I assured her. She smiled and promptly gave me a date.

I liked her because she asked pertinent questions about *Mihailo*, about the Orthodox faith, about guilt. But I was not sure about a date for number two. However, she succeeded in making me come to terms with her definition of a writer. I owe her for that.

All through this Ted Berkman, himself a writer of considerable experience, had taken me in hand and given me Instructions For Use about publishers. Ted had been my boss at United Nations Appeal for Children at Lake Success. He was a fine craftsman and an excellent journalist who had spent the war in Cairo where he headed a US government radio news service. He came from a family of overachievers. His aunt was Fanny Holtzman, an elfin dynamo of a lawyer who had been Adlai Stevenson's boss at the San Francisco Peace Conference where she represented the government of China, the conference which had established the creation of United Nations. Almost everyone in the Holtzman family did something exciting, worthy or newsworthy or, in Ted's case, both. That time in New York he decided that I should be taken in hand, which amused me.

Ted had imagined himself in love with me when I was very young. Though anything but a matinee idol—he was actually quite ugly—he had great success with beautiful and often accomplished women. We were close friends for the rest of our lives. Fanny, his feisty name-dropping lawyer aunt who was close to the Churchill family, to Noel Coward, who had a long correspondence with George Bernard Shaw, and his sister Helen who in this galaxy of stars claimed to be the first woman to drive a trolley car in Washington, D.C., and who then repaired to Nova Scotia to rid herself of galloping hay fever, and her English husband who taught at Columbia and with whom Ted wrote film scripts for movies that won serious awards, were the family he was so close to. And Bertha, his elegant and serene mother, were all part of the condition of being Ted's friend. He was something of a walking social club. When I told him so, he looked up at me, astonished.

"But I think of myself as the last Loner in New York," he said. Which says something about how cross-eyed people get in looking in the mirror.

Among the many occasions he invented to introduce me around town to help the book was a launching party given for Larry Collins and Dominique Lapierre by their New York publishers somewhere elegant down in Murray Hill. The first person who came over to say hello was Gerold Frank whom I had known at Lake Success when he was covering the General Assembly for I forget which newspaper. Gerry now gave me a pleasant smile and took Ted's hand. Ted slowly turned his eyes to me. Gerry followed his gaze and then, in a second's hush, his eyes lit up and he remembered me. It had been well over twenty years since Lake Success so I was enchanted that he remembered me at all.

Ted went on to muster a clutch of ghosts like Gerry into a corner, oblivious to Larry Collins who was telling the assembly that several Israeli leaders assured him that they had learned more about what they had been doing by reading O Jerusalem than when they were doing it. Ted gave me a quick glance and murmured, "You don't have to be Jewish to have a modesty problem, after all."

Ted had written several excellent books on Israel, including a biography of Mickey Marcus, the American-born Israeli general who had been killed by accident by one of his own sentries who mistook his white shirt clad figure for an Arab lurking in the shadows.

He had also written a much-discussed piece in the American Mercury on the wisdom of creating a State of Israel at all. Coming from a family of active, public minded New York Jews—his grandfather had been an educator of the poor in Brooklyn and a friend of Teddy Roosevelt—this caution was not always well-received.

At a party for the birth of Israel given by the Jewish Agency in May 1949, to which I had been invited for my generosity in getting press seats for Israeli journalists whose claim to that profession might have been at best tenuous, Ted said to Moshe Sharat, the head of the delegation, "What are you going to do with the Palestinians? Put them in more camps? And create an army of outraged Arabs whose land you claimed after an absence of 2000 years?"

I remember the moment now, the cold shock I had felt at the time. There was no answer then to that question. Not then, not now. And the ripple of unease that cut through the air then is as alive to me now as it was then, and as unsolved. Ted was a good Jew, in his own words, and labored for a just and equitable Israel. Which, he claimed ruefully, was a contradiction in terms. He was not the only Jewish intellectual to face the problem squarely nor was he the only one to reach the conclusion of no conclusion. But he was the first one I knew to say it out loud and I have always been grateful to him for his lesson in faith.

He thought that was very funny when I told him. But, then, he associated the word faith with the wearing of ashes on your forehead on Ash Wednesday which he saw me do once. Or so he claimed. Catholics have faith, he countered, while Jews have a race, in all senses of the word.

I wonder.

Talking about *Mihailo* and the mysteries of faith came easy to Ted, who was an atheist and therefore a bit jealous of faith. He enjoyed telling everyone to buy the book. And they did.

Chapter 19

The Watergate scandal and the vigorous protest movement against the Vietnam War were part of my perception of a return to New York. Caroline Pezzullo, my militant old friend from the '50s, was one of the leaders of the Catholic Left.

She had had an admirable career in Young Christian Workers of which she had been President and dropped in on us during the ice age spell in Paris when we must have looked like a dosshouse on the rue Condorcet.

Caroline had just founded the first all-woman run and owned bank. I was awestruck. She was still beautiful, funny, tolerant of others, and a great cook. She asked me what I would like most that she could give me as a gift. I said Daniel Berrigan, deciding against asking for a full bank account in her new venture.

She organized a dinner at short notice and the great peace priest, the remarkable poet, the prelate who had done much to reconcile me with a faith I had had problems with since my cousin Mono was killed in the war. Twenty years of frequently unthinking anger.

I had come to know the evolution of the Church through the years and the courageous stance of a part of it in the protest years in America. My anger was blessedly dissipated. Or almost. There was no way I could tell all that to Father Berrigan during a sweet dinner at Caroline's apartment but I was grateful for the occasion to hear him talk about The Movement in America with such conviction and a total lack of anger. That must be the ultimate mark of a real Catholic, an absence of anger and a genuine trust in redemption. He dedicated a copy of his book of poems I had just bought with one word: Thanks.

The American peace movement in France was a cross-section of everyone from mild Democrats to Marxists who had nowhere else to go. I was fond of the latter because they were mostly New Yorkers and we had dissidence in common if not Marxism itself. The Catholic Left was far more visceral for me than Marxism.

There is instinct in Catholicism, there is love as well. One does not just drift away from Catholicism, one breaks away noisily slamming doors and shattering glass. My break was full of fury, which probably was simply a display of the incomprehension I felt at what I saw as injustice.

The Church, of course, had changed and so had I. What I had taken away from Incarnation was no longer the Church as it stood in the 1970s. I thought back on the little homily the young priest who had officiated at my mother's funeral in the West of Ireland that had given me an unexpected glimpse of the breadth of change that was ruffling through the Church since I had stopped listening. The peace movement, the bravery of the peace priests, the emergence of la Teologia de la Liberacion in Latin America, the work and valor of priests like Camilo Torres of Colombia, all had repercussions on my perceptions. I felt a timid sensation of coming home.

Caroline gave me a Cheshire Cat-smile over the dinner table that evening. Later on when I went to Chicago to see Ann and told her about my tip toe return to the fold, she burst out laughing and said, "I told you so!"

I look back on the time when we first became friends in 1945 when she would come up and spend the weekend at my house. My parents loved her, my father enjoyed taking us all to Forno's for Saturday lunch and Mother thought she was a good influence for me. We were sent out to 12 o'clock Mass on Sunday, rain or shine, and rain or shine I made her walk around Washington Heights to fill in the hour we should have been at Mass. Ann was Jewish but didn't mind the liturgy. She did mind wandering around windy streets, however. We compromised on a soda fountain my mother didn't patronize.

Growing up was taking me a very long time.

On another of those trips home in the 1970s, a friend in Washington offered to drive me to the court in Lancaster, PA, where Father Philip Berrigan, Daniel's brother, who had since left the priesthood, was on trial with several others for his anti-war actions. There had been a spate of peace priest trials since the outset, but this one was perhaps the most prominent. The courthouse corridors were full of Catholic Peace people, some of whom I recognized from Caroline's crowd.

I caught John Grady's eye and he obligingly came over to talk to me. We talked about the combativity of the Church in the US and traced it to the stewardship of Dorothy Day. She had formed a generation to ask questions and demand answers. Her message refused to go away, which is what the Church, as I recalled it, wished it to do. She did not get lost, she went forth and multiplied. The face of the Church in America was altered. Complacency, as I knew it, was no longer the norm. Obedience was questioned. Dumbing-down was out.

"Everyone is acting like a Presbyterian," I ventured to Caroline.

To which she answered, "You are a snob."

Perhaps.

Trying a Catholic priest in a US Court was an exercise in degradation. I was almost physically sick at the sight of the tall athletic Berrigan being escorted into the dock in handcuffs.

What had gone wrong with my country that it had fallen so low? Even the southern Baptist journalist friend who had driven me up to Lancaster and who had but only mild curiosity about this scene, was discomfited.

The Catholic Left came out of those years reinforced and with a voice now listened to with new concern. It was a price to pay, a painful one for those who went to jail. But they came out as winners. Latter Day Saints, in my view.

My trips home in the 1970s were not all as emotional as that one, nor did I do nothing but wave peace banners and look pained if anyone mentioned Nixon in my presence. There was much more. There were friends to catch up with and places to make sure were still there. Change, I had to admit, was not what I was looking for. Yet it was around me everywhere I looked. I liked some of it, though my buddies complained here and there that change is what I was screaming for on one hand and what I was screaming against on the other. I must have been a royal pain in the ass.

To my itchy dismay, on my first visit home I had to leave New York and go to Chicago to see Ann. She brushed aside my pleas for her to come to see me; I had to see her new life and of course, she was right. And I even liked Chicago, though I was not expecting to.

She met me at the airport with her new man, Ted. I immediately called him Bob which made him smile slightly but made Ann furious. "I don't do it, you shouldn't," she snapped. Ted didn't mind, thank heaven. He thought I was like a new brand of mother-in-law.

Ann had been tied to Bob emotionally and physically since she was nineteen. They had been closer than any other couple I have ever known except Juan and me. They moved from New York in the mid-1950s to their tiny hamlet in a forgotten corner of Chesapeake Bay which was pretty and quaint but culturally nowhere. True, in New York they had few friends but they were surrounded by people who did have friends, who had conversation and a variety of interests from which they could or could not, as they chose, nibble on. Nourishment does not only come with the oysters that piled up on the local skiffs. The library in Cambridge, MD, did not have the keys to all their needs. (I was horrified to hear, later, that Cambridge erupted into a racist cesspool in the race riots of the late '60s. Ann was more horrified than I, of course.) But they had been happy in their locked in marriage, they created their own universe and they thrived. She was now in her forties and shakily alone.

Not quite alone, of course, because Lorraine, her sister was in Chicago. She was the dean of the Erikson Institute, Bruno Bettelheim's graduate school of social sciences. Lorraine welcomed Ann, brought her into her circle of auspicious friends and she soon got herself a job at the University of Chicago Press as head of publicity. She claimed that everyone, including the janitor, had a PhD.

Bob would have thought that a giggle. I was awed.

Chapter 20

Tom Donahue was now a notable in Washington which gave me immense satisfaction. Friendship is one of those elements in life that make one blush when trying to define it.

Tom was my buddy, my comrade in arms from another planet... a planet from which we were among the few survivors, I thought.

He had taken away the lessons learned from the Free Europe years in Paris and put them to good use in his career in the Labor Movement. The Johnson administration did well to have him on board. He was Assistant Secretary of Labor. Those were uneasy years for liberals. The progress in Civil Rights, which was manifest, was seen to have been compromised by the multiple divisions brought by the Vietnam War. It not only seemed like two countries but it also felt like two different administrations. Tom and I managed to sit on opposite sides of that fence with both grace and tolerance on his part.

I never laid claim to either.

On one of the early visits there was a sit-in on the Pentagon grounds. He knew I wanted to go so he offered to drive me there and come by and pick me up later. I did not want to embarrass him; he was a public figure, after all, but he assured me that it would be fine. Tommy, his teenage son, came with us. At the corner where I was to get out and find myself a patch of grass, Tommy said, "Can I stay with her?"

My heart sank.

"No," replied Tom calmly. "You can come back with me to pick her up, though." I thanked the Good Lord for the gift of diplomacy, not the most Irish of attributes, that Tom was clearly blessed with. And the sit-in was peaceful—a truce had been signed in heaven that day.

The Donahue kids were personable. They asked questions and gave me interesting insight into what my children's' American counterparts were like. Of course there were differences between being brought up in Paris or in Washington, but they were all you could want in kids their age. They

187

had curiosity, that most precious of qualities. The one that never goes away. And they weighed differences, they did not pass judgment.

"Whatever it is," I told Tom, "You are doing something right." Which is by no means faint praise for the father of a pair of adolescents.

Each of my trips home was distinct, but as of the early '70s they took on another color. Christy was in New York. He had grown up, gone to the University of Geneva, graduated and had gone to New York to maintain his American citizenship. In those dark days all children born of one American parent abroad was obliged to spend five consecutive years in the US to conserve his American nationality. This amounted to second class citizenship. It was pointed out that anyone could go to the US, spend five consecutive years and become a citizen, one did not need an American parent for that.

Years of hard lobbying in Washington by Democrats Abroad France and the purposeful determination of one American abroad, Phyllis Michaux, who founded a group called American Wives of Europeans, in Paris in the early 1960s, changed the legislation.

But, in the early 1970s, the change in the law had yet to be achieved. In Chris's case he could have opted for Spanish nationality but we were still in the Franco years and he would have had to do two years of military service in the Spanish army for that. The notion did not appeal to him. Or to us. The alternative would have been to ask for French citizenship but the military service clause was mandatory there, too, and just as unpopular.

But most important of all was his own sense of who he was, a sense of identity. He was American. He was an American abroad, but an American. There was no question about it. He had to go to the States at the earliest opportunity if that is what the law obliged him to do.

There is a God in heaven who takes care of our particular frailties. He works overtime with me. True, I give Him more challenging quandaries than most and that might possibly appeal.

Christy also wanted to be a journalist, not anything else. A foreign correspondent, preferably.

Just before he was to graduate from college and depart for the US an old friend of mine, John Donahue, whom I had met on the ship going back to New York after my first stay in France in November 1949, and with whom I had kept up, came through Paris and dropped in. He had married a lovely French woman and they had six children. Most of the children were with him and Christiane on this visit and they were headed for lodgings in the French Alps for the whole tribe over the whole summer. I asked him if he knew of a job for Chris on his beat in New Jersey, not really thinking he would.

John, who was tall and skinny and looked like a professor even when he was young, said, "Yes. I can give him a job."

I gaped.

He smiled a little because when we had met he was a fledgling reporter himself headed to a paper in upstate New York. And I had fallen into a job as editor of a trade journal called *Travelling In France*, published by the French National Tourist Office. That would have been 25 years earlier.

He said, "Send him over, we'll see what happens. And don't worry. You and I managed, didn't we?"

So, off he went. With a full address book, college diploma from the University of Geneva and a job in New Jersey waiting for him. Who says there is no such thing as luck?

Chapter 21

Then came Millie, who was to teach us lessons in the diversity of our native patch and the time warp we live in while living abroad. Nothing stands still, not even New Jersey.

Millie turned out to be something new to us, a Jersey girl. New even for Barbara Grosset who was from Teaneck, not far from the George Washington Bridge. But that was not the Jersey Millie was talking about. This, of course, was long before The Sopranos. We could have written a couple of episodes with no great effort, after Millie.

This small dark-eyed bundle of electricity burst into our lives with the flair that characterized most things she touched. In coming to Paris she had changed worlds but not gears. I wondered if she had had any relatives who went to Textile High School when I did. She reminded me of a half-dozen Italian kids in my year who intrigued me with their bravado, Sinatra style.

She proved to be in awe of Juan. She admitted to me that she had never met a man who was an artist full-time. Like with no day job, as she put it. And she thought I was some kind of saint for encouraging him. She was especially fond of Suzy. Suzy, at fourteen, could slip into four different languages without a glance back. Millie gazed at her in deep admiration. What a gifted child I had, she sighed, shedding a silent tear for her lack of language skills. She could barely say Oui understandably.

But that did not get in her way. She had met Joan Dupont while waiting in line at the post office trying to register a letter in what sounded like pidgin Italian with an American accent. My friend Joan was next in line and, hearing the insane babble she quelled laughter and offered to help.

Millie was ready to hug her in gratitude. The letter that had to be registered was important. She took Joan to the nearest café and ordered champagne. They both lived in a pretty fringe suburb of Paris and Joan instantly became Millie's best friend. Until Joan introduced her to me. Millie's enthusiasm for new friends in this foreign landscape was slightly overwhelming, but she touched me and I enjoyed seeing her quite genuine pleasure.

She had been in Paris for several months with a new set of in-laws, very middle class French, who found this American confusingly different from Debbie Reynolds. She was by then ready to turn tail and run back to Jersey City when she met us. She introduced us to her young husband, Gerard, making me wonder why girls like her always picked on men whose names they could not pronounce. I did not give her long in Paris and I was right. But she managed to get around while she was here and she blossomed once she got started.

Not long after we met Millie got a job with a student travel organization run by a friend of mine. I did not realize that I had had anything to do with her getting the job 'til much later.

One day she and I were having a drink after work and she turned to me and said I should check out New York to make sure Chris was as well as he said he was. I smiled and said yes, remembering idly how important families were to Millie and her warm interest in mine.

"I like New York in June, how about you?" she let out. We were sitting at a favorite bistro of mine off the Champs Elysées, which she found particularly classy. She grinned naughtily and handed me a ticket for three weeks in June, a limo included.

"Go check it out, it's on the house," she said impishly. I stared at her. "Nobody counts," she murmured, with a shrug of the shoulder. "Except me and I won't tell."

And so I flew off to New York for free and was met by a limo and Christy said mournfully, when I told him, that the part of New Jersey he was in had no Italians, not even third-generation.

Millie did not stay in Paris forever as she thought she would. She returned to Jersey after a few years, leaving Gerard and a handful of friends like me behind, wondering whether we had just dreamed her up, feeling bereft without her.

More importantly, no one has given me a free ticket to New York, including a limo, ever again.

There was much more to the Sopranos than they let on.

As usual I went to Washington on my freebie trip. By Greyhound bus, this time. Everyone laughed at me, but I love Greyhound buses. They bring me back to my yearly pilgrimages to New Brunswick when I was a half grown child during the war. I felt like Ingrid Bergman then crossing the frontier. My imagination goes a long way even now though stopping at

Howard Johnson's on the Turnpike has not quite taken the place of spies in the night at the age of fourteen during the war.

There were changes in Washington, too. Tom had a new wife. Would I like her? What would I do if I did not like her? Drown her, perhaps? Like a nuisance cat? It did not happen. She turned out to be blissfully New York, frighteningly accomplished and very much in love. Best of all, she was Jewish. I adored her.

She had all the right likes and dislikes, she was an amazing cook and I was enchanted to see she was a little overweight. My Tom had lucked out. But so had I. Rachelle Horowitz walked into our lives and has been a brilliant part of it ever since.

Her background was dazzling to someone like me, who admired a good brawl. She worked with Bayard Rustin on the March on Washington, she had been involved in left wing politics since she was a teenager, but not just in handing out leaflets or voting against Nixon. She had been in the fray. She had been in the clink. She had scars. I loved her. I envied her for having been there at the right time and done the right thing. My wars were all foreign. The closest I ever came to the Home Front was one peace march down Broadway and my sunny sit-in at the Pentagon.

Rachelle had gone on to work as political officer for the Teachers' Union, one of the most stalwart unions on the floor. Tom was, by then, Secretary Treasurer of the AFL-CIO. Between the two of them, I decided, they were running the world. And they looked it, too. It is comforting to see your friends happy. Comforting and, I fear, not all that frequent.

Wherever she is, Millie has kept a special corner of my heart. My free trip was a treasure.

Chapter 22

I was about to begin with "everything changed in the '70s," but it is not true. Everything changes every day. What seemed outrageous in 1948 was commonplace in 1956. It is the giant steps that make the changes. Like Franco's death.

How many years had we waited for it, how ghoulish we felt when putting it into words, yet how easy we imagined how it could be achieved. When I first visited Madrid in 1949, I had harbored fantasies of a quick gunshot to a pudgy figure standing on a balcony waving to a docile rent-a-crowd. I had no notion of the police protection that would appear out of nowhere whenever El Caudillo came into view. Which was not all that often compared to De Gaulle or Churchill or Adenauer. So, I waited through the years for the deliverance of the country that I had come to love with the romantic love of a teenager who admired bravery and lost causes more than might and the sound of whips.

I even had a secret little fantasy that I would be the first in our house to hear of his demise. Or overthrow. Or both. And I would rush to the studio to tell Juan and I would remember the expression on his face forever. He would say Por fin: At last. Then the image would fade into the sunset where such images belong in the first place.

The odious Generalissimo had been either the smartest dictator in Europe or else the luckiest. He had won his rebellion over a duly elected Republic in 1939 with the scandalously visible aid of the Nazi German Air Force, which bombed civilian populations with impunity, and of Fascist Italian troops and planes sent out to gratify Mussolini's almost comic aspirations to reign over the Mediterranean, Mare Nostrum.

Martyred Spain was, when I first knew it, poor, dusty, starkly beautiful, and short of food except on the flourishing black market. One of the first words I learned was "estraperlo," which means black market. Ann and I brought art books in our luggage, when we took the train with Juan, for his friends who were not able to buy them in Barcelona. Picasso, along with most of modern art, was vilified then, in the 1940s. It was decreed as decadent.

When we visited in the summers during the late '50s we were asked to be cautious by Juan's father. Later on, massive tourism modified the air on the streets but the Guardia Civil in their tri-cornered patent leather hats were not just picturesque. It took time and the arrival of vast numbers of tourists to modify the rules, as well as an exodus of another sort that changed them altogether. Millions of Spaniards left their poverty behind and migrated to France and Germany. The Spanish maid and the Spanish garage mechanic became commonplaces—everyone had one. Many of them were called Dolores and Juan, I point out in passing. My friends giggled at that.

But Franco lived on. And lived on. The entire face of Europe would change before my little secret dream would come true and I would be able to say, "Franco is dead" to my long-suffering Spanish love.

I was about to turn off the radio one November night in 1975 when I heard a BBC voice say that reports from Spain were coming in about the Generalissimo's condition, now described as critical. I turned off the radio, ran for the 68 bus which brought me to an art gallery near the Seine where I was to meet Juan. I found him deep in conversation with a solemn faced American painter, Shirley Jaffe. As I all but ran up, Shirley held out her hand to stop me butting in. I gaped.

"Give me a second," she said, "this is important." And she continued to elaborate her theory on the necessity of a gallery in the life of an artist. Juan did not have a gallery then; he worked principally with architects and showed in a few major Salons. It was a subject of such minor importance I could have clobbered Shirley but I waited, feeling the air seep out of my balloon with every passing second.

He must have noticed because, while keeping his eyes on Shirley with his usual courtesy, he gently put his hand on my shoulder and drew me closer. When she had finished he looked at me slowly, and said, "Good news?"

I think it was because of moments like this one that I love him. "Franco is dying," I said quietly.

Shirley looked abashed. Well she might. Juan's eyes widened and a nameless expression suffused it with light. We are brought up never to exult at any death. But there are exceptions. A buzz went through the gallery and someone called out, Mazel tov, Palà.

That was the sort of change that mattered. A sea change. A total reversal of the way it was. To coin a phrase.

There were many of them on all fronts. Music changed, sexual mores changed, what was allowed and what wasn't changed. The notion of patriotism changed. The definition of family changed. We were poised on a see-saw of our own making without a viable Directions For Use.

Without Franco, Spain came to life like a Sleeping Princess and turned into A Fun Place instead. The black-clad clergy slowly melted into the past and there were guitars and bag pipes at Mass on Sunday. It was the moneyed middle class, not as large as in most European countries but a lot more observant, that ushered in the new era. They were young, they were eager, they were hungry for what was on offer in other countries. They had the ambition and now they had the front stage. Spain changed almost overnight. But it had been long years in a dress rehearsal.

And they had a card up their sleeve which took us, at least, by surprise. The king. Without his cool that most volatile of countries, that most divided of nations, would not have come together as it did under the gentle iron hand of a young man who had had a divided childhood but whose father, the ousted monarch, had bequeathed a steely notion of the possible.

We were the first surprised. But change is a strange concept and surprise is a prime factor in it.

Chapter 23

As I write this memoir, the fiftieth anniversary of the Civil Rights March on Washington has been celebrated and applauded, even, on both sides of the Atlantic under the quiet eye of a young American President whose father happened to be African. If I did not object to the word as it has become, I would say, "This is awesome." But that is exactly what it is, awesome.

We were in the country that summer, out of touch with the immediacy of what was taking place in Washington. There had been a small delegation that presented a petition to the embassy showing support for the movement at home signed by Americans in Paris, which was a beginning. Much more was to come.

That autumn I was part of a group that met informally and put together a little core called PARIS which was sort of an acronym that meant Paris Americans for Racial Equality. It proved to be the only a partial beginning. The movement protesting the Vietnam War moved in and suddenly there were two fronts, not necessarily drawing the same adepts. Civil Rights was one thing, but the Vietnam War was another.

Jim Jones, for example, from the start defined his sympathies. He criticized the government, not the soldiers who did the fighting. He was, of course, true to the sentiments that had brought him to write *From Here to Eternity*. Therein lay the difference between the two American movements in Paris which, of course, mirrored what was happening at home.

It was not all that difficult for an American teacher or businessman or woman to be against racial discrimination. A petition for civil rights was easily signed and there was more pride than prudence in taking such a petition to the Embassy and presenting it to a posse of officials who were, for the most part, eager to receive it. Those who opposed civil rights, if there were any, must have stayed home. Taking a petition to stop the war in Vietnam, however, was touching a very different set of values.

Thus, the creation of a chapter of the movement so vociferous at home was merely a question of time in Paris. I joined it readily, and so did most of my friends who had come out staunchly for Democrats Abroad, the first such grouping.

As the scale of the war in Vietnam widened and the hostility toward the administration mounted, the tenor of our efforts in Paris changed. It was then that the Anti-War Movement came into its own. At the same time the bi-racial group that PARIS represented quietly faded out. Civil Rights was no longer the only battleground. The Vietnam War was eating us alive.

The urgency of putting an end to that misadventure brought together a broad spectrum of Americans in Paris. Enduring friendships were made among people who would never have run into each other under normal circumstances. And there were unlikely patriots, too, those who lost their jobs when they spoke out. Foremost among those was Lawrence Wiley, then Cultural Attaché of the US Embassy who soon felt compelled to resign his post as Cultural Attaché at the Embassy.

Larry Wylie was an endearing scholar, a homespun American from Indiana, a Quaker who had been a conscientious objector during the World War II and a pioneer in a new science, social ethnology. His books on rural France are brilliant as well as delightful classics, *A Village in the Vaucluse* and *A Village in Anjou*.

In all conscience he could not endorse what his country was doing nor, even less, represent it. He resigned his post as Cultural Attaché in sad protest to the government's pursuit of a war he could not condone. Having someone like Larry Wylie as an American spokesman in Paris was by way of being a passport to legitimacy. His presence, like his gesture, was indicative of what the divisions within the country over the war were like, what they were doing to our image abroad and, more importantly, what they were doing to the nation as a whole.

That was just the beginning. All through the 1960s Maria Jolas, then in her late seventies, was the core of the Peace Movement in Paris. It seemed only fitting and proper at the time. She had been in Paris since the 1920s and, in her unobtrusive way, was the quintessential American in Paris in terms of achievement, involvement and, indeed, longevity. She had come to Paris in 1919 before the smoke had cleared after the end of the First World War. She was from a prominent St. Louis Kentucky family and a descendant of Thomas Jefferson. Instead of making a career in music she married Gene Jolas, a handsome Franco-American newspaperman-cum-writer-cum-editor, who, with Eliot Paul, founded *Transition*, the first of the great "little" magazines that changed the face of literature in the magical '20s in Paris. They were the original Americans in Paris. They set the aims, lent the color, marked the goals.

I had heard Maria Jolas speak to small audiences about those years but never imagined we would become friends. We did. Close friends. And I will be eternally grateful to the tricks of fate for letting that happen.

The group we formed was called PACS for Paris American Committee to Stop War. It was a loose grouping of Paris residents of a variety of backgrounds, though a great number came from the periphery of the arts. Juan claimed that if you scratched an American you would find a would-be writer and Paris was their Mecca. Perhaps. A number of them came forward and were counted in PACS. But there were others, too. Women who had married Frenchmen, for example, students, professors, doctors, temporary residents, others who had come after the war and just stayed on. All kinds of Americans with one major concern. Something had gone wrong with our country and part of our heritage was that we felt obliged to change it. Maria's grandmotherly stature which was the other half of her firm resolve to have our dissident voices heard, contributed to our stature.

The upheavals of May 1968 resolved the French police to put a stop to PACS. The official at la Prefecture who had handled our permit to assemble peacefully convoked Maria, then well into her eighties. She was imposingly tall and distinguished. The slightly cowed police official demanded that the organization be disbanded and not reconvened under any other name. Maria gracefully accepted. "I accept your diktat," she said, using that word assertively. She added that she would be obliged to inform the members and affiliates of PACS abroad and, of course, the international press. She nodded politely at the policemen and took her leave.

I would love to have been there.

Around that time I was also convoked to the Prefecture by a chill policeman straight out of a spy movie. He ushered me into a dimly lit windowless office with one bare desk and two chairs at the entrance and a smaller desk with a man at a typewriter in semi-darkness at the other end. The touch of Maigret made me duly uncomfortable.

I must interject here that, for all their faults, I cannot altogether blame the French Prefecture for calling me in. I was a very unruly foreigner and any other country would have at least fined me long before. To explain, I must go back to the Free Europe years, the '50s.

The Committee preferred its employees not to take out French residence papers. Go figure why. An American tourist could remain in France for three months without needing residence papers. So, every three months the office gave us the equivalent of a first class round trip plane ticket to Brussels and a night's fare at a top hotel but we were asked to maintain our status as tourists. I cannot imagine what bit of nonsense prompted this silliness but the result was that I had lived in France since 1955 without a permis de séjour, the green card equivalent. This was all the more insane when we traveled as a family because only Juan had legal papers. The children and I were wetbacks, so to speak.

I could hardly get outraged when they finally took me to task in 1977.

Quite sternly my interrogator in his creepy office began by telling me to get myself straightened out, to stop agitating for peace on French soil, and a handful of other chastisements.

Then he let one word too many drop between us and I realized he knew where I lived. He knew my house. Clearly, he had checked us out in the neighborhood and even knew that, at that particular moment, we had two cars. I felt chilled to the bone. And I must have showed it for he suddenly changed tones. "You would not make a good agent," he said laconically. "You don't recognize me yet? I have been to a dozen PACS public meetings and have often taken the same bus as you to go home afterwards."

I was dazed. It is true that I have a poor memory for faces but still...

"I live on the rue St. Yves," he added, smiling broadly. "Of course I know your house."

I had a terrible fear of throwing up but fought it off and tried to smile. I did not cry, which was a major miracle. I cry when I am angry and I was very angry then. Flamingly angry. With myself. The rue St. Yves is around the corner from my house. We were neighbors.

Some time later Susie Ovadia was introduced to a friendly face in the Prefecture who facilitated both our statuses. Hers was not due to excessive subversion in the Peace Movement, it was simply because renewing resident cards was a nuisance. Her man turned out to have a normal office with a window and several chairs. He was cordial to me, possibly because my second book had just come out as well as a short story in the French edition of Cosmopolitan. The title of my book *Trumpet for a Walled City* was translated into French as *Une Américaine à Paris*, an idiotic choice of the publisher's, not mine. But it sounded just right to the Prefecture chap who presented me with a three-year card while I gave him an autographed copy with warm thanks. I have been "en règle" ever since.

Maria Jolas lived well into her nineties and hers was one of the most treasured friendships I have ever enjoyed. She and her husband published Joyce's Finnegan's *Wake in Transition*; they published Ezra Pound, Hemingway, Scott Fitzgerald, Kay Boyle, Anaïs Nin and anyone else of value at that amazing moment in Anglo-American letters, the between-the-wars period. They were the ones who had lighted the way, they were the reason why we came.

In addition to being a friend of James and Nora Joyce and the partner in *Transition*, she was also the mother of two remarkable daughters. Like many American mothers of small children she thought their French schools unnecessarily harsh. Thus, she founded the first ever bilingual primary school in France.

"That would have been in your spare time?" I asked her.

Her blue eyes widened and she turned to me, "What would I have done with spare time, my dear? Just what?" And she laughed out loud. There was never time for spare time in Maria's remarkable life.

Chapter 24

If the seventies stick in my memory as a time of continued conversation, of dialogue without punctuation, arguments twisting around unconscionable events that turned the tables without warning, it is only normal. The world spun in its orbit as if there would be no tomorrow. And how close that seemed.

President Richard Nixon proved to be as unscrupulous as my Democrat mentors had predicted, possibly worse. The Watergate scandal had reduced the Presidency to a smoke filled room.

The idols had fallen and the general nakedness that resulted was uncommonly bleak. The only way was up after that. And up we went.

I remember theater erupting in a half-dozen directions, not only in Paris but all over. Especially London where it was habitually superb but in Austria and Germany, as well. Brecht had left a handful of hot coals and we looked on in admiration. In the brand new air after Franco's death new, insolent young voices tumbled over the frontiers and everyone in Paris spoke Spanish for awhile. We had always been avid theater-goers here in Paris or in London. It seemed only natural. Theaters were not outrageously expensive as I found them in New York, and their quality was a matter of almost personal concern.

Everyone had an opinion on Jean Vilar, the visionary who created the TNP, a difficult repertoire for a popular audience at low prices in a huge theater seating a huge audience. His genius was as contagious as it was outsized and the TNP became an institution as French as the Eiffel Tower. I don't imagine we missed many of its productions in Paris and only regretted we could not get to Avignon where it performed in the breathtaking space offered by the Palace of the Popes in summer. Jean Vilar was, in my lexicon, the spirit of post-war theater, not only in France but all over the western world. He reached out from the Classics through to today, having ripped through the century's treasure trove of European and Americans like Tennessee Williams, Eugene O'Neill, Sherwood Anderson or Federico Garcia Lorca in Spain. At popular prices, which was part of the movement.

Theater was not for an elite but for people at large. Vilar's concept of theatre has marked several generations and a half-dozen other troupes followed his. The bigger and more impossible the locale, the more challenging the theater. Perhaps the most daring was the medieval Chateau de Vincennes on the eastern edge of Paris. Turning it into a vast arena was a perfect example. And the booming productions that were put on there by Ariane Mnouchkine were worthy of its magnificence. Where else but there to stage the French Revolution and make you squirm a little?

No matter how broke we were we managed to see most of the theater of the day. But so did all our friends. I look back and wonder about the scene today. The theater has grown quiet and that makes me squirm a great deal more urgently than the sound of galloping hooves in a reconverted citadel. I can only conclude that we made up a particularly talkative generation.

At the risk of wallowing in clichés, I have to admit to having enjoyed being forty. All things considered.

Suddenly being able to take trips to New York easily was a strong point. There were bargain flights that made it tempting and, once on the other side, my delightful friend Philip Goodman—playwright, film director, my most generous host in a dream apartment on West End Avenue a few blocks away from where I had lived as a small child on Riverside Drive— made me welcome a half-dozen times. I will never be able to thank him enough.

My mother used to lament the loss of her sunken living room in moving uptown. Not everyone knew what a sunken living room was but the depth of her sigh, when she bemoaned its loss, sufficed to elicit a gasp of sympathy. Philip has a huge sunken living room on the 15th floor on 80th Street and West End. As soon as I saw it I offered her, surely in Heaven, a silent apology... it is indeed a pretty dramatic way to situate a room. New York does that to me... it unearths little corners of my life I had forgotten and pours sunlight where there had been none before.

I loved visiting Philip, I loved his hospitality, his immense joy in sharing the city he loved with me. We traded secret corners, special views, dusty landmarks only we knew. He was the perfect host for this ever-reluctant expatriate.

To my surprise, and with thanks to that doctor in Barcelona whose magic pills did wonders for my waistline, I liked being forty. No wonder.

Juan was doing interesting work and it was proving interesting to other people. He had a regular stream of commissions from the State which he used not to make money on, as most other artists did, but to do seriously expensive pieces he could not afford to do otherwise. He was right. They constitute a group of major works, the only large-scale pieces he was ever able to afford to do. And, as it happens in his work, one piece prompts, or triggers off, the creation of the next.

These commissions engendered shock waves and one creation carried the germ of the next. It was fascinating to watch the progress. In a way it was like deciphering a text to measure the distance between one piece and the next.

The fact that he poured a sizeable slice of the budget he was given to actually make the sculpture raised a few eyebrows. But he knew he would have little opportunity to do more and no one could guarantee how long the French State would be building new schools that would require works of art to be included in their budgets.

He was to have nine such commissions. Somewhere toward the end he calculated that if he had the two new commissions he had just been given made in Barcelona, where metalworkers' salaries were lower than in France—the sculptures are made in a foundry under his supervision and in his presence—he could ship them back to Paris by rail and, at the same time, spend a little time with his mother who, though in good health, was ninety. He would even make a sizeable profit. Or so he thought. It seemed to make financial sense.

Needless to say, it did not. Labor was not that much cheaper in Barcelona, it took longer to make the pieces, the two foundries that did the work were at an awkward distance from each other in different industrial suburbs of Barcelona, and it took more time than he counted on to get from one to the other. Predictably, both ran over their budgets. Then, shipping the pieces by rail to Paris was extremely complicated, as was finding transport the instant they arrived in the Paris freight yard because the railroad began charging storage the minute they arrived… financially it was something of a flop.

However, before leaving Barcelona, one of his fans, an interesting woman who promoted art shows as a bit of a hobby and had a small collection of her own, liked his work and invited him to show one of the pieces in a salon she directed and thus reintroduce him to Barcelona after an absence of over 25 years.

It all happened quickly, before he had much time to think about it or to discuss it with the few artist friends who were around. Which was just as well. On the opening night of the Salon, then, the space in the center of the gallery was taken by Juan's monumental piece in burnished steel, a sphere that stood imposingly on a plinth creating a sense of silence and solemnity. The piece was breathtaking. Surrounded by smaller works and a variety of paintings, it appeared to be totally alone and distinct. It claimed attention and held it. And tomorrow it would be gone, for it would be shipped to Paris.

There was magic in its presence.

I was overjoyed to see it and to see the reaction among the attendance. Barcelona is an exceptionally art-conscious city. There are groups, coteries, cliques within cliques. Juan was, in many art circle eyes, the local boy who had made a stir when he was very young but then went away and did not come back. Apparently, a house in Mallorca did not count. Then, too, having married an American, in those post-war years, implied a rich American.

I never did anything to dispel the notion in the beginning, when we first met. I did nothing to dispel it later on, either.

I was proud of my Barcelona boy with his sculpture breathing life in their midst. He deserved a rich American.

Chapter 25

Meanwhile, back at the rue de l'Aude, almost without our really noticing, the children had grown up. Christy left for the States in 1974 and Suzy, our delicious sweet tempered baby, almost without our noticing it, had become a young lady… or was it a teenager? From being my welcome poppet, running off to see Granma in Ireland several times a year with me, or going on a wild flight to abundance in Geneva at a moment's notice, she had become someone who had previous appointments, new ears to whisper to on the phone if we were around… a young lady. It took me time to recognize the change, let alone admit it was happening. My Suzy had grown up.

She had done it so gently that we hadn't quite noticed. True, during the Mallorcan summers she got us used to disco hours and the presence of boys in our patch of the beach. But she and Karina, who spent those adolescent summers with us, got us used to their version of adolescence which was, because there is a God in Heaven, nothing compared with her brother's. She did not sulk, she did not run away from school, she did not fail every exam in sight except the finals once a year, like her brother. She did none of those things. She was still pleasant to live with and smiled easily. So it came as a shock when from one minute to the next, she began saying no. "No, thank you," to be exact; she always remained polite.

The best way to turn your parents upside down in France is to fail the baccalauréat exam. The French Bac is the indispensable key to the rest of your life. It is worse than the class barrier left over from besieging the Bastille. Of course there are alternatives to the Bac, but they are expensive and usually second-best.

Even Christy passed the Bac. He passed it brilliantly, in fact. But Suzy did not. She told us that she had come back after the lunch break a few minutes late and the doors to the examining halls were closed. The afternoon subjects were Spanish, English, German and Geography. The morning had been Maths and other hurdles. Suzy is a born linguist; she would have passed brilliantly, had she taken them. Now, something like thirty years later, she tells us that she went swimming that afternoon with a boy from the Rugby team.

Even now I am dumbfounded. Adolescence is clearly a form of insanity. Swimming?

We lived through it, she lived through it and everyone has survived. It gives me no end of pleasure to add, as a post scriptum, that Suzy went back to college at forty, did the Baccalauréat exam, passed it with honors and then did a BA as well as a Masters in English at the Sorbonne. After that she took up a teaching career.

Finding that a new kind of life really does begin at forty appears to be a family study in genetics.

But I jumped around a bit there. While Suzy was finishing her growing up, Juan was getting a little restless. The rue de l'Aude was all house and very little studio, he pointed out. That was true, of course, but there were other ways of dealing with studio space than leaving my beloved little house in the 14th, I would protest.

He said, "Name one." Of course he was right.

The house had been the nucleus of the way we lived, the friends who came on Sunday afternoons or for dinner, or for parties at the slightest occasion. The privacy the little house afforded was enviable. We had a big sunny bedroom at the top with a glassed-in solarium bedecked with plants which caught whatever sunshine Paris was giving and poured it through the house. The kids had their own rooms and I squatted Christy's when he left for college in Geneva. It was my pad. The living room was a floor through with two fireplaces, and double exposure.

There was a little patio, grandly called The Garden, where we ate out in good weather. True, the studio was small but perhaps he could find a second studio nearby that would augment…? He had tried that, but he had worked at home all his life and found it disruptive to adapt to a different way of life now. That was clear. It would not work. It was getting late, he pointed out; he was in his late fifties. There was not all that much time left to do the kind of work he hoped to do. Sculpture is arduous, particularly in his case where the metal he used was filed and joined by hand. His work is polished, the edges are perfectly shaped. Flawless. The light on the surface of the piece is as important as its size, in his work. He needs room, space to find the forms and dimensions he aims at. His studio at the back of the patio was no longer viable. We would have to move on from my beloved rue de l'Aude.

In those years I had been doing translations of film scripts and enjoying it. I also translated a novel about Alain Delon, which was easy to do and paid well. The two novels I had written were doing reasonably well financially and even better than that for my sense of self. I had thought we were sailing along pleasantly at the time. Christy was working for UPI in Puerto Rico by then and enjoying himself. Suzy had found her way without benefit of higher education with a good job and a jaunty social life. She had not spoken of getting a flat on her own yet and I was enchanted with her adult presence at home. On slow evenings we would play Scrabble in four languages. I thought we were living charmed lives.

Looking back, we were.

The situation was clear, then. My lovely little house on the rue de l'Aude was going to have to be sacrificed. But, no I would not live in the 19th arrondissement, a run-down area that I find charmless but which was just becoming "in," along with the 20th, which I actively disliked. Everyone was telling us that that was where we would find great space. I glared. When pushed too far I would say through my teeth that there was always New York if the Left Bank failed. I was firm. I was not going to leave the rue de l'Aude for just anywhere. I had a cabal of friends who had been staying overnight on the living room couch for decades who backed me up.

The rue de l'Aude was a small street with small buildings that ran for just one block and ended in a staircase lit by an iconic lamppost which brought you down to the Avenue du Parc Montsouris, crossing the rue des Artistes in the process. You turned to your right and you walked half a block and entered the Parc Montsouris, which happens to be one of those secret treasures Paris is so foxily graced with. When you come upon it unexpectedly you think it is a Garden of Eden no one else has ever shared. Henri Rousseau, the amazing painter of exotica among the Impressionists, lived next door and painted his wild jungles right there in the Parc Montsouris, not Africa. Braque lived off the Park and used to sit on a bench for a bit every sunny afternoon after lunch. Paul Eluard's widow lived two blocks up the avenue.

There were more artists' studios per square meter here than anywhere else in the city, including Montmartre. I knew the streets by heart. I wanted to keep my boundaries, my shopkeepers, my much loved markets. I needed to be within a reasonable distance of Montparnasse to be able to walk home from the Select of a late afternoon. I wanted to be able to walk to the

Luxembourg Gardens or the Place de la Contrescarpe in the heart of the Latin Quarter. This was my patch of Paris and I was not going to emigrate twice.

Moreover, it had to be a house. We had lived on our own since 1959. I would not take on neighbors over my head or under my feet at this late date. It was too late for me to take on French concierges.

So, with that cheerful mindset we began looking. I don't remember how long it was, but I saw very few ateliers and even fewer apartments. Early on, one of the agents, used to artists, said to Juan: "How would you like to build your own house? I have a vacant lot on rue de la Butte-aux-Cailles, just up a bit from the Parc Montsouris?"

Chapter 26

If my memory seems amazing at times, it is flagrantly fragmentary concerning the eighteen-month period between the end of the rue de l'Aude and our entrance into the Butte-aux-Cailles. There was, of course, a lot that that was eminently forgettable.

Moving house is a terrible disruption under most circumstances. Moving from a house you have restored yourself, added a floor to, brought up your children in, wrote two books in, and which you loved deeply, was a horror. I understood the reason for leaving, I acknowledged that it made sense and I was the first to agree that Juan needed more space as well as the fact that we, as a couple, could make do with less.

But it was a horror. To compound the horror, building a house proved from the outset to be more of a nightmare than anything I had ever imagined.

To take things in sequence, we sold the house after several months of negotiating. We sold it to a charming French university professor with a wide variety of American cousins and a brother who collected art. It was being passed to friendly hands. That was the easy part.

Juan bought the vacant lot, a small one, at the foot of a picturesque hill on the other side of the Parc Montsouris. It was in the 13th arrondissement, as opposed to our 14th but, roughly speaking, it was similar in feeling to the corner of Paris we had come to call home.

The choice of architects to build the house was the beginning of the many mistakes we made. Juan had been working with architects for the past sixteen years and could trust them. I forget why but he chose someone he did not know.

I had little to do with the entire project. That probably has more importance than it might seem. For one thing, Juan has never worked on a team. He has worked alone all his life. He is the most generous of men in all domains except that which have to do with his work. You do not touch unless invited to do so. His studio is his domain. Even I am a guest. It took me some time to realize that the building of the new house was going to be like the building of a sculpture. It was his project, not mine.

He did not think this was an unusual point of view, either. After all, he was the one who designed things; I only described them.

So, we began by finding someplace to live while the building took place. We put our furniture in storage, packed a mess of clothes and went off to Normandy. Rather than rent an apartment in Paris, we decided to rent someplace in the country where we could have Paris at easy access but be far enough away to not be pressed.

It was the only good idea that had come out of the whole show. I love Normandy, I love the coast and the inland roads, the houses, the food, the castles, the sea gulls. In the years that we had our thatched cottage not far from Pont-Audemer and Honfleur, I dreamed of coming back. I felt good in the quiet and the presence of the sea. We rented a cottage for the winter in a town close to where our old one had been. We were fully convinced that the Butte-aux-Cailles would be finished according to schedule and that we would move in by summer. It was to be a three-story building with big bay windows and a roof garden. If I ever saw the plans at that stage, I don't recall it. What I do recall was worrying about finding a suitable apartment for Suzy. I am not absolutely convinced that she ever found one but there was a series of small abodes which, I suppose, is part of growing up. She was quite happy on her own, of course.

I wasn't. Without her I felt as though I was missing an arm. This whole house adventure was a lot to get my head around, cutting myself off from every shred of my life as I knew it... beginning with my daughter.

The Honfleur area is a joy to explore, of course. We wandered around to our heart's content, coming back after long rides to the very pretty cottage with its huge fireplace and cozy open beams we had rented. We were on an extended little honeymoon. I had several film scripts to translate, which was welcome, and our city-bred little Scottie required walks into the town because he liked peeing against car tires, not trees. All I needed was a wardrobe of tweeds, I thought, to be the prey in an English thriller, just waiting for the body to drop.

Those first months of autumn and winter were charmed.

But by February there could be no turning a blind eye, the work on the house was way behind, the architect's promises were hollow, the bills were outrageous and no one was respecting deadlines. Juan had been told a hundred times not to sign any architect's contracts without a clause covering penalties for lateness. Everyone reminded him.

He neglected to do so. No one can figure out why.

The rest is predictable. And my memory flags. In any case, the details were too appalling to remember now. It was simply a long, nerve-wracking tight rope. Juan was in Paris most of the week, on the site or doing something related to the construction. He was, of course, tense and on edge. I tried to make his time in the country pleasant and relaxed. It was not difficult to do. The most arduous decisions facing us up there was which fish to buy on the quayside when the boats came in.

We made new friends in Honfleur, by magic, who were good company for me. There came a juncture in our exile when their support would become vital.

At one point we had to move from the first cottage because it was rented annually to the same people and our time was up. We found another one easily enough just as pretty, but with fewer amenities, unless one counted the neighboring cows who liked to poke around our backyard that they clearly thought was pasture. The cottage was at a crossroads just at the cusp of a hill that led down to Honfleur on a woodsy back path. There was no phone, unfortunately. It was on the damp side, too, so I had a fire going all day long, which I quite liked. The green of the Norman grass, greener than anywhere else outside of Ireland, came up freshly minted after massive snowfalls. Spring had arrived with a mini heatwave and we were enjoying a long weekend on our own.

I had been getting nervous because Juan was clearly showing the strains of this adventure. Though our half-built new house was already beautiful, the delays in finishing it were monstrous.

That beautiful Sunday, then, we were taking sunbaths as though Mallorca had travelled north. He was in the front patch of garden and I was watching him fiddle with the rose bushes when he swerved around and called, "Dolores, I think I'm sick," and collapsed on the grass.

We were alone, and we had no phone. There were neighbors down the road and I screamed. I did not know what else to do. Holding his head and shoulders in my arms, stroking his forehead I was there in my bathing suit, my mind racing confusingly, thinking of the comfort of one's own language in times of danger. Half-naked on the grass I felt no confidence calling out "A moi" or "A l'aide." I was not sure anyone would come.

Bending over him on the ground cursing semantics and yelling ineffectually until finally a young woman and a couple of children ran up the road and through the gate to my side, calming me, putting something soft under Juan's head. He was now smiling awkwardly, saying something about putting them to such trouble.

A man appeared and told us he had called for an ambulance. "I suppose you have no phone here?" he asked gruffly. It then occurred to me that the local farmers probably thought we were very strange, living in a small cottage in the middle of a patch of farmland, on our own. At least very strange.

The ambulance people were amazingly thorough and kind. One lovely man assured me that it was not a heart attack. He said he knew what heart attacks looked like and they did not look like this.

And it wasn't.

According to the Honfleur Hospital doctors, it was the sun. Despite the fact that Juan was Spanish and was used to the Mallorca sun in August? I asked, incredulous.

The cardiologist smiled indulgently. "Un concours de circonstances," he added, to convince me. The sun is a fickle friend, I knew. Juan had been running on ragged nerves for over a year.

His house on the Butte was nowhere near finished. None of the deadlines had been respected. The doctor told me to take him away for a week or so, somewhere different. A friend in Oxford urged us to take one of the cross-channel ferries and come to her. Lots of healthy food and late mornings, the doctor said. Late mornings but early nights, he meant. And fresh cream teas but no Scotch, he warned. Seriously, NO Scotch. And he gave me a long dark look.

Not a heart attack, no. But a warning. And Scotch was the operative word.

We had a lovely calm time in Oxford with dear Unity Evans who adored fussing over Juan. We saw Richard III at Stratford, we had teas at The Trout, we visited a couple of dons and Juan got better. We eventually went back to the cottage in Normandy and even down to a by-now summery Paris and the house on the Butte grew by inches, or so it seemed to me.

We finally moved in in November 1982. It was extremely beautiful, light poured in through the two story bay windows, the space was graceful, the staircases going up to the two loggias was of African wood and were made by a carpenter just down the road from one of our rented cottages in Normandy. There was light and grace and charm. The ground floor was officially the garage but it was his studio and it was about twice the size of the old one on the rue de l'Aude.

I looked at it all calmly and thought that it was the perfect house for a sculptor. He would work downstairs, with enough space to move around. Once finished creating, he would go up the stairs and come into a cathedral of his own: the living room and dining area and the super built-in kitchen with a rich wooden counter, then he would look up at the first loggia, fitted with book cases and a desk, then a few more steps and a bedroom, painted raspberry and white with a bath with a high window at your elbow to let the light pour in. Then up a few more steps and a third loggia, with a guest bed and second bath. And, finally, a few more steps upward and, wow... a glass door opening onto a roof garden. And what a view—all over Paris. It was heaven for the sculptor who loved open spaces, who had his privacy on the ground floor, who would come upstairs and survey his realm in deep satisfaction.

Writers are not sculptors. They need to be alone with their heads and their typewriters or quill pens. They do not welcome people coming up the stairs from the studio, putting on the TV news or a record or simply casting a shadow. However beloved he may be, it is not an all day long option. I had nowhere to hide in that house. Even the bedroom was shared.

But Juan thrived in the new house. All his ills subsided as the first months went by. Our doctor in Paris had him undergo a dozen exams, brain scans included. He came to believe that indeed, it was the sun that triggered off something passably ominous, but whatever it was it went away.

Our doctor, who loved him and who admired his work, warned that booze was not the best thing for him. Gently does it, doucement, he said. I was a little shaken. Juan was sixty. Was he going to start having an alcohol problem at sixty? Or was it there already and I did not know it?

The friends we made in Honfleur played what turned out to be a pivotal role in the rest of our lives. It is astonishing how the rest of your life can sometimes be traced back to, so to speak, the head of a pin.

We had just moved back to Paris and into the brand new Butte. Moving into it was something on the order of fitting into a sleek glove. The house was pristine, slim-lined, and uncluttered. It looked nothing like a house of mine, at all. The living room had a couch and our two Voltaire chairs. An eighteenth century chest we had bought for the rue de l'Aude stood in front of the stairwell looking handsome and preventing anyone from falling down the stairwell. There was a row of glass bricks in that wall allowing more light in, though the bow windows did that handsomely. The interior was never dark. When it rained it was magical.

Freddy and Connie Gore were the first to come and see it and Freddy stood in the center looking upward at the two loggias overhead and he said, congratulating the sculptor, "At last, a Palà house! A single sculpture was not enough."

It was just that. It had the sobriety of his work, the sharp lines and use of light. The simplicity that was never simple. Freddy was his most astute critic.

Shortly after moving in, then, we went to dinner at the home of friends, an American sculptor and his Australian wife. They had an unexpected visitor, a youngish French art critic who was on the board of the purchasing committee of a government agency that bought art for Regional museums.

Briefly, France has several such organisms on national or regional levels that supply museums and keep the national art collections up to date. They also give artists in France the notion that someone out there is interested in what they are doing. Juan had pieces in the national collection and in the Ville de Paris collection, as well, but not in the regional one.

I am not at all sure he realized that evening what the young man, Patrick-Gilles Persin, actually did for a living. He does not always listen to the small print in conversations and I was doing most of the talking to the young man, anyway. It was not about art, however, it was about Protestants. Patrick-Gilles turned out to be Protestant and from the southwest, still a Reformation stronghold in France despite the Saint Barthélémy. I mentioned that we had been saved from boredom in rural Normandy thanks to Calvin's brood, and he opened his eyes wide and said, "No, you don't mean the Ullerns?"

Helene and Sylvain Ullern were the friends we made totally by chance when one day, early in our exile near Honfleur, we were out for a drive and passed a field where I noticed a cow doing a strange dance and emitting bleats of sheer agony. The cow must be calving, I thought, alarmed. The New York girl who thought cows needed obstetricians, instantly assumed we should inform the farmer. The nearest house was just down the road and quite grand, but that did not stop me because Normandy farmers can live in chateaux, after all. We drove into the driveway and I saw a slender gentleman of a certain age with a bunch of garden tools in his hand, wearing an apron. The house, a manor, had a handsome staircase on either side of the front door, a fact which warned me that perhaps we were in the wrong courtyard…? I stuck my head out the window and apologized for the intrusion but I thought he might like to know that there was a cow over there in great difficulty. The gentleman gardener's very blue eyes were by then extremely amused but he smiled politely and told us that he was not the cow's owner, the farm was down the road, but would I by any chance be American? I felt myself coloring and, feeling like a total fool, I admitted I was.

"Because," he went on, "my wife went to Mount Holyoke and we have American family connections. Won't you please come in, I am sure my wife would love to meet you."

I looked toward the house and there she was, small, electric and commanding, Helene Ullern. They were in their seventies but still active and alive and interested in everything around them.

They helped make our residence in the neighborhood an adventure. Within a few minutes Helene had told us that her sister was married to Jacques Davidson… did I know him? Jo Davidson's son? She peered at me as though I was passing an entrance exam.

I said, "No, not Jacques. But I have known Jean Davidson for years because I was a copy girl at AFP when he was bureau chief in Washington and we met and became friends again in the anti-war movement in Paris and, and, and…"

Jean Davidson was married to Alexander Calder's daughter, Sandra. We had gone down to Saché with Suzy in tow and spent a weekend with them not long ago.

We were in gales of laughter standing in the middle of a country lawn with the Seine flowing toward the Channel just yards away from us, knitting a precious friendship thanks to a cow calving noisily in the distance.

Helene and her sister Elizabeth had both gone to Mount Holyoke. Their mother, a young widow, had been something of a Paris hostess during the pre-war years. They were part of that interesting minority, Protestants in France who maintained a prominence and a difference that

I found intriguing. They made me think of Catholics in Nova Scotia and my aunt's prickly snobbishness. Helene's younger brother along with her mother, had been part of the Varian Fry Resistance network that got so many foreign artists and writers out of France via Marseilles during the war. And all this little world was Protestant, like Patrick-Gilles Persin, the young art dealer in Paris.

So, when we met, so freshly associated with the Ullern crew, it was like a school reunion.

Shortly after, he came to see Juan's work. He was visibly astonished that he had not seen anything of Juan's work before but, he said, in a way he was glad because now he could claim that he was the critic who discovered Juan Palà.

And he was.

The rest of our lives began there. In the beautiful house on the Butte-aux-Cailles, at the age of sixty. Suzy and I had taken him to the Ritz bar to celebrate that one. Good luck had done the rest. With the help of a Normandy cow.

Chapter 27

If the seventies were mine, the eighties were Juan's, but in spades. La Butte was easy to entertain in and was an oddity at the same time. We didn't know anyone else who had actually built a house in Paris, so curiosity was a strong attraction. It was sometimes fun to notice which ones… the old buddies from Barcelona were particularly curious. Others, too, whom we hadn't seen in years suddenly replied to change of address cards and dropped in.

As though in perfect timing, Juan had pieces in several interesting salons which always caused a ripple. But it was Patrick-Gilles, who came over with Edda Maillet, the curator of the Fonds Régional d'Art Contemporain de l'Ile de France, who instantly struck a change. She loved his work at first sight. Down in the studio she went through every piece of sculpture, all his collages and pastels on paper, a stack of the most recent paintings. She looked at each of them quietly but with care. He had her full attention. He looked pleased.

Edda Maillet, a slender woman somewhere in middle age, had an elegant face and a quick smile used sparingly but which lit flares in her brown eyes. On that first visit there was something of the gold miner who had found a new vein about her.

When she finally left the studio we went upstairs to have a well-merited cup of tea. She looked around at the open space, the sense of captured light and she gazed at me with admiration. I made a gesture disclaiming any responsibility. This was Juan's house, not mine. All his. She raised an eyebrow at that. A bit later she went upstairs to the bathroom. She looked around at the first loggia, book-lined and with my long cluttered desk, then gazed down at the light and grace of the living room below and said over the railing, "I like what you do, I like how you live."

Which, I gathered, was French for "I am now your sponsor." And she was. Edda Maillet was also the curator of the Musée Tavet in Pontoise. Pontoise is a small town on the Seine about ten miles upriver from Paris. It had been a summer retreat for the kings of France and was next door to

Van Gogh's village. The Impressionists all painted there, and there is also a museum of Impressionist art with a major collection of Pissarro. Pontoise is the heart of nineteenth century French art country. Her museum is a jewel. She had built up over a couple of decades a superb collection of abstract artists, but particularly constructivists.

It was as if she had been waiting for Juan.

Chapter 28

I recall that it was Pierrette Gargallo, daughter of the great Picasso contemporary Spanish sculptor in Paris, and his longtime friend, who came to see our house and, in passing, his recent work, who said something about Juan's trying for the Prix Bourdelle, the biannual French sculpture award. Juan looked blank and said, "What's the Prix Bourdelle?"

So there we were… off on another sprint. I wonder from time to time if other people's lives are flipped like a coin as much as ours, arbitrarily, casually and frequently, miraculously.

Our life in Mallorca hung on the thread of a garrulous bore on an ocean-crossing bragging about his clever purchase, or better still, our own meeting because I went along reluctantly to a dance with a boy who wanted to dance with another girl. These haphazard brushes with luck seemed particularly relevant to us and the unlikeliness of our lives.

That day I had a tingling feeling that, though he might not know what the Prix Bourdelle was, others did. I remember gazing up quietly at the three open levels of his house and forgave it its lack of privacy. He had endowed it with grace, which, in his eyes, was far more worthy.

I suppose he must have made up a dossier of sorts, a C.V. and photos, and he might even have brought it over to the Musée Bourdelle in Montparnasse. I asked him if he had ever visited the museum. "I must have, when I first came to Paris," he answered, which meant he hadn't. I had the feeling he knew as little about Antoine Bourdelle as I did but was slightly embarrassed by his oversight. Well he might be.

Bourdelle was, of course, a noteworthy French sculptor of the earlier part of the century, who had not quite broken new ground but who brought imposing public statuary into the twentieth century, much as Gargallo had. He was another facet of the star-studded cast in Montparnasse before the First World War. After his death his studio was turned into a museum.

The Prix Bourdelle was awarded biannually to a sculptor whose work merited more attention than it had been getting. There was a purse of 2,000 francs, which inflation had made into a joke, but also a retrospective exhibition in the museum of the winning artist's work. That was the real prize. The jury was entirely made up of other sculptors which was, I believe, unique and meaningful. No considerations touching upon money or other interests were involved; it was a case of peers: sculptors judging other sculptors. The Prix Bourdelle was unique in its category. And it carried clout.

I went with Juan when he brought over his dossier and a couple of small sculptures as entries. I was left to chat with a pair of delightful elderly ladies, one of whom was Bourdelle's daughter and the other his niece. Both caught my accent and instantly switched to fluent English. Their mothers were Greek, they told me, as though that was a logical explanation. "We had an English nanny." Of course.

We were sitting in a cluttered office overlooking the garden. Her cousin, now an aged lady bent over with osteoporosis, was still beautiful. They had been Antoine Bourdelle's models. The cousin pointed out the window to a set of stone figures against the wall. Surprisingly, I recognized them in the stone carved likenesses, which pleased them and somewhat startled me.

When we drove home Juan said, "Forget it." And, I think, he promptly did. He had been instructed to wait at the corner café with the other postulants on the day of the vote. He did no such thing.

On the day of the vote I was in the bedroom getting ready for a lunch with Mary Kling, my dear chum and agent, when the phone rang. It was the museum and the voice was frantic.

"But where is M. Palà? He is the Winner. He should be here." Le lauréat, she said. I managed to ring off and rush downstairs to the studio to tell him. But he was at the kitchen counter, having a coffee.

And he was smiling like a boy.

Chapter 29

Here the moments rolled into each other and our lives rolled with them. The award-giving was a forgettable affair at the museum where several dignitaries made blessedly short speeches praising Juan's work. A few convinced me that they had actually seen it. Dignitaries from any Ministry are expert at passing for knowledgeable about work they had only met firsthand an hour before. There was no reason to believe the Ministry of Culture would be an exception. However, courtesy is a balm and they were all past masters at that.

The presentation was followed by a late lunch at the Coupole. We were ushered down the restaurant's main aisle by one of the waiters whom I had known forever and who now looked surprised. "I did not know you were a sculptor," he whispered.

And there we have the problem of Juan's name. It is Joan, as in Joan Miró, and a million other Catalans; not Juan. The waiter was reading Joan as in Crawford. I quickly explained. He raised his eyebrows and suppressed a giggle. He then led us down through the restaurant toward the rear where a large round table was set for ten. We passed Sartre and Simone de Beauvoir's table on our way, the one they lunched at for so many years. I glanced at it with a terrible desire to nod at their ghosts. I am sure they would have been pleased at the occasion.

But there was nothing to fault in the Prix Bourdelle. It opened doors, we might say, both here and abroad. The abroad bit was interesting. Barcelona suddenly cocked an ear.

I mentioned before that I sensed a certain reticence toward Juan's work in Barcelona, if not toward him personally. Perhaps reticence is too strong a word, but it serves my purpose. Nothing was ever said, of course, but there was a sense of exclusion which could not be ignored though that was principally what he did, ignore it. Eventually we spent less time in Barcelona going to and from Mallorca but we were there nonetheless twice a year for at least a week. We were available if anyone was interested. The only fellow artist who ever was, was Joan Josep Tharrats. A painter of renown, a man of influence, and an old friend, Tharrats was the only one in Barcelona's tight little art world who was interested.

At the time of the Prix Bourdelle, another boyhood friend, Josep Estanis Boldu, said to him, "Why don't you have a show at the Institut Français of Barcelona, which gave you the chance to go to Paris in the first place? They would like to do it. What do you say?"

Of course he said yes. But a little hesitantly. I could see that he could sense a touch of double or nothing about the venture.

But that would be next year. First there would the big exhibition in Paris at the Musée Bourdelle in Montparnasse. As would be expected, the museum's space is perfect for showing sculpture, big pieces and small pieces alike. High ceilings and tall windows. There was one room at the end of the main hall which would have been fine for the crown jewels. It prompted him to do a sculpture consisting of several separate elements which one can walk through. He called it "Ariane's Wall," "le Mur d'Ariane." He was able to make that in the studio at the Butte-aux-Cailles with the help of a young Japanese sculptor, recommended by Sugai. It stood on its own, made of wood and painted off-white. It was overwhelming at the back of the main exhibition hall, like an emblem of victory. It was acquired by the Musée de Dunkerque, which sent a truck to collect it on the last day of the exhibition. The truck proved to be too small and they had to hire a second on the spot. I loved that.

The Bourdelle Museum made a catalogue for the exhibition which remains one of the best he has ever had. Freddy Gore wrote a remarkable introduction which has often been reprinted through the years. He ends his analysis of Juan's work with two words: "It is." And it is.

Chapter 30

The Prix Bourdelle, we soon learned, wielded a certain clout in official French circles: among museums both national and provincial, and in the sphere of new purchases. He had several pieces in national, provincial and Paris museums already but there was definitely room for more. That was pleasant, for starters.

All sculptors are keen to have state commissions, Juan was no exception. He had done seven or eight by then but a few more would have been welcome. And so it went. This was the predictable fall-out of a national prize.

But the big retrospective at the museum itself was the essence of it. Paris streets were dotted with giant posters announcing his exhibition, featuring a picture of a rectangular sculpture called "Beckett's Wall," in a photograph taken by Robert Doisneau, the great French photographer who was always very kind to us. Doisneau was the jewel in the crown of the Rapho photo agency founded by Raymond Grosset who, with his American wife Barbara, was our close friend.

The sculpture is called "Beckett's Wall."

Samuel Beckett came to the house one day with a mutual friend, Gloria McGowran. Gloria was the widow of Jack McGowran, the wonderful Irish actor who had been the first to play *Waiting for Godot* and who went on to play the rest of the Beckett repertoire before his untimely death. Beckett was extremely generous to Gloria, who had a young daughter to bring up. He was generous with a whole brood of Irish poet friends who, like Jack, had made up his odd family.

I forget why, but Gloria stayed at our house when she was in Paris which happened to be a few blocks away from where Beckett lived on the Blvd St. Jacques. When he walked her home one evening not long before we moved from the rue de l'Aude she convinced him to come in and meet us, assuring him he would at least like the sculptures. Beckett's reputation as a curmudgeon was not unearned. As it turned out, he did like the sculptures as well as the sculptor and he asked if he could come back one day and look at the work quietly. He did come back, shortly afterward. Alone.

I left them in the studio but could hear their conversation, what there was of it, in the kitchen with the window wide open. Their voices and their silences. Halfway through Juan's presenting the works, Beckett stopped him at the sight of a long rectangular brass piece and, after a bit, he asked in his distinctive and intimidating Irish voice, "When did you start reducing?"

I froze. This, from the man who reduced theater to one long "ooooh" from a spotlighted mouth on a darkened stage… this was daunting. After a moment and very calmly Juan answered, "Probably from the very beginning… though I did not know it at the time."

I think I stopped breathing.

So, the photograph was reproduced on the poster and printed against a red background and for several months it stood at busy corners throughout the city and, if the Prix Bourdelle had done nothing else, that made me seriously proud. There was a poster right in front of Le Café Flore.

That had to be just for me.

The opening of the exhibit was an event. We invited all the friends who had put up with us through the lean years and they turned out to be a record number. The usual Musée Bourdelle openings, we learned later, would involve perhaps thirty people. There were over 300 at Juan's. Friends brought friends who brought friends. Some came from far away to celebrate with us. Robert and Elizabeth Gabor changed travel plans so they could come. The Gores came and camped out on the living room couch despite the fishbowl feel of the living room. We had names to drop, like Mary McCarthy whom we had met not long before and who, with her husband Jim West, was open and friendly. Christy had married a charming American violinist, Leslie, and had just returned to Paris, which was an added pleasure.

I remember being moved watching Juan's face as he looked around the very crowded museum hall. He is capable of an immense calm when something essential happens to him, which comes as a surprise to most people to whom he appears excitable, volatile. When the chips are down, however, he is absolutely still. On that particular occasion, he was calm, confident and quiet. He has always found a way of astonishing me; he did then.

The museum opening spilled over to a party at our house on la Butte-aux-Cailles. Several people wanted to see the studio, which was locked. For good reason. The studio was empty. There were fifty sculptures at the Musée Bourdelle.

It was his whole life that was on show.

Chapter 31

There were repercussions from the exhibit, direct and ongoing. All sorts of people took notice of it in the art world and beyond it. Edda Maillet and her crew at the Musée de Pontoise was untiring in her effort to promote him. She included him in a series of prestigious group shows in France and abroad. I was particularly impressed with her.

Then someone new came into our lives and has remained a key figure ever since: Eva Maria Fruhtrunk. An imposing figure on the Paris art scene, with a network of galleries and museum throughout Europe, she was and still is totally committed to constructivist art and to the artists she sponsors in an international group that she has created, based in Paris, called Repères. It was then located on the Place des Vosges, which did nothing to detract from its promise. Eva Maria, its creator, is a German-born art historian, divorced from the late painter Günter Fruhtrunk. She has devoted most of her adult life to the furtherance of constructivist art. Not just any constructivism, either. She has strict, sometimes even rigid, norms and she is amazingly eloquent in explaining her choices which are not always that evident to a less practiced eye. I have fallen short of accurate judgment of other artists' work from time to time and have felt the sting of her wit. She takes teasing nicely, however, and just puts up with what she must see as my failings without taking offense. She loves Juan, she loves his work and the way he lives his work, and she has devoted long years and enormous single-minded effort on his behalf from the first time she came to the studio.

She was sent by an unlikely mutual friend, Edie Ardagh, with whom she did ceramics somewhere in Paris. Edie had just retired from a demanding job with UNESCO and was free to do the things she had had no time for during the previous thirty years, such as Japanese-inspired ceramics, to the delight of her friends. To delight them even further, she bought a roomy sprawling house outside Vaison-la-Romaine and invited us down frequently. Her old friend and close neighbor a village or two away was an extraordinary woman called Dijour, a former journalist, a Russian Parisian, who had been everywhere and knew everyone and whom I instantly took to.

It is wonderful for me now, so many years later, to look back on that spiral in time which we just sort of fell into lightly, enjoying the company, the drives around the villages of Provence, drinking the wine, eating the food, talking endlessly as though in a time sphere of our own. While in Paris on la Butte-aux-Cailles, Juan produced a series of strong new works. The '80s were a productive span for him. They were a talkative time, too. I was out a lot, oddly at loose ends. Free.

Eva Maria gently advised Juan on directions to take, very gently. Not in terms of his work but rather of what to do with it. She has been doing that for some thirty years with other artists and much of what has happened to him and his work since then is thanks to her. From the time she met him she has been of extremely wise counsel. That was true of Edda Maillet, as well, and, after her retirement, of the young Christophe Duvivier, her successor at the Musée Tavel in Pontoise.

It was then in the 1980s that Juan began to see the first shadings of recognition. And what a sight that was.

After the exhibition at the Musée Bourdelle closed, he began working on the next which was to be at the Institut Français in Barcelona. It was this noble institution that allowed him to leave Spain and go to Paris in 1948.

It is hard to picture it now but in Franco's Spain, a Spaniard could not leave the country without an exit visa and exit visas were not easily given. It was much like the Communist countries of Central Europe, though no one took much notice of the dereliction of civil rights in Spain as long as Franco remained a bastion against encroaching Communism. Entrenched fascism was not a worry to the West during the immediate post-war. Be that said in passing.

In the mid-1980s, however, with a handsome young king and a freely elected parliament, Spain was another country. Barcelona, ever an art capital, was bright and light, high-heeled and well-heeled, back in the circuit of arts, letters and haute cuisine.

For the first time, Juan ignored the summer heat and actually worked during that summer of 1985. He set up a studio in Suzy's room at the top of the house in Fornalutx and produced a wonderful series of gouaches and pastels and even a few collages for the Barcelona show. The sculptures were a selection of those shown in the Musée Bourdelle but the graphics were new.

In Fornalutx, Bob Ochs, a history professor at the Univeristy of South Carolina and an art collector of the post-war American school—he was a friend of most of the stellar painters but particularly of Jasper Johns whom, I think, he taught—began buying a couple of pastels.

So did Elena Davis, a New Yorker settled in the Sóller valley since the 1950s and everyone's favorite person because she ran an English language lending library niched in a café in Sóller where everyone literate in English gathered before lunch, coming from up and down the coast to borrow or return the week's reading matter. Elena is remarkable for her astuteness, her taste in books, her love for Spain and things Spanish, her courtesy in learning Mallorcan and fluent Castilian with a New York tinge, and for providing a hearth as well as a heart for what became a community. She is still with us at the age of 99 and we are all making reservations for her hundredth because the hotels are bound to be overbooked if we wait.

Elena said she would come to Barcelona for his opening. And so did Elna Ernest, a stunningly beautiful Swedish painter-cum-hospital psychiatrist in London with a house in Sóller. Splendid. Then came Jenny and Chris Strickland, who lived in a big house with a pool midway down to the coast which they had bought from Tony Johnson—they came, too. And Mary d'Espinay, who also had a pool on the Sóller side of the Palma road, one of the few French denizens of our very Anglophone valley. Mary said she would not miss it. Edie Ardagh said she would join us in Barcelona, driving down from Vaison-la-Romaine.

And this contingent of beautiful great ladies became known as Juan's "Les Girls." It set a tone for the whole adventure.

Jenny Strickland instantly bought a sculpture for 800,000 pesetas. All the others bought gouaches. Before the show had even opened, Juan had made a million and a half pesetas.

I took a certain pleasure in hearing out a few leftovers of Juan's apparently distant past who would come up to me and gently weave their way into why they could not buy anything in these troubled times. Whatever.

The little red dots that were stuck by each painting sold, or by the brass sculpture in its glassed-in stand, spoke volumes.

After the exuberant Musée Bourdelle opening, the Institut Français's handsome exhibition space looked empty to Juan. It was by no means empty, but it was not crowded either. There were notable absences.

He saw it that way and was hurt, even though he would not admit it. I could measure the hurt. He is a man without guile and finds it difficult to deal with guile in others. Nor is he jealous. The absence of a handful of old friends who should have been there hurt him. He did not need them to buy his work, Les Girls had done that, without prompting. He did not need their recognition, he had had that from Paris where it counted.

He sought their presence, their interest, a gesture to their shared past. Except for a few like Bulou and Joan Josep Tharrats who wrote a delightful text for the catalogue, it was not forthcoming.

Some dribbled by the exhibition during the time we were in Barcelona. Here and there one would drop in and sign the attendance book, chat a bit and nod at the work in approbation. But it was in driblets and, actually, it no longer mattered. He had made a brilliant show and got a few good reviews in the press, but it had not mattered. It simply no longer mattered.

Chapter 32

Aside from preparing exhibitions and living through their opening nights, the 1980s were vividly distinct from the '70s as I recall them. Living at the Butte-aux-Cailles was different in itself. I had fumbled through a novel set in Vienna which I was not sure about. It had a mixed reception from my various agents and the euphoria one feels when one thinks a book is finished soon evaporated.

My agent in Paris, Mary King, who had been a friend since the early '60s, long before she was an agent and I a writer of novels, was always frank about my work, so I listened carefully to what she said. She urged me to rework it a little but not to give it up. There were one or two characters whom she found vivid and endearing and she claimed that I had caught a whiff of Cold War Vienna that I should not let go. Work on it, she said. I did not. Not then, at least. I put it in a drawer where it stayed 'til 2003 when I reworked it for the last time and then published it in the new fashion, online.

It managed to get half a dozen reviews from a variety of readers who remembered the Cold War and the way it worked itself into some of our lives. But that was later. In the 1980s our particular lives were on quite different paths.

There was a less than happy trip to The States in 1982 when almost everything went wrong: my wallet was stolen when it was full and I was on my way to the bank the day after I arrived, for starters. Then, lugging a sculpture to Washington for friends gave me a case of sciatica that would take painful months to get over, and, to top it all, a damaging row with Christy in Puerto Rico almost as painful as the sciatica… everything that should not happen on a trip home seemed to happen in spades.

Except for the lost money everything else eventually worked itself out, but for the time being I lost the taste for "going home."

Fortunately there was a new buzz in Paris. The Mitterrand years were upon us. And they did bring in a new sense of… call it adventure. It was a kick to see the changes set in. Not that a pragmatic French Social

Democratic government was going to nationalize the air we breathed or do much else in terms of affecting everyday life but there was a buzz and it was exhilarating.

And on a personal level, Juan and I had a sort of new springboard in the glass house built for one. Suzy stayed with us whenever she was short of funds and saving on rent, which was blissfully frequent, but in theory the house was just ours.

The artist was in his element, at last, and much-concentrated on his work. The result was that he had a one-man show every year for five years running during the '80s or else took part in prestigious group shows in Paris and elsewhere for the other five. Eva Maria and her group kept him in shows and galleries not only in France but in Germany and Switzerland, as well. The galleries he showed with in Paris were dynamic and, though he did not sell as much as he would have liked, his work was noticed in the right circles. Painters have it easy compared to sculptors. Everyone has walls, not everyone has a place to show a sculpture. They are not household words.

Fortunately, I had a steady stream of film translations to do and I got a kick out of being on the fringes of the film world without taking it seriously. I did get to do a documentary on Angkor Wat, the great temples of Cambodia, and was invited to a showing at the Quai d'Orsay, by the Minister of Foreign Affairs, Claude Cheysson, which was something. And when Mikis Theodorakis, the brilliant Greek composer who just escaped from the wretched colonels' jails in Greece, arrived clandestinely and gave a sensational press conference, I was the interpreter sitting on the stage between him and Francois Mitterrand—not yet President, of course.

Without trying and mostly by chance I had made a bit of a name for myself that I was never quite sure what to do with. It did bring me one absolute delight, however. I was the interpreter for Tom O'Horgan, the Broadway musical director, who came to Paris to direct the musical comedy *Starmania*, written jointly by Luc Plamandon, a Canadian, and Michel Berger, a French songwriter. Musical comedies are American by nature, a few are English-born, perhaps, but the French, Canadian or otherwise, are not on the same wavelength by any means.

I love musicals. Cole Porter, Rogers and Hart, Hammerstein and all the others are on my list of who to look up in Heaven. To see a musical actually come to life was a marvelous, if exhausting, experience. It was a scenic railway ride that I relish in retrospect though it was nerve-wracking to live through.

Tom O'Horgan was one of the most endearing, the most generous and certainly the most patient man I have ever met.

The whole caper was worth it to have seen him bring something pleasurable and frothy out of the mediocre talent and questionable charm he had to work with. Over the years I have run into a host of very odd jobs, but *Starmania* had to have been the oddest.

During the '80s, I found it easy to hop on a train and run up to Amsterdam for a few days to visit with Ruth Froma, who had married a Dutch colleague of hers at Bonds for Israel, where she worked in the Paris office. She was a New Yorker, a little older than me, with a smile that I took to as soon as I met her. It seemed to come from a million miles inside her; it lit up her face and yours and everything around. She had been one of the victims of McCarthyism at UNESCO, forced to resign because she would not tell Cohn and Schine, the disgraceful tandem of truants McCarthy and the US Senate had sent to clean out Communists from UNESCO.

Ruth had been a Depression youngster. She got out of college in the late '30s and, as a science major, managed to find a miraculous job as a travelling saleslady for some cosmetic company. She couldn't drive and couldn't afford a car anyway so she did her traveling on Greyhound buses and local trains up and down the East Coast.

When I asked her if she had actually joined anything "subversive," she said with her eyes flashing, "I joined everything in sight in 1938… Only a fink wouldn't have!"

But the Cohn and Schine boys were not asking about her past, they wanted to know about her parents. What she was refusing to answer was that: ratting on her immigrant parents.

The ignominy of that makes me livid even now.

By then Ruth and Joel were retired in Amsterdam and enjoying the world as it was. In one of his mellow moments, Joel said, "You know what, Suzy should meet Pascal."

To which Ruth acclaimed, "Of course, of course! What a wonderful idea." Apparently it was. They have been married for more than 25 years since then.

Pascal Loir was the only son of their friend Nono Weitzman, a pretty blonde Parisienne. Her name was Fernande which she shortened to

Fern, because Fernande was on a par with Dolores for user-comfort. I sympathized. Her old friends called her Nono, however, and that is what we called her. She became a friend within minutes. As small as her son was big and husky, she was blonde and slim. She was also Jewish. Her parents had emigrated from Warsaw in the 1920s, settled in Paris, became French citizens, prospered in the leather business and lived in Belleville, then something of a French version of The Bronx. Her story is a prototype of what happened to Jews in Paris under the Nazi occupation but thanks to the Vichy French rulers, who tried to outdo their German bosses in terms of horrors.

One morning the police threw a dragnet across Paris and arrested all the Jews they could, children and the aged alike, and parked them in the Vel' d'Hiv, the Paris vélodrome. Nono, her mother, and her sister were miraculously saved by the waiter at the café next door who hid them in the cellar. The father, however, was caught. From the Vel' d'Hiv, he was sent to a detention camp near Paris, staunchly convinced that he would be released because he was a French citizen, not a stateless person or even a Pole. He was naturalized French! And he apparently believed almost to the end that they could not do this to him because he was a French citizen.

Nono, who was eight at the time, and her mother and sixteen-year-old sister were hidden in the café 'til alternative safe lodgings were found. Her sister, a Resistance heroine from that moment on, ended the war with enough medals to open a shop, yet she was modest and unassuming.

Nono grew up like most survivors, with a skeptical eye cast darkly on the world around her, along with a sense of humor to make up for it. I liked her especially because there was something familiar about her. She could have been someone I might have met in High School, had the world been different. She had a New Yorker's kind of humor, which says a lot about her, about me and about New York, as well as the times we lived in.

We all got on and Pascal and Nono slipped into our lives comfortably. Then one day Suzy came and told us that she and Pascal were pregnant and they hoped that we would be as happy about it as they were.

Well! Of course we were. We had everything else, didn't we? Galleries, museums, a house of glass with a roof garden where the forsythias bloomed?

We all cried with happiness and laughed with joy. I think that only a woman who has experienced it herself can understand the special happiness she feels when her daughter tells her she is going to have a baby. It is the most intimate of emotions, the most heartfelt of all.

I can look back at that moment now and only marvel at the intensity, the purity of the love involved. My baby, my babies.

But there was something else gnawing at us, though, not our progeny. It was the eternal double-edged problem of space and money. Once again, there was not enough of either.

Juan was selling, but not enough, and the state commissions had dwindled. More disturbing by far, though, was my newly discovered problem. The film script translations which I had thought of as a sinecure for life, were tapering off. Admittedly, I charged a little more than the crop of youngsters that had turned up since I began, but the directors knew my work, I had a bit of a reputation and was, after all, a published writer.

What I had not realized was that my English was as dated as it was erudite. Ronald Coleman was long dead and I had a hard time entering the new nasal world of Seinfeld. I did not even like it, if truth be told. I could not stand their diction, either, so I could hardly expect to emulate them. In dismay, I was forced to admit that my world had changed while I was not looking, or listening, more to the pint, and I was being swept away without a whimper.

No one talks like me anymore. Imagine not having noticed.

We would have to give up the beautiful glass house built for one, in splendid isolation, in a choice corner of swinging Paris. It would be more of a blow to Juan than to me, of course, because it was his creation.

There was no way out. My translation earnings were the bedrock of our ever-chancy exchequer. I was getting too old to run off to Geneva, or anywhere else, to plug the failing dykes again. That caper was almost twenty years ago. We had no alternative but to sell the house. But where would we go?

I rather liked the idea of a house in Normandy somewhere near Honfleur and a small flat in Paris as a pied-à-terre. I forget why we did not pursue that quite charming notion, but we did not. Instead I spent a lot of time sulkily looking in the very near suburbs of Paris or at outlandish places in the city which real estate agents insisted were perfect for sculptors who worked in metal… like third floor walk ups in derelict corners on railroad yards.

Robin Juan Bradley Loir was born in Paris on June 24th, 1987, la Saint Jean. St. Jean is the patron saint of Spain. It is Spain's national holiday, too, because the clever young King Juan Carlos made it so, thus dislodging the 18th of July, a day marking Franco's power, which divided poor Spain for some forty years. St. John's day, on the other hand, is celebrated with bonfires throughout the world, it is a day of light and happiness, of dancing in the streets and our most remote ancestors would have celebrated it first for being the summer solstice.

Our Robbie chose to make everyone in sight even happier by being born in time for a cup of tea. Just like his mother. Also like his mother, he was delivered by Dr. Etienne Oudiette, who, with his wife, was among our closest friends. It was uncommonly touching to have Etienne deliver the baby he had delivered himself some twenty seven years earlier.

That is surely what is meant by dynasty.

Finding a house at the end of the '80s proved more difficult than selling the Butte-aux-Cailles. We sold it to a young opera singer and his Colombian painter friend. They chose our house for its privacy, as much as for its charm. Practicing scales is not something that endears you to neighbors.

It was finding them that turned our luck. Juan came upon the miracle. The house on the edge of a forest where Sarah Bernhardt had lived, the hunting lodge set in a garden as though afloat in hydrangeas, the house with a terrace off the main bedroom, a staircase on either side, edged with the red and white brick much favored in this Forêt de Sénart where wild boar and foxes still scare drivers and strollers some 45 kilometers from Paris.

This house where the feisty George Sand visited is a few minutes down the road from where she met her husband, at the Mare au Diable, the Devil's Pond, an experience then but another one now. It is now a splendid restaurant in an enchanted garden, a treat.

Exactly thirty minutes by train from the Gare de Lyon, with a little railroad station just around the corner but with enough woods in between not to hear the rumble of trains in the house, Juan tumbled on The Miracle. No doubt in a state of grace.

But it was a touch of magic that made 24 Avenue de Quincy, Combs-la-Ville, turn out to be a fairy tale three-story, nine-room house with stables attached that would make the dream studio of the century, with all the storage room needed and then some. All this plus a rambling landscaped garden of 1500 sq. meters. The property was walled and dated from 1830 when it was a hunting lodge and the Sénart Forest was all around it, decades before the railroad was to cut through the woods and separate it from the delectable river Yerres.

Yerres is pronounced the same way as hier, or yesterday. Thus, a river called yesterday flowed just down the road from us, quickly becoming one of our favorite spots for a stroll. It was like walking through Alice's byways and I often looked out for glimpses of the White Queen, for instance, and never failed to catch a sniff of her perfume on the water's edge. It was only to have been expected in a river called yesterday.

Finding the house totally by chance and deciding to buy it almost immediately has been one of Juan's favorite stories. It was as random a choice as any other in our lives, so checkered with random choices. We have been lucky in many things from the first moment, but the star among them all must have been finding Combs because it has brought pleasure to just about everyone who has brushed through its many doors. We spent 25 years saying thanks. Not long enough, of course.

And the first festivity produced after moving in was to have a wedding. *The* wedding. Suzy and Pascal were married one sunny February day in Combs while we all danced to their happiness. Robbie danced most enthusiastically of all.

It was true, living on the Butte-aux-Cailles was different. Things happened. Not the least of them were the trips to medieval towns in Germany where the intrepid Eva Maria sponsored Juan's work and we went to openings in fairy tale galleries or museums where the starkness of his metal angles were set off splendidly by the aged open beams everywhere in view. I loved driving through the Black Forest. I all but told myself fairy tales about witches and pumpkins while gazing beyond the museums and galleries replete with constructivist art in all sizes and colors, half wondering whether a gnome or an imp would pop out of woodwork and laugh at us all.

It always has been difficult for me to understand Germany, much less to feel comfortable for any length of time there. Much as I enjoy its beauty, the reminiscence of fairy tales in its nooks and crannies, I remain a child of the Second World War and it looms, still an unresolved problem in my heart. The more attractive the town, it would appear, the more of a quandary I find myself in.

German critics liked Juan's work, and he was treated respectfully in galleries. Eva Maria worked hard for him and her efforts were fruitful.

I had learned a long time ago that prejudices of all kinds were booby traps. Generalizations are as mindless as they are interchangeable. Belgian jokes in France are the same as Newfie jokes in America.

Since my only Collins family in North America is in Newfoundland, I take instant umbrage at the dumb jokes and I grow very Irish indeed in London when arch British accents belittle the Irish. My scowls deflect the conversations within seconds. Spending my entire adult life as a foreigner, I have learned to sink into icy silences at ill-mannered anti-American quips in France so I am careful of what I say in Germany. I wish I had been able to come to terms with all this because I realize I am the loser, but there are problems that have no solutions and that is the way I must leave it.

But I heartily recommend driving through Germany and Berlin is one of the great cities for the imaginative, much like Prague or Dublin.

Things happened on the Butte-aux-Cailles, indeed. To get back to Pascal Loir and our Ruth's skills at match-making: Suzy, too, agreed he was a nice chap. Tall, heavyset, he was a sound engineer at RTL, France's biggest independent radio stations. He liked doing music mostly but he also covered the Elysée Palace, admired Mitterrand and voted Socialist.

I had fiddled with radio reporting when I was eighteen at the UN in Lake Success. The head of UN Radio was a friend, Cesar Ortiz, who remained in our lives 'til he died in London a few years ago. Cesar let me do a few interviews under his careful scrutiny. He thought I had a good voice and what little Spanish I spoke had a good accent so he fed me lines and questions I more or less parroted, but we got away with it. It did not hurt being the niece of the Ambassador of Colombia at the time, no matter how Yankee my Spanish was. I did a little more later on in Paris working with a tired Polish technician called M. Jelskski who followed me around with a heavy load of radio gear in tow. I would have loved to have had a career in radio and so was pleased to talk with Pascal about his work.

Chapter 33

There we were, then, living in the country. Of course, Combs-la-Ville is not really the country but to our very city-bred eyes, it might have been situated anywhere in rural France. Except that it is the only town we know that doesn't have a beautiful church in the middle of a graceful square with a café on one side and a patisserie on the other. All French towns are so constructed. Instead, the main road that runs in front of our house also runs in front of the church and there is no pretty square around it.

The church was begun in the twelfth century and the priest has a stone on his desk to prove it but it was finished the day before yesterday, as he put it. Even that was done on a budget, he added. He was a charming priest who welcomed us at a beautiful candlelit Easter Mass that first year when we were all present: Christy and Suzy, Robbie in arms, and Juan and me. Christy was back from two years as bureau chief of AFP in Nigeria and staying with us 'til he found himself a flat on the Ile St. Louis, which he did quickly, and, as usual, Pascal was working. Radio technicians, unfortunately, often work on holidays.

We rediscovered the pleasure of seasons in Combs. The life of the garden mesmerized me. The previous tenants had migrated from the fashionable western banks of the Seine, Montfort-l'Amaury, which resulted in exquisite floral touches like placing lilacs next to winter jasmine and something else with a bright white flower, thus bringing out the colors to advantage. The garden was petal perfect and we did our best not to wreck it.

Crokie and Frank Allen came over to see what we all assumed would be the Last Chapter of Palà Poverty Properties, this side of heaven. We had been close friends since 1956, well over thirty years. I can see us in my mind's eye, scampering along London streets in the early years to catch a tube for one last drink at one last memorable pub before the long trek back to Whipps Cross Road and their magical Georgian house. I remembered them in Mallorca climbing spiky mountain sides for a better view of the sea and, once there, having to make a disgruntled about-face and return to the house because what I had was galloping hepatitis and not just a case of Majorcan tummy, as they called it in their fruity English accents.

And I can see Frank on another occasion winning at the Trouville Casino and preening a little, not because he had won but because a local press photographer had snapped a picture of him. His great mop of wavy white hair and bushy eyebrows to match… Frank himself was the point, not his rather modest win. I don't think he actually realized how striking he was. Crokie did, though, but she just smiled.

They came to give their seal of approval on Combs. We saw them only once more in London. Frank died far too soon, and all of us felt shocked because he was that rare breed who are not supposed to die, they are the monuments of other people's lives.

So, we took up residence in what we called the country with good spirits. Juan's studio was huge compared to the others. He worked in what had been the manège part of the riding school the previous owners had run there for years.

Outside the studio itself, the rest of the area was storage space that, amazingly, managed to get filled within what seemed like days. There was room for the lawn mower and several large sculptures, piles of precious magazines, bags of earth, machine parts for which the whole was long forgotten, in addition to an office with a pretty desk I instantly decided to restore one day but never did. There was also a toilet and sink and still lots of room for much more. Paintings were safely stacked where grain bags had been and extra garden chairs were piled in mounds for different seasons of the year. A battery recharger was added for the parade of cars that we parked outside under the rain. That must say something about Juan as a driver but I am not quite sure what since I never learned to drive at all.

A huge double door protected this treasure island. I lost its huge iron key early on. No one knew it, but the studio remained unlocked for the next 25 years.

Chapter 34

There was a charming wine shop in Brie-Comte-Robert, our next door village which had the exquisite thirteenth century church we had hoped for in moving "to the country." Along with the wine shop there was a pastry shop to go with it, an antiquaire where we bought irresistible things like an eighteenth century whale oil lamp, and then there was the charcuterie with amazing smoked salmon and Hungarian salami. All this as well as well as a pick of cafés, including one overlooking the ruins of the medieval chateau of le Comte-Robert and its churning moat, swans and ducks included. Brie was our favorite corner in an area rich in favorite corners. It was our picture post card.

When Robbie was one year old we gave the first St. Jean party in the garden. We set up trestle tables in the garden for drinks and food, put out the chairs and tables for all seasons and invited all our friends. Once they learned to cope with finding Combs on the map, once they accepted that there would always be a bottleneck at Villeneuve-Saint-Georges, once they got used to going through the forest without watching out for wild boars, marauding deer, or Rumpelstiltskin himself, they arrived happy to have found us, after all.

Parisians are even worse than New Yorkers when it comes to venturing into the hills. Hugh Weiss, my much loved painter friend who came from Philadelphia, not even New York, arrived each year as though he had hacked his way through the Northwest Passage to make it. That first time he gazed around at the manicured rockeries with their flowers in bloom, and then at the imposingly handsome house in brick and stone, and ultimately at the size of Juan's studio which he could guess at by the number of its windows, he shook his head. "I give you three years… Three years and you'll come running back to the city."

Hugh, who painted flying elephants with roguish expressions, whose fantasy ran to Jabberwocky, who had been in the Navy in the Pacific in 1945 and guiltily welcomed the atomic bomb because he would have been in the front row of an invasion of Japan… Hugh with a conscience as big as a house, and who really should have been a Catholic, would call me late at night to discuss Joyce or wonder, with me, why we remained so American despite all our adult years spent abroad.

"Maybe they were never that adult?" he murmured idly late one night toward the end.

We were talking around what we always talked around: being here, being who we were. He and I shared a secret little identity problem. Living abroad is done at a certain price, we both felt, somewhat shamefully. Of course it was secretly because we both knew how fortunate we were, how clearly ear marked. We could claim to be the Happy Few. Yet, were we? Really? We each had that niggling doubt, which was our own little secret bond.

Hugh's funeral at Père Lachaise was like the most brilliant of his very brilliant vernissages. Faces from all the decades of our lives in Paris were there. I could have mused about how old we had grown but I did not. Instead I wondered once again at how distinct we were from others. Gershwin was right, there is such a breed as An American in Paris, after all.

Losing friends is to be expected but losing them early is an acquired skill. I have never learned to tame grief or to live with absence. When Barbara Grosset died at 59 I felt angry. Anger was the only defense I seemed to be able to manage. I wanted to pull her back from wherever she was, physically, by the arm, my hand rough on her wrist to yank her back into our lives, her life, theirs. Hugh's death was nearly twenty years later and at our age was more acceptable, yet my reaction was much the same.

Do not go gentle into that good night, our generation's bard said, no doubt in a Welsh accent. Dylan Thomas was the voice I thought I heard in times of need such as this one.

Moving to Combs brought me into my sixties. I had enjoyed the fifties, rather despite myself. Acknowledging age is an acquired grace I admire in others but find lacking in myself. Men seem to approach the question less self-consciously. On my sixtieth birthday we found ourselves in Combs rather than in Mallorca, where we had been on all the August 1st's since 1964.

"What shall we do this afternoon?" I asked Juan over cups of China tea in the garden. We were sitting on roomy soft lounge chairs enjoying the scent of jasmine, which I recognized, mingled with a half-dozen others I did not, feeling like Sarah Bernhardt and George Sand indulging in arcane conversation in that nineteenth century setting, perfectly secluded behind the laurels and the high garden wall.

He looked over at me with those fine-browed eyes and smiled a slow special smile, inching just a tiny bit closer, he took my hand.

"I can think of only one way to make it a perfect birthday," he said lightly. He was, as usual, quite right.

But Combs has its little ways and we found, to our amused dismay, that the local restaurants mostly close in August and do not accept latecomers after 8 p.m. if they are open. Ravenously hungry, we managed to have my sixtieth birthday dinner at restaurant in Paris's Chinatown, not far from the Butte-aux-Cailles. They sent out for a bottle of champagne.

Chapter 35

It did not take us long to realize that one acquired children in a variety of ways. You have them on your own, of course, but you can also pick them up along the way. When they are little the latter tend to be the ones you take to the beach because their parents are too busy, like the divine little Teresa Browne in Fornalutx who almost made our Suzy jealous when she was seven because Teresa's huge, tender Indian eyes obviously had me mesmerized. Then, all through the school years there were others. But later on, they would be young adults... and, all of a sudden, you have a new kind of affection. The chords are different... not quite the same as for your own, but they are touchingly there for you. Like Karina, like Kathy and like Brigitte Boucher, who had been a girlfriend of Christy's for about fifteen minutes, and then became a symbiotic daughter of ours from the moment she first turned up for Christmas dinner. And Adrian. Adrian is the major case in point.

When we moved into Combs I called around to friends asking if they knew anyone who would like to help us paint this slightly overwhelming house in exchange for room, board, interesting conversation and pocket money. We were beginning to feel our age, ceilings were out. The doctor had warned Juan off ceilings after his strange little episode while we were in Normandy when the house on the Butte was being built. No painting murals, he was warned. So, no ceilings either.

Gladys Berry, a great chum from the anti-war days and a fine actress, instantly said, "Yes, there is that young nephew of Diane's...You know Diane?"

To this day I am not sure I do know Diane, but we made arrangements for Adrian Lees to come out, stay with us and help paint the living room, dining room and the entrance hall, all of which had high ceilings full of ornate Victorian moldings. For starters. It was a big house.

I went down to the train station to meet him, looking out for a tall young man wearing a Kenyan scarf. I was the foreign lady with the frisky dog. We couldn't miss each other. Nor did we.

He was indeed the tall, slender, very handsome young man, straight out of an English movie with Hugh Grant, peering around 'til he spotted George, the dog. Once I saw his smile I adopted him for life.

He has charm, he has humor, he has patience and, above all, he has indulgence for others. Adrian, just out of college in Capetown, South Africa, came into our hearts and installed himself. Now, some 25 years later, it is he who is running our administrative affairs, not to mention everything else in our roller coaster attempts at achieving an elegant exit. He and Suzy plus the handful of other close beloveds. But he has the reins and the ultimate business instinct, not just the overflowing heart.

You call on family at certain times of the year, for specific rituals, and without them at those ritual calendar dates, you are bereft. That is a chilling prospect.

Our Christmas dinners in Combs were worthy of Dickens. We had a carload of Loirs, most especially Robbie and Thomas, the bouncing little newcomer, who arrived in 1990, as well as Nono who reminded us all that this whole fiesta started with a Jewish family. There was Christy some years, there was Michael Kidner, the eminent English painter and Marion, his New Yorker wife, from London, who had lost their only son and for whom Christmas would otherwise be difficult. There was Brigitte, from the start, and, quite soon, her Spanish husband, Jose, who became an instant beloved addition, and there was Adrian.

Juan and I sat at either ends of the table on those splendid Combs Christmas nights, in a raspberry-colored dining room that Jose painted, in between theater engagements, amid a sea of tinsel and bits of shiny gift wrappings strewn about, the polished de Soto silver serving dishes, dripping with Catalan stuffing, and platters of plump French turkey, Yankee sweet potatoes and cranberry sauce as well as all the other multicultural goodies that make the holiday ring out, the most important of it all being the sense of love. And it arms you for the rest of the year.

Shortly after moving in to Combs there was another Paris one-man show for Juan. Once more it was in the Place des Vosges. This time it was in la Galerie Philip. Much was expected of it because the gallery owner was close to the curator of the Musée de Pontoise, Edda Maillet, who had done so much to sponsor Juan's work.

The skies were clement on opening night, no horrendous storm bit into the festivities and the turnout was good. They were, I noted, almost all our friends. This time he showed almost as many paintings as sculptures, or so it seemed. The show looked elegant and did quite well, though there had been little effort on the part of the gallery owner.

It is a sad truism that artists and gallery owners more often than not find themselves at daggers drawn. This show was no exception. Juan would never work with her again, yet, looking back, it could have been worse. All the pieces sold were bought by our friends, true. However, not showing at reputable galleries, the artist withers on the vine. So the spiral continues. He had had a startling number of shows since the Musée Bourdelle in 1983, he did not have to think of another for a while.

That was without counting on Eva Maria who exhibited his work for him in group shows in a variety of German and Swiss venues. By then he had started a whole new vein of pieces in black and bronze that I found stunning.

Then one winter day in 1991, I went into the garden for some pretty branches to make a bouquet for friends who were stopping over before driving back to Torino after a few days in Paris. I slipped on a wet patch in the garden, fell clumsily and broke my ankle. Little Robbie stood staring at me not knowing whether or not to cry. Bravely, he did not. I did, though, 'til I was able to call out for Juan to help.

It was not just a break; I managed to pulverize the bone. That was bad luck but even a badly broken ankle does not usually change your life. This one did. I developed something I had never heard of, called algoneurodistrophy. There is not a great deal to be done about it, either. If it gets too bad, as it did in my case, they give you a treatment of injections which relieves agony slowly 'til you get to the point of being able to hobble a little with crutches but not really walk. I was in a wheelchair for six months and hated it.

It is a fallacy to think that wheelchairs might be fun and you might whizz through traffic and pedestrian knots like a Keystone comic. You cannot. And they do not whizz, they creep. Crossing streets means that oncoming traffic looms at you scarily and headlights blind. You become a rabbit. But a clumsy rabbit. You can seldom get properly seated at a table and, despite the kindness of strangers, you remain uncomfortable in public and always feel in the way. There are no saving graces in wheelchairs, or none that I found.

For a bunch of medical reasons which made sense at the time, I agreed when the surgeon at a reputable clinic near Melun suggested that I would benefit by a change of knees. It was true, I had had trouble with my left knee for some time, suffering from what is called a "mouse." A mouse is a bit of cartilage that is loose and scoots around inside the kneecap, causing havoc. A jab of the mouse as you are crossing the Etoile, for instance, may cause you to fall and trigger off the worse traffic disaster in history, if your imagination runs that way. An unruly mouse can indeed cause you to fall. Or grab on to a total stranger who happens to be next to you. My mouse has done both. So, when the persuasive surgeon suggested dumping this knee for a brand new American import, I said yes. Most medical friends agreed that knee surgery was advanced and so, why not?

A year after falling in the garden, a year of either wheel chair or painful hobbling around with a crutch-cane, I went in for the operation. It was a total flop. There is not much of an explanation for it, it is just bad luck. I have since learned to walk with a cane.

I walk more than most normal people I know and for the first fifteen years, or so, I out-walked most of my friends. Once into my eighties, however, my marathon propensities began to flag. Now, at 86, I hobble with the aid of my crutch-cane. That has less to do with the accident in the garden than with the ravages of age. However, the tumble on the wet grass turned out to be one of those dumb things that changes your life.

Nevertheless, that life still held a number of agreeable corners left to explore. There was still time.

Ann had come over to spend our fortieth wedding anniversary in 1991 and I had been to Chicago twice to see her but I still missed her closeness, perhaps more now that I was incapacitated and feeling slightly sorry for myself in the wretched wheelchair. At the same time Kathleen and Maura Collins, my Irish cousins from Castlebar, came over, too in June 1991. We put them upstairs in the attic bedroom and Ann in the room next to mine, known as Granma's Pad, which was my office.

I had been a bit apprehensive about that full a house, but I need not have worried. It was like a holiday camp and we all turned very young. Juan drove us around the countryside. We went to Chartres, we visited the fabulous cathedral at Meaux, we showed off Melun, our market town, and also Provins, a miraculously well-kept medieval walled town not very far from Combs. We took them to dinner at a particularly attractive restaurant in Barbizon after viewing all the vistas still extant painted by the Barbizon school of painting that just preceded Impressionism.

It was easier to visit the countryside than traipse around Paris with me in a wheelchair but we did that, too. I remember a fit of uncontrollable giggles in trying to get the wheelchair into the ladies room at the posh Gare de Lyon restaurant, Le Train Bleu. Blocking traffic expensively, Ann put it. A corpulent gentleman on his way to the Messieurs lent a hand by extracting me out of the chair, helping me inside to the nearest stall, then calmly leaving us all to get on with it. His smile and an elegant bow of the head did the rest. The French are unbeatable when it comes to class warfare.

Chapter 36

It was at this time that we began to use separate bedrooms. Rather gingerly, at first. Then deliciously. There is considerable literature on the ticklishness of separate bedrooms and I soon understood why. It was forced upon us because I needed the bed to myself and my cast. But, to our delicious surprise, it proved to be the ultimate in luxury. The house actually had two master bedrooms, each with a bath. Mine was on the first floor and it had the terrace which dripped wisteria, summer annuals, elegant ancient roses and vintage geraniums. The wisteria often blocked the shutters of the tall windows and French doors, but I found that so attractive I did not mind and only reluctantly cut it back. Our nineteenth century brass bed facing the wall of windows and glass door had made being in bed all those weeks tolerable.

The second master bedroom had a white marble fireplace and several built in book cases. Juan added two trestle tables which became instantly invisible under an assortment of papers, books with frayed corners, loose drawing pads and trays with paid bills which, when required, he could actually find his way through. By the time I was agile enough to clamber up the eight steps to go visit it, it looked lived-in and very much HIS. And you could hardly see the white marble mantelpiece for the doodads it held.

Forty years of marriage seemed like an amazing achievement as I bumped along the garden turf watching not to run over anyone's feet or, more importantly, the small scampering bundle called Thomas who had learned to speed crawl for the occasion. He was ten months old and had the time of his life during our fortieth wedding anniversary weekend. A head of fair curls, chubby cheeks and a triumphant little laugh whenever he could avoid parental hands outstretched to pluck him from disaster.

Suzy's new baby was the star turn. Two grandsons made us feel like millionaires.

Everyone had come to celebrate that fortieth anniversary, which coincided with la Saint Jean. I remember Raymond Grosset, who had married Barbara the same year, turning away after he raised a glass of champagne to us. And I remember the stab of rebellion I felt because there was something wrong in the dealing of the cards.

Ann, too, holding on to my hand as we laughed over Juan at the altar saying he would take this woman as his Awful Wedded Wife ... while she, John Kenton, our best man, and I managed not to laugh out loud at the Swiss-German priest's face hearing him.

The Awful Wedded Wife of forty years could only thank the spirals of luck that had made it possible. It was only fair, I thought, the early years had been rocky enough. Or it was not fair, as children say when they lose. But fairness and luck are two different levelers. I recall looking over at Juan talking volubly to Raymond and thanked the heavens for our amazing luck, holding my breath for a moment to make sure it was all real.

Wheelchair aside, of course.

Chapter 37

And then the world we lived in fell on its head while we were looking the other way. We were all involved with getting old, breaking bones, feeling fussy when, with no more than a spy's sigh, the Soviet Union vanished from the board. It even lost its national anthem, which made it awkward for the International Games a few months later. Off the board! Even Francois Mitterrand admitted to being taken by surprise.

The East-West divide had colored my entire adult life. From the age of eighteen at the nascent United Nations, by chance in my early twenties with the Christian Democratic Union of Central Europe and, ultimately, to the Free Europe Committee in its Paris office, I had been closely conversant with the East-West conflict. It had become part of my baggage.

At no point did I ever imagine the Soviet Union spreading its armored grip over Western Europe, but neither did I ever imagine it would belly flop one afternoon and never even try to get up.

The fact that I did not see it coming is one thing, the fact that no one else managed to foresee it is quite another. Of course there had been signs and there were many ponderous evaluations by pundits about the fissures resulting from Glasnost or other doctrinal slouches to the West on the part of their leaders. But these came after the fact. No European chancery was ready with a Plan B. This is hard to believe, in retrospect. Washington was bombastically left with its mouth open and not much to say.

The effects of Glasnost had been misjudged, but so had the importance of the Polish hammering at the gates, and, specifically, of Pope John Paul's often pugnacious stand-offs. I had mistrusted the Pontiff at the time because in my mind he had no sense of the need for social change beyond the East-West divide. He dismissed the South American cries for help with his indelicate dismissal of their Church of the Liberation. "Liberation from what?" he had said flatly. He listened to their pleas laconically in silence. He saw only one tyrant. I saw many.

That, perhaps, was another reason why the fall of Communism so amazed me. And it fell without a net, at that.

That year we had a red Lada, a Russian station wagon that was half the price of a Western European counterpart. It lacked the little niceties French cars offered but it had space, was reasonably comfortable, and Juan liked it. The first thing we did was to call Susie Ovadia and say, "Let's go to Budapest." Her bag was packed in a minute.

It was a memorable trip, the one that began by Juan not finding Germany. He did find Austria, however, and we had a hard time in getting him to leave it. It is true, Vienna is one of those half-dozen cities which has an aura of its own, whose past and present seem to curl around you as you walk through the imperial gardens or along streets like the Graben or the Franziskanerplatz. It is a city whose past whispers in your ear and somehow reassures you that everything will all work itself out and the streets and their lamps will still be there when you need them next time.

I saw Vienna first when the jeep with a British, French, American and Russian soldier patrolled its nights, not long after the war, when peace was still an uncertain concept. Now, forty years had gone by and, still slightly dazed, we felt that perhaps we had finally won the Second World War.

We had a hard time getting Juan to leave Vienna. But Budapest was a serious temptation. I had always had close Hungarian friends; it would be like visiting distant cousins in their family seat, I thought. Susie had been to visit Budapest when she was a child and had vague-but-vivid memories of this and that. I was distracted because I had mislaid the paper on which I had written the name of Robert Gabor's hotel in Budapest and the dates of his visit there. I was trying not to show the other two my distress. Imagine seeing Budapest with a Hungarian patriot who had fled it at the last minute four decades ago? Imagine losing the piece of paper? I tried not to show my confusion but it took the shine off the Danube and, I think, put a hex on the weather. It did nothing but rain 'til we left.

Even after Vienna, which is hard to beat in its genre, Budapest is a jewel. A glorious timeless bijou with domes and spires, the Danube curling around it and the bridges like fine meshed silver toys. And all over it, a penchant for red flowers. It is a Hollywood set for a musical comedy.

It is also a tough-fibered city with scars on its walls from the shooting spree of October 1956. It is broad esplanades in front of the museums and crowds filling the cathedral of St. Matthias on a Sunday morning. It is a leftover grandeur in a framework of recent betrayals. It is mean streets and verdant boulevards. It is the anger of a people who felt they had been held hostage for too long.

The Hungarians were not gracious hosts to the eager Westerners we were. They were icy in their bruised dignity. "Where were you in 1956?" was thrown at us like glasses of cold water. At me, especially, I felt, because Susie spoke German and was identified as Viennese and Juan had a Spanish accent. I was easily identified as American.

Everyone spoke German, I noticed. That figured. I dared ask a ticket-taker on a bus on Margaret Island if people also spoke Russian, having learned it in school. "No!" he retorted, "We learned not to speak it in school."

And he laughed. I remember him vividly because he was about the only one whom I made laugh. Most of the people we ran into did not smile, let alone laugh.

We were made to feel unwelcome. I would like to have stood in front of the museum and shouted at them… it was not our fault… but even through the veils of my fantasy, I knew that somehow they would never believe me. It was the West's fault. They saw no truth in the logic that the roots of the '50s were in the '30s.

I was disheartened because that was not how I saw the past, and I became concerned for the immediate future if that resentment were to take a grip on the country in the post-Communist years. Democracy is a fragile accomplishment and it has as many definitions as we have dictionaries.

Beautiful Budapest was also brittle and her people kept scores. We owed them and they did not seem in a rush to wipe the board clean.

We stopped on our drive to Graz in Austria on a mountaintop café looking at the rich Hungarian countryside behind us and I felt that we had stumbled on a troubled truth in making a short visit like that. Had Robert Gabor been with us we would have been spared the hostility, the rancor. We would have met the proper people. Later, when I told him about our reception, he was pained and agreed that it would have been different with him guiding us. But that was deplorable in itself.

As it turned out, he had been there staying in a hotel just a few blocks from the Elisabeth Bridge, which we took every day to visit the city under the rain.

We had been staying in a hotel that had seen a vastly different past because it had been the Habsbourg Ministry of Finances. Its black wrought-iron staircase outshone the one at the Paris Opera. That was the jewel we had been looking for.

The past is a weathering present in Budapest. I count on that to keep it imperial in its heart.

Chapter 38

Living out in the country, or what we called the country, inched in on our way of doing things. We were a little more organized, in one way, in that we went shopping by car and stocked up sensibly. That made me realize that we had done things a little erratically most of our lives. If I had needed a stick of butter on the rue de l'Aude or la Butte-aux-Cailles, I would have popped out, bought it and come home. Now, at sixty, I was getting organized. It was a minor point but, I thought at the time, a telling one. Change of life? It was about time.

I remember in the early '90s coming into town and meeting Susie Ovadia, who had at last retired after a lifetime of being a journalist by going to Bulgaria with Mitterrand in the press cortege, not because it was breathtaking but because it would be the last press junket she would make. Lasts are prickly, more solemn than firsts and frequently less joyful. She quite liked Sofia. And she quite liked retirement, after a while.

We walked all over the city on those afternoons which I look back on as moments of precious leisure, thought provoking meanderings, poking around the city's secret corners and our own favorite places, privileged onlookers with our French progeny always a bit of a surprise, comfortingly close because of our odd-man-out-ness. There were other things to do, yet the sense of my being free to wander around on my own or with someone I was especially fond of peppered those first years at Combs. That despite the acquisition of a permanent crutch-cane. That and discovering parts of the countryside we had not known before, collecting favorite churches, chapels, castles, moats, turrets, street markets and antique fairs to keep us delighted… like permanent tourists. Being a tourist is charming under the right circumstances, and ours were particularly auspicious.

All this time Juan was working. He was edging up to what would be a very important show at the Musée Tavet in Pontoise, which was a giant step in his career. There had been a connection between him and Edda Maillet and Christophe Duvivier, the very young assistant who was later to become curator after Edda retired. Complicity between artist and museum verges on marriage bonds. It is a joy to see it develop, to progress, to flower. It has little to do with money because neither ever has much; it has to do with faith, and faith is a subject for reverence. Juan has been fortunate in having had the support of the Pontoise group and their ramifications.

They have not made him rich but they have made him proud. Pride is priceless for an artist.

Chapter 39

Of course, something in the calendar had to give. Time for Mallorca seemed to shrink or alter in the seasons. One year I stayed on past the summer 'til November, but the next year we were only there for six weeks. Or we dropped in for spring rather than the long hot summers we all had loved so much. Suzy and Pascal came down with the two little boys, making me feel like the Queen Mum, but we all did not fit in the house so we staggered dates. Eventually they went off to easier summer places, like the Alps or the beaches outside St. Tropez where Pascal's aunt and uncle were on hand to eat them up. Who would not want those two delicious little boys to bathe in their lagoons? I was jealous, of course. There is no jealousy like a grandma's. How we both delighted in those little boys. Having them in Mallorca was a treat, like the cream on your strawberries. I'm sure we bored our friends to tears.

Living in Combs altered our schedules because the garden was delectable in spring and early summer, so we stayed on 'til autumn approached and we suddenly turned into what I used to call September people in Spain, those who could afford to avoid the excessive heat of August and yet turn up on the beach with a smashing suntan.

Also, we had to rent out the Combs house because not only did we need the money, but burglars loomed if we left it empty. We were burgled once, at the beginning. An unsavory experience which robbed me of my only diamond ring, a legacy of my mother's, and a feeling of desecration of our bedroom with underwear scattered all over the floor and the bathroom cabinets emptied. The burglar turned out to be a local lad, a tall, blond blue-eyed junkie and a chronic offender who did not remember where he sold the ring. No one at the local police station got very excited about it. We were given what seemed mingy compensation from the insurance company but it made us resolve not to leave the house visibly vacant for more than a weekend. We must have done something right because it never happened again.

We had been emotionally attached to Mallorca for decades. Its beauty, its pleasures, our friends were all a major part of our lives. Without really putting it into words, however, we both sensed that this was a chapter that was slowly leaving us behind.

I had always been fond of being there on my own. It was never for very long, but here and there I would spend a few weeks by myself and take on a different schedule than the one we had when we were together or en famille. The car, for starters. Fornalutx is a couple of kilometers up or down the mountain from Sóller. Sóller is a lovely little town where the shops and market are, where we bank, where we sit at cafés and chat with friends from Sóller itself or other towns down the coast. It is our hub. There is a magnificent 1930s tramway to take you to the beach and an electric railway that takes you in to Palma. It is a national monument, the train, and the tramway to the beach is a treasure. With my capacity for walking up and down my mountain road unpleasantly curtailed, I had to depend on taxis or friends. That was as unexpected a disaster as was the onset of age.

Then one day Juan said, "I don't want to be old in a place where I was young," at a dinner table with Spanish friends, stopping conversation. Our friend was a colonel in the Spanish Marines and an outspoken liberal who had miraculously weathered the Franco years without sanction. He was taken aback by Juan's words. So was I. It had never occurred to me to give up Mallorca, nor had the notion of how geography fits in with accepting old age.

But when I looked at him, he was quite serene and just as firm. It is true that he is far more physical than I. He does not lie on the beach like I do, he swims. And he swims elegantly like an ad for summer. He skims the surface of the water and slides gracefully in and out of grottos. He is the boy on the dolphin. He also goes for walks in the mountains among the orange groves or the ridges overlooking the sea that no one else tries to access. He explores the mountain trails above Fornalutx before dinner while everyone else sits on the patio waiting for the rice to boil.

Juan loves Mallorca. What he meant then was that he did not want to be there when all he would be able to do would be to sit and wait for the perfect sunset. That prospect sent a chill down my spine and jostled our military friend, who clearly had never questioned it before.

I forget when we decided we should sell the house in Fornalutx. Toward the end of the 1990s, I suppose. I was convinced of its wisdom at the end of one season when I had increasing trouble getting a taxi to go up or down to Sóller. But there was more.

Imperceptibly, our corner of the island had been changing. Our tiny mountain village had become a tad too fashionable for our taste. Also all of a sudden, there were different new faces and new cars in our midst. The thing about small, secret jewels like Fornalutx is that they do not take easily to foreigners. And foreigners seemed to have been parachuted down one night when no one was looking and suddenly everyone at the café was German.

True, Mallorca has always had a German colony. In the late '80s, however, it exploded. Really exploded, though, even to the point of trying to form a political party with the connivance of one of the greedier right wing political parties that did not mind an influx of Deutch Marks.

More to the point, Mallorca has had a large and discreet English-speaking resident colony with good manners and low voices, the opposite of the new German summer people. The English-speaking foreigners had been installed in Fornalutx for so long that they now felt like victims of marauders from the east. Without really noticing it happening, they were out-voiced at the café terraces, the three village restaurants, its two groceries and, worse still, the few available parking places. The road was infested with Mercedes, the cafés suddenly had no tables, the talk in the village square was Teutonic and the local pecking order, installed for half a century because Balearic air made us all live long, was toppled like a house of straws. Fornalutx had changed. Village houses were being swept up at amazing prices. All of a sudden.

Just five minutes after we had sold ours to a Mallorcan couple, he a university professor and she a school teacher, from Palma. We sold it at a pre-invasion price. We thought we had performed a miracle in passing our Spanish house to another Spanish couple. They, like the wily Mallorcan buccaneers they stemmed from, promptly sold it for considerably more to an English teacher the year after.

There, in a nutshell, is the story of our flair for finances and the quite different story of how an island in the Med stays afloat... a study in opposites.

But I did one uncharacteristically clever thing. It was I, because Juan thought I had gone mad, who bought an apartment in Palma. "An apartment in Palma?" he had echoed. "You are out of your mind."

For forty years we had avoided Palma. He would race off the Barcelona boat as soon as it docked and head for the mountains, ignoring what he considered to be a small hot city full of sunburned foreigners in shorts. Whereas I liked Palma.

I bought us a small modern apartment on the edge of Palma which means on the edge of the sea as well, that consisted of two rooms, each with a comfortable terrace, a kitchenette plus two full baths and the very beautiful beach which we shared with the King and his household. It is called Cala Mayor. The beach was literally downstairs. We heard the lapping of the waves at night. I got a kick out of that.

We had arrived on the island when we were young and our children were small. We spent bountiful years in a magical setting among people of substance and those who imagined they were of substance. The island had not quite been turned into a monster mockery of The Perfect Resort that Spain's criminal rulers of the Franco era, which lasted 'til the first free elections in 1977, had claimed. Not quite but almost. We had been blessed with the proper timing there. Every generation has its summer luck, we were all round winners for the time and the place.

I loved the little flat on the cala, I loved the difference it brought me in terms of living in Mallorca. It was mine more than Juan's because he was busy working in Combs and I was free to run down for a couple of weeks at a time whenever I felt like it. I liked feeling free in my late middle age. It was one of the few things I found positive, to put a fine point on it. But even that came to a standstill or a tapering off.

We sold the little flat for three times the price we paid, some six years after buying it. Serendipity. And heartfelt thanks.

We left Mallorca for good in 2006 after 42 indelible years. Juan was nearing eighty so he was not quite old in the place in which he had been young. Just in time, so to speak.

Chapter 40

Crossing the avenue of the new century sent shivers through me. I needed to take lessons in old age. Not only did I feel old and fat, walking with a cane and drifting out of touch by living in the country, but all of these things came to me as disconnected surprises. Others might slide into decrepitude but not the girl from Incarnation, I would tell myself, deep under the covers, looking for a way to circle reality. But not me. How do others cope with reality, I wondered. Looking around me, I saw that some ignored it. Others denied it and looked silly, but the sensible ones accepted it. I could think of no way to do any of these things so, aside from avoiding mirrors, which I do to this day, I decided to high jump it. Like those Spanish horses of Vienna.

And I started to think of those misty people I had created years ago but left in boxes in the cellar. Ghosts of '60s people who squirmed under the heat of the new sun. Women who took the wrong decisions and had to run to catch moving trains. Women whom I might have resembled had it not been for... had it not been for...

Juan came up from the cellar one day with a carton of papers, saying, "Wasn't this supposed to be a book one day?" in that detached voice of his when it came to my books. He claims that is my imagination and that he has always been involved with my books. Perhaps.

He held out a messy manuscript and said, "You put them in Vienna... I remember," almost convincing me. I took the unloved bundle to my desk and that was how we began the century.

It takes no time at all to write a novel but it takes years and years to rewrite it.

And Juan remembered accurately... it was indeed set in Vienna, and it was also a fragment chipped off the rock of the Cold War.

But I was interrupted by a whack of reality no one expected. I suppose everyone is guilty of the illusion that he or she is exempt from the blow that cancer carries. I certainly was.

It came one February day when I was to meet Susie Ovadia to do the last day of the Paris winter sales. She was to pick me up at the clinic where the test was performed. She found me looking no doubt like a ghost, standing with an uncomfortable doctor who was busy telling me that it was easily reachable and would be nothing to take out.

Susie, who had gone through moments like this herself, guessed instantly what the test showed. We just looked at each other and I recall smiling at her reassuringly. It will be nothing, I said confidently, they will take it out and throw it away. And maybe I'll lose a kilo or two. We avoided each other's eyes and headed for a tea room she knew, where I ate a particularly rich raspberry tart, just for the road. And, what with one thing and another, we missed the sales. I have never done the Paris winter sales again.

The operation for breast cancer is a remarkable medical victory. I was only slightly angry that they had to take the breast with it but felt that surgery to implant a replacement was ridiculous for a lady of 75—my vanity did not reach that far. I only regret it in summer when being lopsided is so difficult to hide.

But I am eternally grateful to French medicine and the remarkable health care program that makes it possible. I can't emphasize that enough.

This episode made me a little more aware of my mortality than I was before, which in turn made me do something I should not have done. I foolishly chose to use a private publisher rather than go through the fuss and feathers of waiting with my angelically patient agent, Philip Spitzer, to tread through normal publishing channels as I should have.

I use the word angelic advisedly. He had handled my two earlier books admirably. We were good friends. He had seen *Run a Hollow Road* when I first wrote it and had advised me painstakingly what was wrong with it and how I might easily put it right. I had not done it at the time but I was ready to do it now. What I could not do, or so I thought, was to sit and wait for a publisher to say yes or no.

One half of me knew that what I was doing was unprofessional but the other half screamed like a frightened child left alone in the dark. I went ahead with arrangements to use an online publisher which entailed handing in a manuscript ready for the printer.

We did not go to Mallorca in the summer of 2003; we stayed home for the first time in decades. I was in the middle of the novel when all of a sudden the electricity in the house went berserk. Lights flashed, blinked, hissed and finally bombed out. My computer did the same. A blitz of strange sounds, flashes of color and suddenly, nothing. The screen was dark. It was dead. With my newly rewritten novel inside.

I had only been using the computer for a year or so and was timid about clicking things. I am a poor typist and even worse editor. Mistakes must be glaring for me to see them and even then I manage to skip over most of them. And, of course, I knew nothing about computers beyond the rudiments of emails and Word.

We were having a heatwave. Now, being a New Yorker and having spent some four decades of summers in the Mediterranean, I did not think much of what turned out to be a murderous calamity for much of France and particularly the Paris area. People died, literally, from the heat. It became a national issue.

Computers, too, were knocked out on an amazing scale. When mine sizzled itself out I called Kathy Grosset, the sweet daughter of Barbara and Raymond, who had taken over the Rapho photo agency and who was brilliant, kind and patient and also one of the few competent people still in Paris in August.

That was a serious consideration. Juan and I were on a desert island in Combs. We were not threatened by the heat because big nineteenth century French houses are built to resist inclement temperatures and, besides, we had a nice inflatable pool in the garden if we were uncomfortable, but an imploding computer was something we had not foreseen.

Kathy and Thierry, her calm, cool, polyglot partner, came out and saved the situation. Kathy is one of these lovely young women her mother and I used to admire because they were serene. Unflappable. Well, almost unflappable.

Enough to come in and sit down at the sick machine, insert what looked like a nail file in its innards and then turn around to tell me not to worry. The manuscript was inside the nail file and nothing was lost. And while we are at it, can we help you do this publishing thing?

She might just as well have said, can we save your life?

Chapter 41

Thierry enjoyed working on the book, and he enhanced it with an imaginative flair for its layout. It looked handsome. None of us was particularly good at typos, however. It was alive with them. My highly critical friend Philip Goodman said he could not see himself give the book a review on Amazon because it looked so unprofessional. I realized then that I had a more sizeable problem on my hands than I had thought. Fortunately, other friends were not as stern as Philip and the book got a half-dozen or so substantive reviews from people I asked. One was reprinted in a Vermont newspaper, which gave me healing pleasure and I have that one framed hanging over my desk, something I did not do with either *In Search of Mihailo* or *Trumpet for a Walled City.*

Run A Hollow Road was like a lame child and I love it still, in a special way. Kathy and Thierry were by way of being godparents.

The first decade of the new century seemed to be marked by clashes of cymbals. Being seriously sick and surviving, giving up our long summers in our Mallorcan house and trading them in for short visits to friends' houses there, bringing out another book and Juan having shows on a scale he had hoped for but was not always sure he would get to do, in the dark years. There were galleries in Germany, also, which were handling his work, almost by magic. Then Eva Maria, in her unobtrusive way, told him she thought it was time he had a retrospective. I blinked. She went on to suggest Le Musée des Ursulines in Mâcon. Now he blinked.

One should understand that in these new days of contemporary art, museums outside of Paris were no longer the small dusty provincial stopovers one might visit between the capital and, say, Marseilles, good for a visit while you are waiting for the ferry to Corsica, for instance. Not at all. They are provincial, perhaps, but that is a function for financing them as much as it is a geographical fact. Provinces and regions and other such geographical considerations all have budgets, their curators have egos, and their collections are often influenced by artists with connections to their whereabouts.

Matisse came from a small corner of the North on the way to Brussels, one might think, but there are now two major museums with world-class collections because he came from there. Cambrai, where Juan is admirably represented because of Eva Maria, is a case in point. Another is Mâcon, in Burgundy, where the Ursuline museum is in what had been a handsome convent. It has a splendid collection of constructivist and minimalist art. Eva Maria decided that having a retrospective there would be perfect. It was close enough to Paris for people to come without making a pilgrimage out of it and almost everyone agreed that a weekend in Burgundy would be a welcome treat.

The show, which Eva Maria hung along with the curator Mme. Marie Lapalus, took pleasure in showing how he arrived at the work he does now.

It is a very special feat for an artist to be given a retrospective for many reasons. But one dominant reason is because it is the only real moment when he sees both where he began and where he has ended vividly placed before his eyes, for his own assessment. I asked him about this and he answered very quietly, "I am sure about what I'm doing now," and he smiled a little. He is never cocky about his work so I was particularly moved by his answer. And, perhaps, I breathed a sigh of relief, as well. He was, after all, eighty years old.

In 1955 we left New York for good as far as he was concerned. He had never returned. In 2005 Kathy and Thierry, who visit New York frequently, said one evening as they were just leaving, that they were going on a little visit. It was the end of October. As we stood by the open door I thought for a second and pictured New York just before it gets really cold and then felt a tug at my heart… Thanksgiving? I let the door close on its own and began to smile.

I love Thanksgiving. It is the one day of the year I am homesick. When my children were small I used to make Thanksgiving dinners and would coerce my French-Catalan in-laws into eating turkey, candied sweet potatoes and cranberry sauce on a Thursday night. I wanted my children to know what it was, to understand its generosity and, if possible, to love the essence of what Thanksgiving means, beyond the Pilgrim Fathers in a new and pristine land. They will tell you if I succeeded.

But whatever it did to them was probably less important than what it means to me. For several years in the new era I had managed to get to Washington and spend it with the Donahues whose adult children I had known as kiddies and with whom I could share the taste of my tattered New York roots.

So, I said, standing at the door in Combs without much further thought but looking hard at Juan, "Why don't you come, too? Why don't we all go to New York?"

He gaped at me in the way he did long ago when I said, let's go to Haiti, or, to Egypt, or, let's buy a house or… whatever. It became clear early on in our life together that the Spanish bullfighter in this family was definitely not the Spaniard, no matter how audacious his work might seem.

But Kathy and Thierry jumped at the idea and we cornered him 'til he could think of no good reason why he should not go, too.

Once every fifty years? What the hell.

Chapter 42

It was worth it to see the expression on his face when we caught sight of the skyline on the way in from the airport. Philip Goodman had come to fetch us to bring us to the Village where the adorable Geraldine Gore was waiting for us in the magical flat she was lending us for Juan's Return of the Warrior. And it turned out to be only a few blocks north of Broome Street, from which he fled in 1955. Two rooms with her father's paintings on the wall, a street view of the kind only New York knows how to do and a splendid elevator for my wretched knee. Philip, with whom I stayed while in New York, took us into the city the long way, giving us a glimpse of Brooklyn Heights for starters.

Welcome to my own my native land. Geraldine Gore, the talented daughter of her parents, was a dream hostess. Not content with lending us her apartment in the Village, she supplied a mobile telephone as well.

It is impossible to describe how touching, how funny, how delightful it was to see Juan's return. Nothing had changed, everything had changed, he decided, quite bedazzled.

Geraldine and Steve, her partner, did everything in their power to make it a stellar occasion, and so did Philip. We managed to peek in at all our private landmarks and Juan was surprised that so much of what he remembered with affection was still there.

Except Washington Heights. He found it shabby and depressing and could hardly wait to take the bus down the Drive and out of what he had remembered so differently. That surprised me, for I was not sure he was justified.

Maybe it was just the red headed ghost of my mother that had flared up and scared him off. I thought back then on what her welcome to him must have felt like to a young man used to the deceits of good manners. No one in Barcelona would have behaved like she did to him. So, we did not visit the Cloisters.

But he enjoyed seeing the colors of the changing New York sky which had always fascinated him. The New York blue, he claimed, was almost tropical in its midnight quality. He says so today, too, that it gives away the game: this is a new world, just look up at the sky.

We did as much as possible in skimming the bright surface of the city... a visit to the Met to see an exhibit of Fra Angelico, and we were a posse of Thierry and Kathy, Philip, Judith Childs, Geraldine and us. But before hitting the Met we stopped in across the street and invaded a splendid Cranach exhibit at, I think, the Mellon, I think, as though for hors d'oeuvres. And afterwards we went back to Philip's for a light four-course snack only he knows how to turn out while discussing Arthur Miller or the possibility of a Third World War.

New York was at its brightest in his 15th floor eagle's nest on West End Avenue a few blocks from where I had been a little girl on 85th Street learning to roller skate on Riverside Drive. The views from his windows make me cry. Once in a while I caught Juan's eye and I could see that he knew what I felt.

Good.

We drove down to Washington for my beloved Thanksgiving, which we would have with the Donahues and their array of granddaughters and Matt, the one grandson, like another part of my family. We stayed with Rafael and Judy Tomero, though, in their big sprawling house in Bethesda where they had spare rooms galore even with the presence of their daughter Leonor's in-laws from Alaska. Now, for exotic... you can't go much further than that.

I looked at us all on the first morning and saw two New York girls and their Spanish husbands alongside real exotics from where the Polar Bears come from. Rafael and Juan were enchanted with these Aliens. Judy, the girl from Far Rockaway who had befriended me in Geneva, raised an eyebrow and murmured, "No one on the Boardwalk would have believed Alaska."

Reunions with those who had been so pivotal at an early crossroads of one's life are tricky, depending how kind later years had been. None of us had been mistreated en route, though none of us had quite sailed through either. The scars we wore were honorable ones, I thought, and we had come through with style. Style counts.

That time in Washington, I was suddenly grateful for the cavalier way fate had dealt out the cards. My upside-down life had been graced by players of substance for the top roles. My friends were my blessings, my love was my bounty. In Washington that year I saw that, though we were very clearly growing old, we had been on a lucky roll for longer than most. Ridiculous to have to travel that far to count your blessings, but why not?

I knew then it was the last trip.

In the meantime, however, Christy had been busy. He had spent the last several years in Kazakhstan for the *Times* and other papers, had visited the North Pole five times and written an excellent book on it called *The Oddest Place On Earth*. He had shared eight years with a precious young lady who had a background similar to his, and even mine. Her father was Colombian. Lovely Silvia Mendes. Gifted, kind, patient, she was a simultaneous interpreter at international conferences. She even went to the North Pole with him. Sadly, however, it did not work out and he married another young lady, a southerner from North Carolina, and they proceeded to have two little girls. They left Kazakhstan for Hawaii—a move that defies comment—but then settled in Washington after a few years and a rancorous divorce.

If marriage did not suit Chris, fatherhood gripped him. He is a resolutely indulgent daddy to a pair of clever and exceptionally beautiful girls.

Unfortunately, they live too far away for us to babysit as we did with Suzy's boys, but we are charmed by their all-too-infrequent visits and their pictures on the walls. Fatherhood becomes him, which is comforting to us.

The early years of the new century were reasonably soft on us. A few bouts with mysterious ailments sent Juan to the local hospital more out of over-care than real necessity. But time ran short around us. My lovely Ruth Froma died quickly and painlessly in Amsterdam while Joel, who had been ill for years, lingered on. We had gone up to Amsterdam to see them in 2006, a little on the spur of the moment because she had seemed harried on the phone.

We found ourselves in the middle of an unexpected heatwave. Air conditioning in America is a fact of life, but in Europe it is a luxury relegated to seriously warm spots and only then in posh neighborhoods. In Holland it is barely a thought since it is rarely hot. Until climate change entered the scene, whether we admit it or not. Amsterdam is hell in hot weather. Even my favorite museum in Europe is stifling in a heat wave. I said a prayer for

Rembrandt and his buddies and hoped the paint they used would survive the weekend.

It was devastating to see Joel, one of the best ferreter-out of special corners in his beloved Amsterdam to show us when we visited, now a very old man in a chair not quite sure who we were or why we all could not go downstairs and sit by a canal. Ruth fussed and protested that she was coping but I had my first piercing glimpse into what I recognized as the end of our lives. I was shaken. No one is master of his fate, except in poetry. Why do we not believe the icy truth 'til it is too late? Why? Because it is easier to say goodbye rather than farewell. It is a question of self-defense. And why not?

We drove down to Spain one last time in 2008, put the car on the Mallorca boat, and stayed with friend Maeve Black for a few weeks. We had sold the little flat I had bought in Cala Mayor, we were rootless where we had been so rooted for so long. It was a little itchy.

A few years earlier Juan had been commissioned by the local art magnate to do a sculpture for his sculpture garden, a museum of sorts on the edge of Sóller. The sculpture had been made in Palma by a reputable foundry whose owner took himself for something of an art expert but whose employees were sloppy enough to tip the sculpture, a large work in iron, on Juan's foot. A horrendous accident. It resulted in a crushed set of toes, a month in hospital, first in Palma then in France near us in Melun. And the amputation of one toe. It was a disagreeable experience on all levels and had been excruciatingly painful at the beginning. There was a financial settlement eventually, but not before lawyers had to be called in, and the whole affair had left a disagreeable note in my mind. The last trip to Mallorca had to be perfect to make up for all that.

And it was. Though the German influx of moneyed summer people had changed the atmosphere of Fornalutx, a change the other foreigners objected to, though it was not the villagers who profited by it, the village was still a jewel. By luck, the restaurant we had favored for so many years but which had closed because the owner was now too old, suddenly reopened and we were able to have our paellas at our old table overlooking the valley under a sky as wide as the poets claim.

I had loved the dinners at the Bellavista. Though the food was slow in coming, was frequently lukewarm, and often lacked salt, the sky was enormous and the bougainvillea only more beautiful than mine because they had different colors—I only had purple. We drove up and had paellas and roast chicken whenever we could and pretended we were young and would go out in the boat again tomorrow morning.

It is dangerous to go back to someplace you have loved and left, but it all worked out as though charmed. Our car started to do strange things as we approached the Barcelona boat, but it behaved as though taking orders from Above and did not actually conk out 'til we were in Barcelona when it chugged to Juan's sister, Rosa's door on the Carrer Padua, where it expired.

Rosa's garage man towed it off to wherever he worked and fitted it out with a new gear box. This misadventure kept it handily garaged 'til we were ready to leave three days later, thus solving the god-awful Barcelona parking problem. The mechanic was used to us, for it was the second gear box he had done for Juan but I did not mention it at the time. Juan does not put his foot down enough, it would seem; at least as far as cars go.

The drive up through France was enchanting, possibly because we both knew it would be the last time. Firsts and lasts are to be celebrated, albeit in different voice tones. We took three days. There was no rush.

Chapter 43

The edging-in process which is a way of describing the weight of age is so gradual that it comes as a surprise one day to look up and say we never go to the movies any more, let alone the theater. Yet to do both is easy for us because Combs hosts one of those remarkable French initiatives, the national theaters outside Paris. Ours is le Théâtre National de Sénart. It is a first-run movie house plus a prestige theater and a library called a médiathèque with TV films, cassettes and records on loan as well as books. We have seen everything from Charlie Chaplin revivals to Carolyn Carlson, Molière, Brecht and the Peking Circus at the Coupole. The building was done by Jean Nouvel, one of Europe's most prestigious architects, something Combs is extremely proud of. We have been avid patrons since we arrived here. But one chilly evening I noticed that it was December and we had not been to the Coupole since returning from the summer. The prospect of getting into the theater seats, difficult for me, had put me off suggesting let's go to the movies tonight, which Juan almost always agreed to. Nor had he suggested it, either.

Imperceptibly our creaky bodies had wormed their ways into our lives, the creaks taking over what had once been our mobility. Just like with the local restaurants.

I should add here that I do not like to cook, have never liked to cook, but have cooked competently almost from the start. So, going out for a little dinner at any one of a number of excellent inexpensive local restaurants was something I usually edged us into almost upon arrival. Our wonderful little restaurants, one on the river Yerres with swans and a fairy tale wooden bridge to gaze at, another with a brook running through it, a third with tables in a garden for all seasons, none of them expensive, beckoned us. Me, particularly. Then, as the new century crept in with its inevitable solemnity, one by one they started closing. First the Moulin whose owner decided to only open for weddings, banquets and presumably High Holidays. This gave us pause. I wonder to this day who feeds the swans now that we have gone.

Then the restaurant with the brook running through it burnt down. How you can burn down a watery place next to a river is a bit of a question, but it was too late to ask. An apartment building, as unsightly as it is intrusive in that tucked away corner by the Yerres just meters away from a millrace was, I suppose, worth the box of matches. The third restaurant remains, thank heaven, but the impetus had been blunted.

And a pizza place opened just up the street a bit, which was not in the same league but served the purpose. We went out less and less. Until at the end, we went out not at all. It was gradual, over a period of a few years but the result was unmistakable. By the end of the first decade of the new century I could no longer take the train into Paris by myself. My left knee never recovered from the accident twenty years earlier. It grew less manageable as time went on.

And my lovely sense of freedom, taking the train and going into the city to meet with friends or just on my own to walk around, a sense I cherished—an almost childish sense of freedom or independence—faded silently without my noticing. Or almost. That is what getting old is. It is stopping things without actually calling a halt.

But there was enough activity around us for me not to notice or to choose not to notice. We went here and there by car. We took trips, which made me realize that I went to London more easily than I went to Paris, which was around the corner. I did not have to walk to go to London and once there either someone had a car or we called a mini cab. My one real regret was the giving up of the London black cab, that superb icon. I could no longer fold my knees properly to get in and out.

That did not stop us from cheering Freddy Gore on his ninetieth birthday celebration at the Chelsea Arts Club or seeing a Tom Stoppard play a year or two later. But it did keep us from going to Freddy's funeral later on. And we have not been back since.

Thinking about our close affection for London it is hard to admit to letting go. One does not admit to it, really, one just does not go. We talk on the phone with Connie, we write newsy emails to Philippa and Ian Fraser, but the Allens are no longer there in their amazing house with all its Victoriana where we had been young and where Crokie had taught Christy to read English.

Our chums had moved on, while I learned to live with problems in moving at all. But everything is gradual, silent, stealthy. It just leaves a wispy little trail of smoke in its place. Nothing at all to do with a greasy newspaper full of fish and chips with Frank on the Isle of Dogs or riding through the Cotswolds making sure Juan was driving on the wrong side of the road. The only time Juan has ever had a problem with being on the Left, as Frank pointed out.

Being on the Left, of course, remained a steadfast preoccupation and one of the few that did not demand the cooperation of defective knee joints. The American political scene remained part of my life so all that happened in this brand new century was of vital concern. I had eyed the tall, dark young man who gave the amazing speech at the Democrat convention with careful interest and kept an ear ready for what he said in the Senate afterward. Of course, it was dream talk to imagine a presidential candidate called Barack Obama in my lifetime.

Wasn't it?

I was good at dream talk, though, and had it not happened once before when an Irish Catholic Senator from Massachusetts, for whom I actually had written a speech in 1954, was talked about for the presidency? Is not America the land of the dream come true?

In 1954 the junior Senator had agreed to give an address to the Christian Democratic Union of Central Europe's first Congress. He said on the telephone, if the organization would write the speech for him, he would give it.

"That would be me, Senator," I said on the phone.

"That sounds fine," replied the young Senator, and he laughed. But he was having an operation on his back on the day the conference was held. His office informed me of this on the phone and then asked if someone could deliver the speech to the conference in his name?

That was me, too. 1954.

Now, I could no longer work on the presidential campaign here at Democrats Abroad France, where I had been a very early Vice Chairman, but I could sit by nervously and watch it all happen on TV. And cheer and cry and believe once more that there is a place called America despite all the Bushes and the Roves who create Halliburton monsters to deviate it and make it somewhere we do not want to go.

Imagine electing a Barack Obama on my computer from the French countryside in the twenty-first century?

I don't know which of those propositions is the most unthinkable. Probably my ever being able to work a computer, considering the fact that I never learned to use an electric can opener.

And I can sit back and say, with accuracy this time, we did accomplish something, after all.

At the back of my head I knew we were skidding on what is known as borrowed time. We were relatively healthy or, rather, used to our ailments so that they didn't get in our way. A trip to Budapest to spend a week or so in 2008 with Robbie Gabor who visited there every spring, seemed an easy option. We arranged to meet Susie Ovadia, who was in Vienna at the time, at one of those Budapest spa hotels with pools and spring water that does things to you and little pavilions on the grounds with fussy hot pools and beauticians who rejuvenate you with mudpacks. I had my first facial and we all splashed around a baby pool with magic bubbles. There was a boat landing on the Danube just next door and we planned to take a boat into town rather than a city bus.

I will never know how, but in rushing a little so as not to miss the boat I lost footing and fell, not into the Danube but instead against a railing. I broke three ribs.

I did not pass out but wished I had. We somehow got back to our lovely room in the hotel and a doctor eventually appeared. After ascertaining that nothing vital was destroyed but that the three cracked ribs needed attention, he sent us to the only ER in Budapest open at night. God bless Susie's German because no one there spoke English or French. Not even Catalan.

Broken ribs are not lethal but there are moments when you would like them to be. We have some sort of insurance that allows us to be repatriated in case of an accident abroad, so an angelic doctor was at the airport to guide us into a handy Austrian Airlines plane and an ambulance was waiting for us at Charles De Gaulle. The doctor came home with us and tucked me in for the night and that was, looking back, the end of our particular road.

Robbie Gabor was devastated. He is a couple of years older than Juan so the conundrum of age and freedom of movement was high in all our thoughts. You can fall running to catch a boat to go down the Danube at any age, I argued, somewhat simplistically.

But when you fall it hurts more if you are eighty. That is the difference. And you don't heal as easily, either. Those ribs are still tender some six years later.

Piece by piece the structure of our lives were chipped away, leaving holes in the velvet of our days. We were cheerful enough, however, and Juan even went into Paris to opening nights of exhibitions he was interested in. I did not. The train proved too unmanageable now. But I did not mind. I was not especially worried about Juan going in alone—though, once in a while, when it got to be long after dinnertime, I grew uneasy, but without much cause. He would have just decided to catch a bite in town after the show. It should be said that he is probably the only man in the western world not to ever have used a mobile phone. I might have been annoyed at his silence but not seriously alarmed.

Indeed, the night it all crumbled I had been having a passing thought about how cozy we were, considering he had just been feted by his gallery with a Homage for Joan Palà on his ninetieth birthday. A handsome show of his works and a lovely party to which we had been transported in a Mercedes limo chauffeured by a stunning young man in livery, to our utter astonishment, thanks to a well-wisher who asked to remain incognito.

We drove into town like royalty, stopped traffic on the rue Guénégaud in front of the gallery as we alighted from the slinky black Mercedes, the door held open by a gorgeous young driver straight out of central casting.

As entrances go, we scored resoundingly. And it was not 'til the end of the evening that Suzy told us the anonymous benefactor was Neely Lanou, a friend from the 1950s who bounced back into our lives enchantingly the year before. She and her husband had visited us that summer, proving that you can pick up a conversation left open five decades earlier if the right ingredients were there at the start.

Neely gave us the touch of magic we needed on that last of Juan's great occasions.

A week later Juan fell on the ground floor tiles late one night and could not get up. I called the firemen, as one does in France, and ran out to the front gate leaving him, still groggy, on the floor, so that they could get into the grounds. They arrived and took him to the hospital nearby.

He was never to come home again. Everything changed places in our lives.

That was August 6, 2012.

He had injured his head and partially drowned his brain. From then on he has been charming and sweet-natured, often funny, but clearly on a different plane. His memory is patchy and so is his reasoning but his affection for us is unaltered.

The way he looks at Suzy or the boys when they are with him shows how he cherishes them. And how he admires the boys' efficiency in dealing with matters now beyond him. He sort of leaned back and became grateful.

So did I. I will never stop being grateful. Juan's accident took place the day Suzy and Pascal flew to Montreal to take a Canadian vacation following in my childhood footsteps in Nova Scotia and New Brunswick. It was an absolutely charming idea of hers, going to Digby which through the decades had become a fantasy land of mine that I had passed on to her, replete with a sparkling lake, a rugged coast, a sweet sixteen party, all the lobsters in the sea and a world long since swept away. They went exploring the scene for me, since I never managed to do it myself.

We were able to keep Juan's misadventure from them for a while but they came back before time. Nono, Pascal's mother, was increasingly ill with pancreatic cancer at the same time. The roof was falling in from all sides. Nono died before Christmas. Pascal lost his mother and his best friend all in one.

We were shaken as well as saddened. It did not seem real.

Next, Juan was sent to a small attractive clinic a few towns away from Combs. He remained there four months, after which he was moved into a nursing home just a few kilometers up the road from us in Combs.

During the course of the next year, the reins of my life slipped from my fingers into the able hands of Suzy and Adrian, with the boys and a still dazed Pascal as ready foot soldiers. Not gradually but sharply, I handed over the burden of decision to their able stewardship. And I sat back and let Lucie do the rest.

Lucie is proof that angels exist. She is the girl who came into our lives as a cleaning lady when we first moved to Combs and she has ended up as another of my surrogate children, like Adrian who runs our finances, like our own Suzy who holds our hands and drives our engine, like Karina who says "Write the story of your marriage" so firmly that I actually did. Like Christy, who had health problems of his own but got over them brilliantly. He would come over and Juan's face would light up and he would tell everyone in sight, Christy is here.

And Lucie kept me company, she drove me to and from the nursing home every day for the better part of a year because it was too short a ride to interest local taxis and I could not have visited Juan daily, as I tried to do, without her. She kept me eating correctly, walking around the garden for exercise. She kept me in touch with others beyond my own small fenced-in world, she kept me laughing at her admirers and she held my hand patiently when I cried.

Without the support of a single one of these, my frail structure would have crumbled. I can never thank them enough, because they don't really know how close I was to not making it.

Chapter 44

There was a lovely nun at Incarnation Grammar School who taught one of the earlier grades, perhaps when I was seven years old. She told us about Limbo, which she must have described in her soft voice as a place specially made for children. It was soft and cloudy and it was where we waited. I came away from her class with the sensation that I was already waiting, without having had to be told to. And the gentle nun was just confirming it for me. I was in a Limbo of my own and I was not to worry, it was what the Good Lord had in mind. I remember being grateful to her because she put me at ease then and for a long time after.

The year following Juan's entry into the realm of care was a year of suspension, a Limbo of sorts. I think it was in some sense thanks to Sister Francis that I was not unduly frightened.

Suzy and Adrian, in concert with their friends whom I called Suzy's army, combed the area just outside Paris where Suzy lived, to find the right nursing home or, as they call it here, residence. In the end, they succeeded. Adrian then proceeded to swing the financial arrangements of selling the beautiful house in Combs and putting our affairs in order. Which to me seemed like performing the most arcane miracles in view.

Neither Juan nor I were particularly careful of the rudiments of life. He had to forage through piles of messy papers to even begin. The Wizard of la Bastille, indeed. He is at least that.

Suzy and Lucie found the Aubergerie, a splendid facility set in a beautiful park that swept down to the little river Yerres, just a mile or two from our house. Had I been my former self I could have walked to see him every day. Had we been our former selves we wouldn't have had to, of course. We were new at being Old.

The Aubergerie looked much like a country club, perched in a glade surrounded by trees on three sides and a bustling shopping center on the other.

When he first arrived he was still able to walk and his mind seemed eccentric rather than damaged. He spoke his four languages without getting them mixed up and was delighted to find another Catalan among the "guests." He found it easy to fit into the rhythm of the place, got along with the personnel and waited for my daily visit. If I could not make it every day, Lucie would go and spend a few minutes with him between jobs. Lucie's other employers knew about Monsieur Palà and his unfortunate accident and allowed for a slightly altered schedule from time to time. I never met any of her other clients yet felt a kinship and gratitude for their neighborliness in allowing me to invade their schedules.

In the meantime Adrian and Suzy were dealing with the real world. Beside the bank, the multiplicity of measures to be taken apart from just selling the house, such as the 'what to do with things?' issue which was predictably sensitive.

There was what I saw as my entry into Limbo the gentle Sister. Suzy's friends from Châtillon, just outside Paris, were more than generous with their cars and their time. Lovely Cocotte and Bernard Rambert, generous and harried Michele Moreau, Brigitte and Jose, Christy who was here, too... I had a standing army of my own. I could not have survived that strange year without them.

Adrian arranged the sale of the house, the ensuing banking part of it, the contracts, everything including, of course, the buyer. Lucie kept me going to the Aubergerie almost every day and kept me fed and sane, rattling around in my house that was shedding its attributes day by day. Never well-organized, I might easily have gone totally berserk watching all my beloved 'things' vanish from the shelves, windowsills, table tops, surfaces from all over my nine-room house. But, thanks to what I called Suzy's Army, we found suitable homes for most of my treasures.

And then came the miracle. There was the horrific question of Juan's work. He had left the studio one night and never returned. Nothing was planned for the future of the sculptures, the paintings, the drawings going back to his boyhood.

And here Sister Francis and her notion of Limbo opens wide. The young curator of the Musée de Pontoise, Christophe Duvivier, and Eva Maria Fruhtrunk, Juan's guardian angel, came and took all the sculptures and most of the paintings and works on paper for the Musée de Pontoise, the Musée de Cambrai, and le Musée de Mâcon. Furthermore, Eva Maria brought along a supplementary miracle-maker who has a large, spacious, and welcoming Art Foundation in Burgundy who took the three very large sculptures that the museums had no room to accommodate. Wonderful, opportune Franz.

Juan and I used to joke about those three awkward but beautiful sculptures. We daydreamed of tipping them into the river Yerres the day before we felt the call of Heaven. Preferably to the sound of trumpets.

Still more astounding, Christophe Duvivier has since produced a magnificent catalogue raisonné of Juan's work, a coffee table-sized volume that is breathtaking in its beauty and simplicity, much like the sculptures within. I know of few sculptors who have had a catalogue raisonné done during their lifetimes. He is blessed.

Sister Francis told us that Limbo was a place that God kept for special cases, like children. Children and artists, I think she would agree.

At the end of the twelve month period, from August 2012 to 2013 I lived on a series of cloudlets, kept in shape by Suzy's private army, by Adrian's patient steering me through oceans of decisions, by Lucie's care and feeding, literally, and just before my 85th birthday the two of us moved into another residence, not the Aubergerie on the river called Yesterday but one similar to it, on the edge of Paris, close to Suzy who can get to us by bus on short notice. The boys, our beloved Robin and Thomas, can drop in easily. It is painless to get here from the middle of Paris. We are no longer the subject of safaris into the hinterland.

Most of all, of course, we are together. We have two rooms, each with bath, adjacent to each other at the end of a corridor with a floor to ceiling window instead of a blank wall. You can see the Eiffel Tower through the window. Juan likes to look at it when they turn on the lights. The director of the residence decorated my room with wall-to-wall bookcases, and before I arrived Suzy had hung a variety of paintings including the superb portrait Juan did of me for our fifth wedding anniversary because, he admitted years later, he couldn't think of what I might fancy.

She also brought along my Ethiopian folk paintings which I treasure: the Queen of Sheba and her priests on goatskins. They came from the Addis Ababa street markets fifty years ago. What more appropriate decoration for Limbo?

Juan's health is more or less stable. He is in a wheelchair now, but he manages to propel himself around expertly. He has a fine appetite and seems alert and interested in all that goes on around him. Much of that, I believe, is just show. If I ask him something about what he appears to be listening to, he says I don't know, confidentially, and with a glint of complicity in his eyes. He has that complicity always at the ready. If anything, it has grown with the strange rigors of these past two years. He relies on me with total confidence, the way a child does and I am touched beyond measure when I see that trust in his face. He also winks and moves to kiss me, leaning forward in his wheelchair, one arm ready to go around my shoulder. He says then, "Like in New York."

He giggles a little then and so do I, though I could cry as well. He is comfortable in this residence where he has a few small sculptures in his room and paintings on the walls and photographs galore chronicling the lives we led and the people we loved. There are dozens of pictures of us and our children and our grandchildren. Suzy's boys were his last great love, which is visible now when he looks at them today, young men going about his business for him… the gallery, the storing, the minutia of his professional life, in his name. Of course he loves them. I see echoes of him in them and I love them a little bit more for that.

Sister Francis did not leave me with a sense of closure in Limbo. It is simply a place where one goes. Waiting, while feeling grateful for the softness of the clouds.

October 2014

Printed in the United States
By Bookmasters